Beyond

Freedom's Reach

ADAM ROTHMAN

Beyond Freedom's Reach

A KIDNAPPING IN THE TWILIGHT OF SLAVERY

CAMBRIDGE, MASSACHUSETTS
LONDON, ENGLAND
2015

Copyright © 2015 by the President and Fellows of Harvard College
All rights reserved
Printed in the United States of America

First printing

Library of Congress Cataloging-in-Publication Data
is available from the Library of Congress

ISBN 978-0-674-36812-5

For Marian and Frances

we'll eat you up—we love you so

Contents

CAST OF CHARACTERS ix

Prologue 1

1. Pointe Coupée 11

2. New Orleans 30

3. War 67

4. Justice 115

5. Reunion 153

Epilogue 187

APPENDIX:
ROSE HERERA'S PETITION 193
ABBREVIATIONS 198
NOTES 199
ACKNOWLEDGMENTS 254
INDEX 257

Cast of Characters

Rose Herera (also spelled Rose Elyra)

George Herera, Rose's husband

Joseph Ernest, Marie Georgiana, Marie Josephine, Joseph George, and Louise Josephine Herera, Rose and George Herera's children

Leocadie (Léocady), Rose Herera's mother

Octave Leblanc, Rose's first owner

James Andrew De Hart, owner of Rose Herera, 1861–1862

Amelie (Mary) Valcour De Hart, James De Hart's wife

Carmelite Roland, an aunt of Mary De Hart and alleged owner of Rose Herera after August 1862

Thomas Jefferson Durant, Rose Herera's lawyer

Benjamin Butler, Union commander in New Orleans, May–December 1862

Nathaniel Banks, Union commander in New Orleans after December 1862

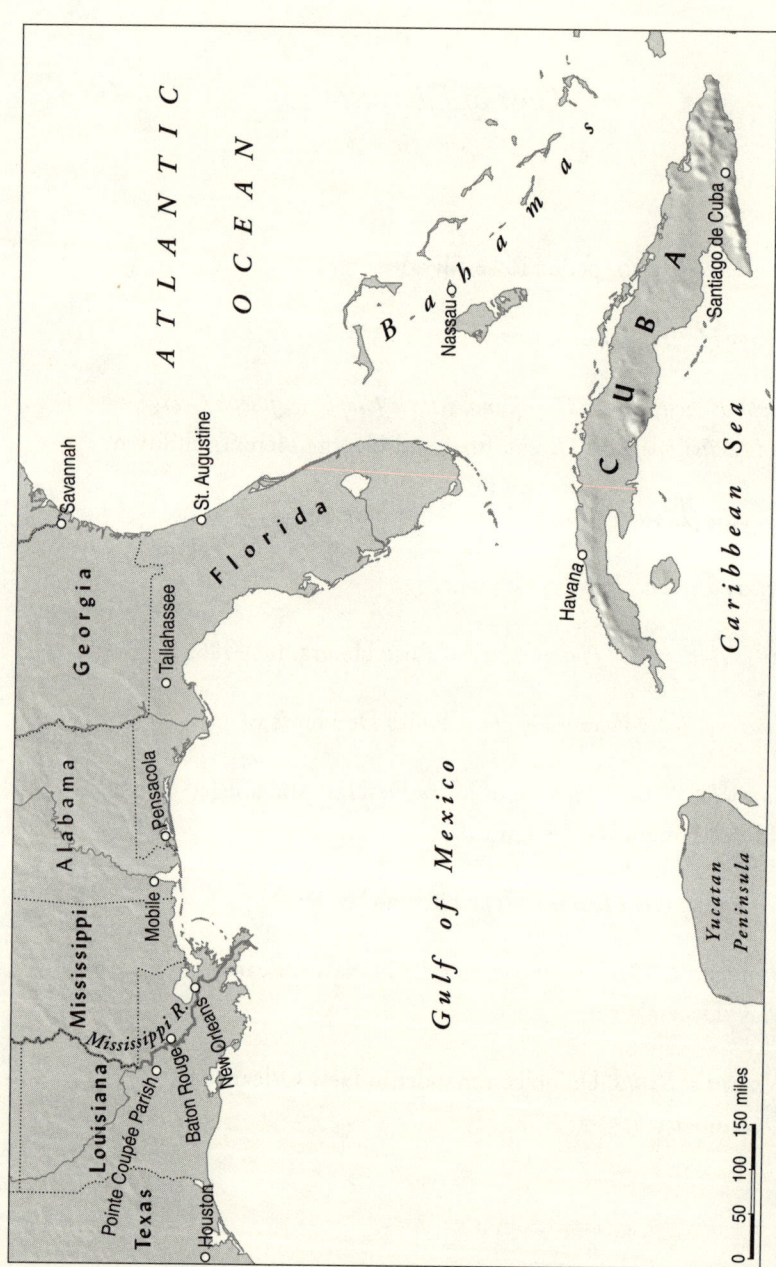

Rose Herera's world: Louisiana, the Gulf South, and Cuba.
Philip Schwartzberg, Meridian Mapping.

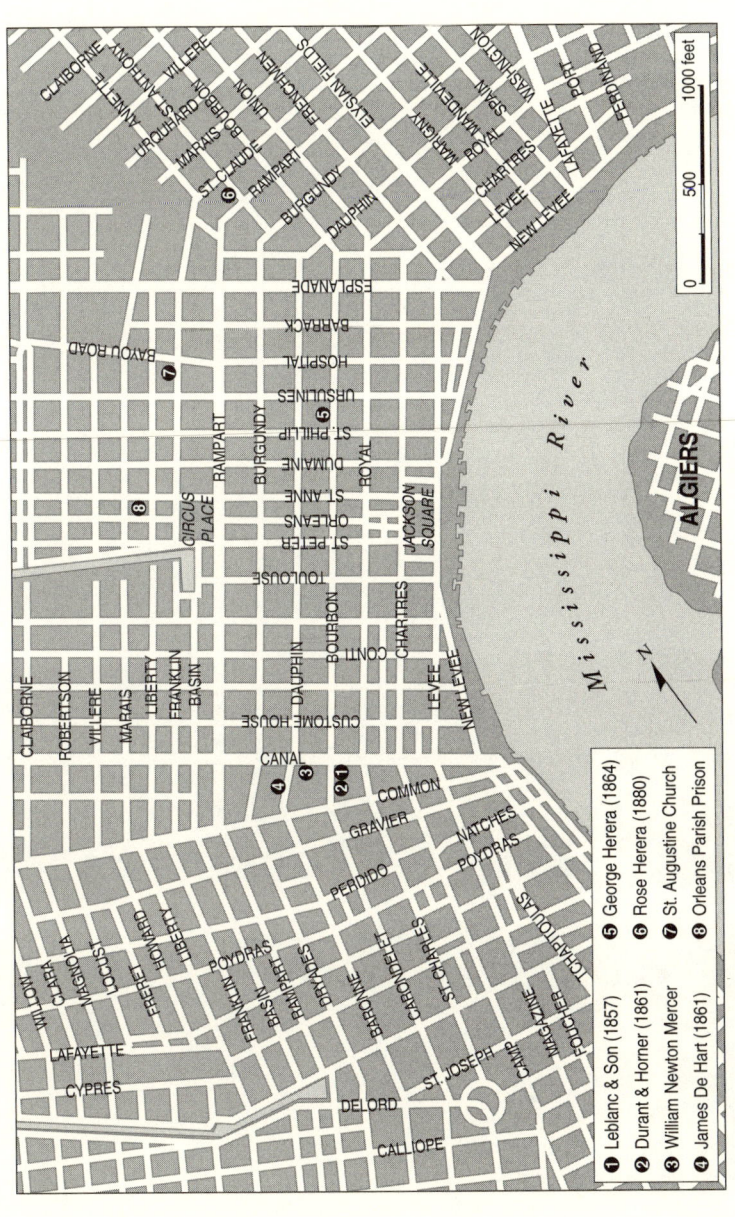

Rose Herera's New Orleans.
Philip Schwartzberg, Meridian Mapping.

Beyond

Freedom's Reach

Prologue

ABRAHAM LINCOLN's tired hand trembled as he signed the Emancipation Proclamation in his White House study on New Year's Day 1863. That act declared more than three million slaves in the Confederate States of America to be "forever free," but it did not end American slavery. The slaves who were freed on paper still had to be freed on the ground in the places where they lived. It would take another thirty months of war to fulfill the promised justice of the Proclamation. Moreover, the reach of the Proclamation was strictly limited. Lincoln exempted roughly half a million slaves in the Union states of Delaware, Maryland, Kentucky, and Missouri, and another 300,000 in Confederate territory possessed by the Union army, including the Virginia tidewater, Tennessee, and southern Louisiana. Those places were not deemed to be "in rebellion," and so the Proclamation did not apply to them. Alternative pathways to emancipation unfurled in those places, each one distinctive.[1]

A thousand miles away from Lincoln's quiet study, an enslaved woman named Rose Herera sat in a clammy New Orleans jail with her infant son. Her life had been an ordinary one until this moment. Ordinary, that is, for a slave. She had grown up in the rural upriver parish of Pointe Coupée, moved with her owner to New Orleans in the early 1850s, and lived in the city for a decade. In New Orleans she was bought and sold several times, ending up in the hands of a man named James De Hart just before Louisiana seceded from the Union. It was in New Orleans, too, that she met her husband, a free man of color named George Herera. She took his last name, and they had four children together. Their children were De Hart's property because by law the offspring of a slave woman belonged to her owner.²

In May 1862, Union troops captured New Orleans and held it for the rest of the Civil War. Many Confederates fled the city. James De Hart was one of them. He joined an exodus of hundreds to New Orleans' sister city, Havana, Cuba, in the fall of 1862, leaving behind his wife Mary and son Edward. In the weeks after her husband's departure, Mary De Hart prepared to follow him to Havana. She asked Rose Herera to accompany her, but Herera declined because she did not want to leave her own family and friends in New Orleans. She refused to play the role of the "loyal slave" that was so crucial to the Confederacy's proslavery rationale.³ Domestic slaves were supposed to happily subordinate their own families to their owners' desires, but Rose Herera wrote her own script.

As 1862 drew to a close, Rose Herera and Mary De Hart found themselves in a crisis. In the words of the twentieth-century Italian thinker Antonio Gramsci, a crisis occurs when "the old is dying and the new cannot be born."⁴ The local practices that buttressed slavery in New Orleans—the auction block and the whipping post—continued to operate, but now that Union troops held sway in the city, it was becoming harder for masters to impose their will. Slaves were running away, finding Northern soldiers to protect them. Some were enrolling in the Union army to fight against their owners' not-yet-lost cause. The great drama of the unraveling of slavery was being enacted in the homes, streets, jails, and courtrooms of New Orleans, no less than on battlefields and plantations across the war-torn South. And it was being enacted by women as well as men.[5]

In mid-December, an altercation between Rose Herera and Mary De Hart's aunt, Carmelite Roland, led to Herera's arrest on the charge of assault. She was thrown into the New Orleans police jail, an annex of the old Parish Prison erected in the boom years of the Jacksonian era, just in back of famed Congo Square (now Louis Armstrong Park.) It had not aged well. "Offensive to every sense and sentiment of reasonable man," complained the nineteenth-century New Orleans novelist and reformer George Washington Cable, the prison was a "massive, dark, grim, huge, four-side block" with weeds growing out of its cracked masonry and bats nesting under its eaves.[6] The four weeks Herera spent in that decrepit place with three-month-old Joseph George took a toll on her body. She could barely stand and walk by the time she was released.

Mary De Hart visited the jail to pressure Rose Herera to go to Cuba, one of the last bastions of slavery in the Americas. Testifying in court two years later, Herera would recollect snippets of their tense negotiations. "Don't you feel like going to Havana? I am fixing to go," De Hart asked Herera on her first visit. "I don't want to leave my mother," replied Herera. But her mistress would not take no for an answer: "You make up your mind, and I will come and see you again." Mary De Hart came back several times to prod Herera into going to Cuba. She finally resorted to threats. She would take the three children in her possession—Joseph Ernest, Marie Georgiana, and Marie Josephine—to Cuba with or without Rose Herera. The children were young. Joseph Ernest was six, Marie Georgiana four, and Marie Josephine just two years old. Still, Herera remained firm. She would not go; she was too sick to go even if she wanted to. She begged Mary De Hart to leave her children in New Orleans.[7]

Finally, on January 15, as the Union army began to carry out the Emancipation Proclamation elsewhere, a carriage pulled up to the jail with Mary De Hart and her son Edward, Carmelite Roland, and the three little Herera children. They were on their way to board the *Bio Bio,* a steamer bound for Havana. One of De Hart's companions entered the jail to secure Herera's release and bring her out, but Herera insisted she was too sick to move. The carriage drove on to the levee without her, where the entourage boarded the steamer. Herera's mother and husband visited the *Bio Bio* that afternoon. They saw the children on board the vessel but could do nothing to prevent Mary De Hart from taking them away. The next morning the *Bio Bio* departed for Havana. From Rose Herera's perspective, her children had been kidnapped and sent beyond freedom's reach.

This book is about Rose Herera's world of slavery, the kidnapping of her children during the Civil War, and her remarkable effort to get them back. Her story has never been told before. It does not appear anywhere in the vast corpus of modern historical scholarship on the Civil War, emancipation, and

Reconstruction. This neglect is difficult to account for because the kidnapping was not a secret, and the subsequent trial of Mary De Hart was a matter of public record. The case was even documented in a congressional report published in March 1866 and then promptly neglected and forgotten. I stumbled into this report by accident while browsing through an electronic database of U.S. government publications in search of material having to do with New Orleans in the nineteenth century. Its heading—"upon the subject of the supposed kidnapping of colored persons in the southern States for the purpose of selling them as slaves in Cuba"—caught my attention as a historian of American slavery. It has kept my attention for five years of research and writing, and this book is the result. Rose Herera's story deserves to be told because it humanizes the history of slavery and emancipation in the United States and dramatizes key aspects of that history.

Historians have tended to write about slavery in the aggregate rather than to delve deeply into the experiences of particular enslaved people. This approach is understandable. It is usually impossible to construct substantial life histories of individual slaves from the meager scraps of archival material that typically document their existence. The exceptions are usually those extraordinary figures, such as Frederick Douglass, who escaped slavery, achieved literacy, and become politically active in the antislavery movement. Recently, however, historians adopting the techniques of "microhistory" have illuminated the lifeworlds of lesser-known figures: the odyssey of a pair of West African dignitaries ensnared in the Atlantic slave trade; the family saga of a woman from Senegambia who was enslaved and freed in St. Domingue and whose descendants turned up in Louisiana,

Mexico, Cuba, and Belgium; the religious revival sparked by a freedwoman in the Dutch Caribbean who preached among enslaved Africans and people of African descent; the liaisons of the Hemingses of Monticello; the career of a North Carolina slave who fought in the Union army and went on to become a legislator. Using microhistory to examine Atlantic slavery and emancipation is to view a hurricane through a pinhole. One cannot see the whole violent storm through a small aperture, but what can be seen comes across with great clarity and vivid detail on a human scale, which can lead to new insights into how people actually lived.[8]

The story of Rose Herera's life, the kidnapping of her children, and her efforts to get them back dramatizes the struggle between slaveowners and slave parents over the possession of slave children. Owners had the upper hand because they had the law on their side. Slave children "belonged" to their owners in formal ways that were publicly enforced by the power of the state and recognized in market transactions. Through the elaboration of proslavery ideas in Southern politics and religion, owners elevated their legal right to own slave children into a moral obligation to protect and rear them up to adulthood. Some went so far as to profess genuine affection, even love, for the slave children they owned. In contrast, the parents of enslaved children had few legal rights to them, and whatever rights they did have were seldom if ever enforced. Even though George Herera was free, he was helpless to keep his children from being taken to Cuba by their owner. Nevertheless, mothers and fathers made claims to their enslaved children through the customary rituals of everyday life that sorted slave communities into families, attached slave children to their parents, and guided children through the early stages of their precarious lives as slaves. Slave children "belonged" to their parents, too. The clash between these two concepts of belonging—one rooted in masters' property rights and the other in slaves' familial bonds—animated the struggle over Rose Herera's children.[9]

The kidnapping of the Herera children dramatizes the mayhem of wartime emancipation. The overthrow of slavery was not linear, orderly, or peaceful. Rather, it was chaotic, improvised, and violent. It unfolded at different times in different places according to a complex interplay of war, politics, and social struggle. Local conditions mattered a great deal. Emancipation in New Orleans, a cosmopolitan port city where slaves composed a small percentage of the population and free people of color were numerous, was bound to be different from emancipation in a plantation district where slaves composed large majorities and free people of color were scarce. But slaveowners everywhere resisted emancipation with more or less vehemence. They chased after runaway slaves. They stashed slaves in remote locations—such as Cuba—where the Union army could not find them. They tried to keep the news of freedom from their slaves' ears. They beat and whipped the wives and children of slaves who enlisted in the Union army, and they murdered black soldiers. There was mayhem, too, in slaves' encounters with Union soldiers and authorities. Slaves were spurned, betrayed, robbed, beaten, and raped by their ostensible liberators, and disease-ridden refugee camps turned into death traps for hundreds, if not thousands, of men, women, and children who went in search of freedom. A realistic history of wartime emancipation must acknowledge these tribulations.[10]

Kidnapping was endemic to Atlantic slavery. Although modern historians debate the extent of kidnapping in Africa and its importance to the Atlantic slave trade, there is little doubt that kidnappers supplied slave marts across the Atlantic world with many uprooted people. The perception that the Atlantic slave trade was a kidnapping racket, moreover, was vital to antislavery discourse and central to the folk memory of enslavement among people of African descent.[11] "Africa has been robbed of its inhabitants; its free-born sons and daughters have been stole, and kidnapped, and violently taken away, and carried into captivity and cruel bondage," charged the pioneering Afro-British abolitionist Ottobah Cugoano in his 1787 *Thoughts and Sentiments on the Evil of Slavery*.[12] As a young boy in Maryland, Frederick Douglass knew many people "who could say that their fathers and mothers were stolen from Africa—forced from their homes, and compelled to serve as slaves." This knowledge filled Douglass with "a burning hatred of slavery."[13] In the early United States, stories of the kidnapping of free black people and their sale into perpetual slavery circulated with alarming regularity. Free black Northerners organized vigilance committees to defend themselves against "man-stealers." The Oscar-winning film *Twelve Years a Slave*, about a black New Yorker who was kidnapped and sold into slavery in Louisiana in the 1840s, made Solomon Northup famous all over again in 2013. But what remains poorly understood is that slaves, too, saw kidnapping in their daily lives. "We are stolen and sold to Georgia," chanted slaves on their way to the Deep South. The song lingered in the ears of the abolitionist William Wells Brown long after he had escaped from slavery. Encoded in the verse was a condemnation of the domestic slave trade as a form of organized kidnapping. From her childhood in Pointe Coupée to her adulthood New Orleans, kidnappers stalked Rose Herera's world.[14]

Kidnapping persisted during the Civil War and into Reconstruction in a variety of forms. The annals of the era are full of stories of slaves and newly freed people who were hauled away by owners or strangers, impressed into military service and public works, or forcibly apprenticed to labor. Very often, critics of these practices explicitly condemned them as "kidnapping" and compared them to the most odious features of slavery. The plight of the Herera children is emblematic of this turbulent history. Moreover, their singular case draws attention to widespread, subterranean fears that newly freed people in the United States were in danger of being kidnapped and sold into slavery in Cuba and Brazil. Rumors of this new threat swirled around the Gulf South in the winter of 1865–1866 and led to the congressional investigation that ventilated the Herera case. The existence of these rumors hints at a sense of the precariousness of freedom for African Americans in a world where slavery endured outside the borders of the United States. The prospect of reenslavement menaced the country's "new birth of freedom."[15]

If the Herera case reveals the perils of the process of wartime emancipation, it also brings the revolutionary quality of that process into focus. It should not be doubted that emancipation was an American revolution, even if that revolution did not achieve full citizenship and equality for freedpeople. Commenting on the progress of emancipation in November 1864, no less of an authority than Karl Marx marveled that *"never has such a gigantic revolution occurred with such rapidity."*[16]

"Revolution" is a devalued word today, but in its most robust sense as the violent transformation of the whole social and political order, wartime emancipation fits the bill. Slavery was destroyed by force of arms, the political power of the antebellum planter class was overthrown for a generation, and the Constitution was permanently altered to embrace people of African descent. "Can we imagine this spectacular revolution?" asked W. E. B. Du Bois in his pathbreaking *Black Reconstruction*.[17] Imagining the revolution of emancipation remains a challenge for historians, but close attention to Rose Herera's effort to recover her children at the end of the war opens up a line of inquiry that connects one woman's struggle to reunite her family, broken by slavery and war, with the profound legal and political changes of the era.

Herera appeared before a magistrate in New Orleans early in 1865 and declared that her three young children had been kidnapped and spirited away to Havana, where they were being held as slaves by her former owners. Herera's bold stand initiated months of legal wrangling in the city's courts to decide whether Mary De Hart, who had returned to New Orleans, was guilty of kidnapping and how to recover the children. The legal battle involved prominent civilian and military authorities in Louisiana, caught the eye of Congress, and finally drew in the U.S. State Department and its Cuban counterpart. The progress of the Herera case from a domestic affair to an international scandal exposes what Herera's lawyer called the "crimes of a departed system" and how one such crime was perpetrated, judged, and remedied in the twilight of slavery.[18]

I

Pointe Coupée

Rose Herera was born in the parish of Pointe Coupée in Louisiana. Like many slaves, she did not know the precise date of her birth. In a petition to the U.S. government in 1865, she guessed she was "about twenty-five years of age."[1] Even the most famous slave of all, Frederick Douglass, lamented that he had "no accurate knowledge of my age, never having seen any authentic record containing it." Douglass observed that slaves "know as little of their ages as horses know of theirs," and he argued that their owners liked it that way.[2] Not knowing one's birthday symbolized what the sociologist Orlando Patterson calls "natal alienation," a defining condition of slavery throughout world history. According to Patterson, slaves have always been denied formal recognition of their family ties, and as a consequence, they experience "the loss of ties of birth in both ascending and descending generations."[3] In reality, American slaves did have families. They had parents and grandparents, husbands and wives, children and grandchildren. They also had aunts and uncles, godparents and guardians, and other people who took care of them when their families were shredded by sale, forced migration, and murder. But they seldom celebrated their birthdays.

Rose Herera differs from Douglass in that an "authentic record" of her birthday does exist. Rose's baptismal record indicates that she was born on December 13, 1835, and baptized on July 19, 1836, in the parish church in Pointe Coupée.[4] That record, written in French by Fr. Jean Martin, described baby Rose as the slave ("escl.") of Octave Leblanc, and the natural child ("enfant naturel") of Léocady, who was also a slave of Leblanc, a resident owner in the parish. The record did not name Rose's father, a standard omission in the baptismal records of slaves. In fact, one crucial piece of information that is missing from all the records of Rose's life is the identity of her father. The erasure of biological paternity was a hallmark, almost a necessity, of slaveholders' claim to wield paternal authority over slaves. Owners not only took precedence over fathers; they often refused to recognize that their slaves had biological fathers at all. Whoever Rose's father was, the phrase "enfant naturel" indicates that he was not married to Rose's mother—or at least that their marriage had not been recognized by the church.[5]

Rose's baptismal record signaled more than her ties of blood and property. It also named her godparents. Rose's godfather ("parrain") was Ludger, a free man of color, and her godmother ("marraine") was Claris, a slave of François Bouis, a nearby planter. In Catholic slave societies, godparentage offered a sacred form of "fictive kinship." Godparents were obliged to look after their godchildren's spiritual well-being; sometimes they provided more tangible benefits, such as protection and money.[6] The ritual of baptism joined people of different statuses—slave, free colored, and white—into a spiritual community, at least for a moment. The designation of Ludger and Claris as godparents suggests that Rose's spiritual community extended beyond her owner's property and into the surrounding neighborhood.[7] Anybody new to the complexities of American slavery might find it strange that a slaveowner would allow his slave to be baptized, a sacrament that recognizes the slave's soul and thus, humanity. Yet caring for slaves' souls had long served as a key justification for slavery. Louisiana's first slave laws, the Code Noir, had required owners to baptize their slaves, and although the sacrament was no longer mandated by state law, the sacrament remained obligatory for Catholic slaveowners who took their religious duties seriously. Leblanc was one of these conscientious masters. The sacramental records indicate that twenty-one children owned by Leblanc received the sacrament of baptism between 1835 and 1849.[8] He seems to have been more conscientious about baptism than many of his fellow owners, for as a priest in Pointe Coupée complained, "Religion is here as one would naturally suppose it to be in a population much mixed, with people of various mores meeting in the same area, with the chief and even sole purpose of making money."[9]

Rose's terse baptismal record offers a point of entry into her childhood in Pointe Coupée, a place one late nineteenth-century novelist called "the most interesting region in Louisiana."[10] A rural parish situated between the Mississippi and Atchafalaya rivers above Baton Rouge, Point Coupée is about one hundred and fifty-five miles up the winding Mississippi river from New Orleans—a day's journey by steamboat. Its distinctive geographic feature, an oxbow lake called False River, served as the

Mississippi's main channel until the river found a quicker route to the Gulf in the early 1700s. Native people lived in the lower Mississippi valley as far back as 2000 BCE, but they fell victim to the Columbian invasion of disease that turned the Americas into a cemetery beginning in the sixteenth century. Tunica Indians lived and hunted in the area when French invaders established an outpost at Pointe Coupée in the 1720s, and a few remained at the time of the Louisiana Purchase. The colony grew into a mixed settlement of plantations and farms owned by French and Acadian migrants, while Africans and their descendants soon accounted for a majority of the population. A "creole" culture emerged: Francophone, Catholic, and rooted in slavery.[11]

Revelations of big slave conspiracies in Pointe Coupée at the end of the eighteenth century showed that the upriver parish, now under Spanish administration, was not isolated from the revolutionary era. A plot in 1791 originated among enslaved Africans living on a False River plantation; it was nipped in the bud, but the will to freedom was not uprooted. Four years later, slaves on the plantation of Julien Poydras, the parish's wealthiest man, conspired to revolt. Encouraged by news of the French Revolution and the slave uprising in St. Domingue, slaves gathered at the St. Francis Church on Easter Sunday to display their strength. The crackdown was swift and harsh. More than thirty slaves were hanged, and some beheaded. Their heads were impaled on stakes planted on the banks of the Mississippi all the way to New Orleans as a warning to others. Dozens were flogged and sentenced to hard labor. Spanish authorities deported three white men implicated in the plot. Two were sentenced to hard labor in Cuba.[12]

Despite these rumblings among the slaves, Pointe Coupée planters ratcheted up their commitment to slavery on the basis of cotton and sugar. They began to shift their operations from tobacco and indigo to short-staple cotton production in the 1790s, tapping into the new demand for raw cotton emanating from textile manufacturers in Great Britain. Sugar cultivation crept up the Mississippi as well, and by the late 1830s, the parish had become the northern rim of Louisiana's sugar bowl. Many planters pivoted to sugar in the late 1830s and early 1840s, as cotton prices fell and a new tariff bolstered domestic sugar producers. Then, in the 1850s, the cotton economy surged. The following table provides a rough guide to the growth of the parish's slave population and its increasing production of cotton and sugar in the two decades before the Civil War.

A key aspect of this growth was the rapidly increasing slave population. Not only did the slave population increase, but its rate of growth increased in each decade from the 1820s through the 1850s as the center of gravity of North American slavery shifted

Table 1 Cotton and sugar production and slave population in Pointe Coupée parish, 1840–1860

Year	Cotton (lbs.)	Sugar (lbs.)	Slaves	% Slave
1840	6,294,726	411,000	5,430	69
1850	6,488,000	856,000	7,811	69
1860	11,578,800	1,218,700	12,903	73

Data sources: Compendium of the Enumeration of the Inhabitants and Statistics of the United States (Washington, D.C.: Thomas Allen, 1841), 240; J. D. B. DeBow, *Seventh Census of the United States: 1850* (Washington, D.C.: Robert Armstrong, 1853), 484, 486; Joseph C. G. Kennedy, *Agriculture of the United States in 1860* (Washington, D.C.: U.S. Government Printing Office, 1864), 67, 69; Historical Census Browser, http://mapserver.lib.virginia.edu. The author has corrected obvious errors in the originals.

to the Mississippi valley.[13] Because the rate of growth exceeded the typical rate of slave reproduction, much of the increase in the slave population, especially in the 1850s, must have come from the local planters' purchasing enslaved people through the domestic slave trade or the relocation of slaves by voluntarily migrating owners. The census of 1850 recorded 131 slave deaths in Pointe Coupée for the year ending June 1, 1850, but only 125 slave births. That year's excess of slave deaths over slave births in the parish was not an anomaly in Louisiana. Slave deaths (5,873) exceeded slave births (4,940) for the state as a whole, in contrast to the excess of births (7,292) over deaths (6,083) among free people. Slavery took a heavy toll. When extrapolated over time, this pattern implies that virtually the entire aggregate increase in the parish's enslaved population during the antebellum era stemmed from forced migration. A cholera epidemic that struck the lower Mississippi valley in 1849 may have skewed the census data, but also suggests the slave population's susceptibility to disease. The statistics reveal the high cost of the mistaken belief that black people's bodies were naturally suited to hard labor in a hot climate.[14]

The pattern of growth in Pointe Coupée suggests a problem in the way historians usually refer to the "natural increase" of the slave population in the United States. The phrase "natural increase" signals an unusual feature of slavery in North America. Unlike most other slave societies in the Americas, the North American slave population increased without continual replenishment from Africa beginning in the eighteenth century. This fecundity allowed the slave population to continue to grow at a fast clip after Congress prohibited slave importation in 1808. Yet the idea of "natural increase" does not properly describe the situation in southern Louisiana, where the slave population suffered from high mortality and low rates of reproduction caused by the rigor of work, a disease-ridden ecology, and a dearth of women. All these handicaps were characteristic of sugar plantation slavery. The slave population of the region thus could only be replenished by forced migration.[15] More deeply, the concept of "natural increase" implies that the growth of the slave population was mainly a natural or biological phenomenon. This implication is misleading because it ignores the legal and social dimensions of the increase in the slave labor force.[16]

Contrary to Aristotle, nobody is a natural-born slave. It was the law that dictated that the offspring of an enslaved woman was a slave and (in a related but separate rule) the property of the mother's owner. This core legal principle of slavery in the Americas is known by the Latin phrase *partus sequitur ventrem*, or following the womb. The principle was stipulated in Louisiana's 1724 Code Noir and never altered. In the case of *Lunsford v. Coquillon*, decided a hundred years later, Judge F. X. Martin asserted that "the issue of a female slave is held to be born in the condition of the mother, the maxim of the Roman law, partus sequitur ventrem, being universally recognized."[17] Hence, the law said that Rose was a slave because her mother was a slave, and that she was the property of Octave Leblanc, the man who owned her mother. That the replication of the slave population was as much a matter of law as biology can be demonstrated by imagining what would have happened if Louisiana had changed its laws so that the offspring of enslaved women had been free. Either the slave population would have been replenished through constant importations of enslaved people, or they would have been slowly eclipsed by free people of African descent. The "free womb" principle was central to laws enacting gradual emancipation from the northern United States to Brazil.[18]

It was a truism of proslavery dogma that the owner's economic interest in his human property gave him a stake in their well-being. A dead slave was a bad investment, whereas a healthy slave would earn dividends, and a childbearing woman would bring capital gains. That logic did not prevent horrible abuse. Even pregnant slave women in Louisiana were subjected to torture. Interviews with the descendants of slaves in the 1930s offer a recurring nightmare of pregnant women being forced to lie face down on the ground with their bellies in a hole as they received a whipping "till de blood come."[19]

The idea of "natural increase" masks the social dynamics of the life and death of slave children—especially death, which was all too common among young slaves. The sacramental registers in Pointe Coupée provide a vital record of sorts for Rose's fellow slaves. From 1834 to 1852, eleven of Leblanc's slaves were recorded as buried. Seven of these were children. Two of the children were infants who died without recorded names. Two others, Pierre and Joseph, were fifteen and sixteen months old when they died. Pauline was two years old. Rosalie and Georges, eleven and twelve years old, were buried on the same day in 1850. The registers shed no light on the causes of their deaths.[20]

Rose was a survivor. She would have turned fifteen years old in December 1850. That year's census provides a more detailed demographic profile of her parish and the plantation where she lived. Pointe Coupée was then home to more than 11,000 people; over two-thirds of them were slaves. Roughly one in four was a free white person, and the remainder—560 people, according to the census—were free people of color. Almost 60 percent of households included slaves (450 out of 760), and just over a quarter of slaveholding households included more than twenty slaves, the conventional line between a "farm" and a "plantation." Most slaves, however, lived on plantations (70 percent). The slave population was fairly young, like Rose, with more than 40 percent under the age of twenty. More than half of the slaves (53 percent) were male, although the sex ratio among children was more balanced than that of adults. Slave buyers' preference for adult male laborers skewed the adult population.[21] The slave schedule for the 1850 census identified 450 slaveholders in the parish and enumerated the nearly eight thousand slaves they possessed by age, sex, and color—but not by name. It is often mistakenly asserted that the so-called ⅗ths clause of the Constitution reduced slaves to a fraction of a human being. It did nothing of the sort, but the census that provided the population count necessary to apportion political power via the ⅗ths clause did something else that is often overlooked. It counted individual slaves but denied them the honor of being identified by name as free people were. This pattern of erasure makes it impossible to identify Rose with certainty in the census's slave schedule, but it is likely that she is the very first of Octave Leblanc's slaves listed in his entry, a sixteen-year-old female marked *M* for mulatto in the "color" column of the census.[22]

That *M* invites scrutiny. The 1850 census was the first federal census to identify people according to a category called "color."[23] Census takers adopted three color classifications—white, mulatto, and black—but when one recognizes that "mulatto" is not a color like white or black, but a genealogical designation indicating mixed white and black ancestry, then it becomes clear that what the census called "color" was actually a racial category. The three classifications corresponded to the conventional understanding of race in the United States in the mid-nineteenth century. A person could be classified as white, black, or a mixture commonly designated as "mulatto," depending on his or her combination of appearance and reputation. These classifications deserve no credence for scientific precision or sociological accuracy. Many people classified as white surely had African ancestry, and even more people classified as black probably had people of European descent in their family trees. (Indians complicated Americans' understanding of the permutations of race, but were generally uncounted in the census or were assimilated into the white/mulatto/black triplet.)[24] Although the federal census slotted Americans into three racial classes, many Louisianians subscribed by custom to a more ornate vocabulary of race and genealogy inherited from French and Spanish tradition. Placed on a continuum between white and black were "griffe," "mulatto," "quadroon," "octoroon," and other esoteric labels designating different combinations of parents, grandparents, and great-grandparents. Lavish attention to racial genealogies was a hallmark of creole society.[25]

Race and status combined in discrete ways. All white people were free, and all slaves were designated as mulatto or black, but not all people designated as mulatto and black were slaves. Mulattoes were much more likely to be free than blacks because they more often got a boost from white consorts and fathers who manumitted them. For this reason, mulattoes predominated among free people of color throughout the Americas and the Caribbean, and Louisiana was no exception. Free people of color were so common in Louisiana that a territorial court held in 1810 that mulattoes and other persons "of color" must be presumed to be free unless there was proof of their slave status, whereas "Negroes" were presumed to be slaves.[26] According to the 1850 census, two in every five mulattoes in Louisiana were free, whereas less than two in every fifty black people were free. To put it another way, 80 percent of free people of color in the state in 1850 were designated as mulatto, whereas more than 90 percent of the slaves were designated as black. Free people of color composed a small but significant element of the population of Rose's parish, and close to Pointe Coupée in West Baton Rouge was a neighborhood known as Mulatto Bend populated by free people of color. Rose's own godfather was a free man of color. Nevertheless it should not be forgotten that most mulattoes in Louisiana, including Rose, were slaves.[27]

The bare skeleton of Rose's immediate community can be discerned in the 1850 census's schedule of Octave Leblanc's slaves. The nameless census data identifies forty-two slaves in all. Twenty-two were female, twenty male. They spanned generations. Oldest were a man and a woman, both sixty years; the youngest was a baby girl, just two months old. The median age of the slaves was twenty-three, but the men tended to be older than the women. Seventeen of the slaves, including eleven girls, were under the age of twenty. The census taker marked only four as mulatto, the rest as *B* for black. A bill of sale for the Leblanc plantation provides the first names of at least some of the Leblanc slaves and their family relationships. In 1853, Leblanc's son sold his share of the plantation and thirty of the slaves to Joseph Stinson. Those who were sold included the men Tiberce, Adams, Robert, Lucas, Bill, William, Richard, Samson, Antoine, Cesar, another William, Pierre, and Paul. Three were listed as runaways, sold in absentia. One wonders whether Stinson ever recovered them. One of the Williams was noted as deaf. The women included Big Rose, Sophie, Jeanne, Ursule, Miza, Clara, Priscilla, and Silvia. Several of these were mothers who were sold with their children. Big Rose had an unnamed four-year-old and a ten-year-old named Marguerite. Perhaps Big Rose acquired her adjective to distinguish her from the teenager with the same name. Sophie had a four-year-old named Sarah, and an eleven-year-old named Therese. Ursule had a seven-year-old named Marie. Clara had a toddler named Denis and an unnamed infant. Priscilla had a five-year-old girl named Adeline. Although acknowledging mothers and their young children, the bill of sale said nothing about husbands and fathers. Buyers and sellers in the slave market rarely recognized those relationships, despite their existence in the slaves' own social world.[28]

Rose's owner, Octave Leblanc, was a sugar planter of French descent. His plantation, where Rose lived as a child, was situated on the west bank of the Mississippi River in a wealthy district of the parish known as the "coast." The plantation is labeled "J. Stinson" in Marie Adrien Persac's remarkable five-foot-long map of the lower Mississippi in 1858, which identifies all the plantation owners along the river from New Orleans to Natchez. Leblanc had sold out to Stinson five years earlier, so it was Stinson's name rather than Leblanc's that made it onto this panorama of property and power.

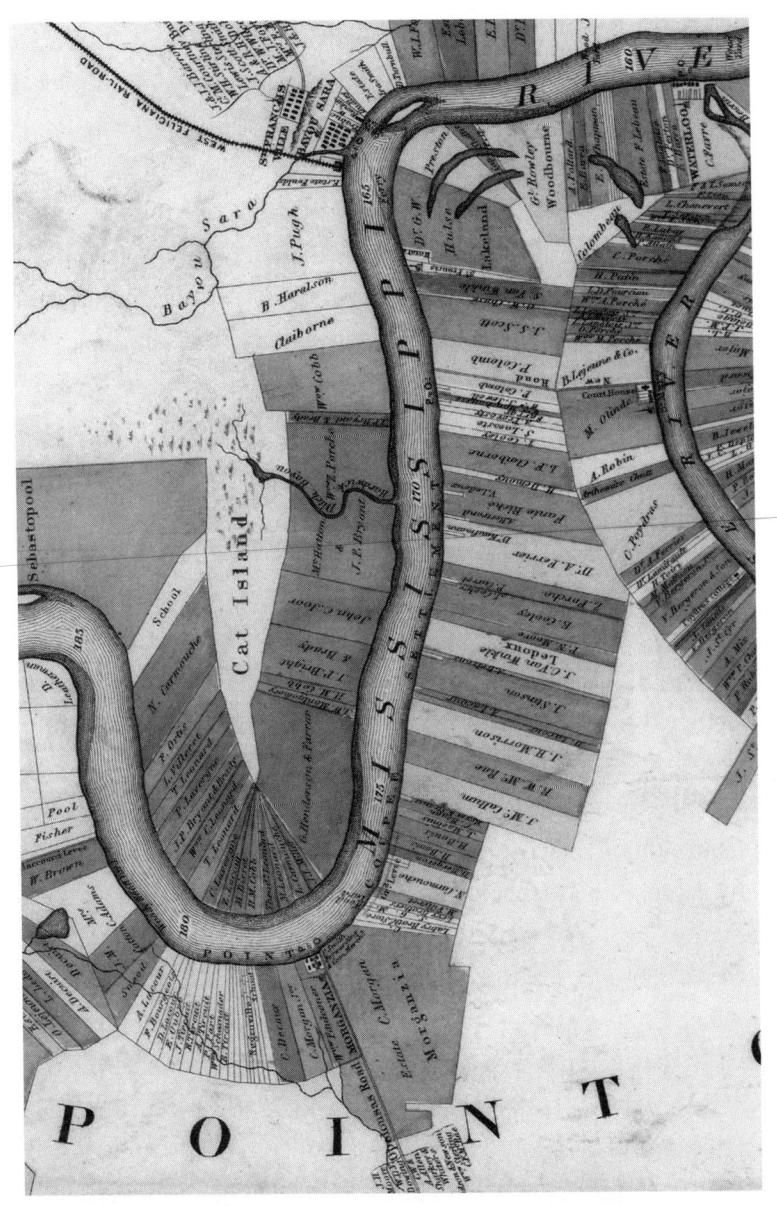

Detail from Marie Adrien Persac, *Norman's Chart of the Lower Mississippi River* (New Orleans: B. Norman, 1858). This map shows the "coast" district in Pointe Coupée parish, where Rose Herera was born. In 1853 Octave Leblanc sold out to Joseph Stinson, whose property fronts the "Se" in "Settlement."

Geography and Map Division, Library of Congress, Washington, D.C.

Leblanc's holdings placed him in the upper 15 percent of local slaveholders in 1850, but he was far from the richest in Point Coupée. Eight planters lived on plantations with more than a hundred slaves. The biggest, Charles Morgan of Morganza, had almost two hundred. Leblanc was connected by marriage to other prominent slaveholding families in Pointe Coupée and West Baton Rouge. Leblanc's mother was an Allain. (The Allains will reappear in Rose Herera's story.) His wife was a Bouis. Such families dominated local society. Their intermarriages created petty dynasties of blood and wealth based on slave labor.[29]

Leblanc's money and family ranked him among the "opulent planters" whom Frederick Gerstäcker did business with as manager of a hotel in Pointe Coupée in the early 1840s. An avid hunter who became a famous writer, Gerstäcker penned a vivid account of the parish in his popular *Wild Sports of the Far West*, published first in his native Germany and then translated into English in 1854.[30] His first night in the area he slept outdoors, swarmed by mosquitoes, on the levee at Bayou Sara on the opposite side of the river. He woke up before dawn to the sound of the "negro bell" that called the slaves to work. The town consisted of little more than a hotel, town-hall, jail, church, and priest's house. As high as twenty feet in places, the levee strained to keep the river in its course at great expense, and it often gave way to the current's constant onslaught. Several times before the Civil War, water rushing through breaks in the levee ruined the cotton and sugar crops in Pointe Coupée. Slave gangs would scramble to repair each new breach. Mosquitoes and floods were not the only environmental challenges the inhabitants faced.

"One great plague of the planters," Gerstäcker observed, "is the coco-grass."[31]

Gerstäcker's view of slavery was mixed. He saw firsthand "the oppressed condition and ill-treatment of the poor blacks" and condemned the cruelty of the auction block. "The horrors of the system were never so evident as when I first attended an auction, where slaves were sold like cattle to the highest bidder," he declared. Yet he admitted that families were not separated as often as they used to be, "at least mothers and children, so long as the latter are very young." Gerstäcker noted that the law mandated that families must be sold together, which was not quite accurate. What Louisiana's legal code actually prohibited was the sale of children under the age of ten apart from their mothers. Despite the law, Gerstäcker complained, "individuals are often sold, and then the most sacred ties are torn asunder for the sake of a few hundred dollars." Still, Gerstäcker contended, "the treatment of slaves is generally better than it is represented by the Abolitionists and missionaries." He parroted the proslavery argument that it was in slaveowners' interest to take good care of the slaves and not work them too hard. Owners supported elderly slaves, he wrote, and the slaves' food was on par with what other poor people ate. Gerstäcker drew from his own experience as hotel manager in Pointe Coupée to make the point: "We had a cook, chambermaid, and porter, all slaves, who never had occasion to complain of ill-treatment."[32]

Other sources provide ample evidence of the devastating impact of the slave trade and the ill-treatment of slaves in Pointe Coupée. A most striking example comes from the memoir of the conductor of the Underground Railroad in Philadelphia, William Still, published after the Civil War. Still told the story of James Connor, who had been a slave of one of the parish's leading planters. Connor had been born in Kentucky, where he was owned by a widow who was "like a mother" to him. She died when Connor was sixteen years old, and as often happened, the death of the owner led to the sale of her slaves. Connor had the misfortune to be sold down the river to "the worst man . . . that ever sun shined on," a Pointe Coupée planter named Vincent Turner: "His slaves he fairly murdered; two hundred lashes were merely a promise for him." When Turner died, his widow remarried Charles Parlange, described by Connor as a "poor man, though a very smart man, bad-hearted, and very barbarous." Connor had the further bad luck of enduring the switch from cotton to sugar in Pointe Coupée, which made for "harder times than ever." He and his fellow slaves were given meager rations and forced to work as long as there was enough light to see by. Connor's testimony furnishes an antidote for amnesia and blindness to slavery's horror: "Many a time I have seen slaves whipped almost to death—well, I tell you I have seen them whipped to death." Connor had been robbed and cheated, and falsely promised his freedom by his owners. He had been shot four times. "I have shot in me now," he told William Still.[33]

Oddly enough, the Parlanges trusted Connor. He was allowed to raise hogs and "hire his own time." They made him an overseer, allowed him to earn extra pay, and then demanded $1,150 for his freedom. In 1857, they invited him to go with them to Virginia on a slave-buying junket and promised him his freedom when he returned to Louisiana with the cargo of flesh. Connor played along. He convinced them that he had "no wish to go North," and so they took him on a short trip to Philadelphia. "My heart leaped for joy when I found we were going to a free State," he confided in Still, "but I did not let my owners know my feelings." Connor activated the city's abolitionist network, which provided him with an "Underground Rail Road ticket" and a passport to Canada, and sent him to the far North. Parlange told the police that "Jim" had stolen money from him and offered $100 for his capture. One abolitionist newspaper, reporting on the event, charged Parlange with "a ruse to engage the services of the Philadelphia police in the interesting game of nigger-hunting." But the game was over, as far as Connor was concerned. Two weeks later, Still's agent in Canada West (now Ontario) reported that Connor had taken "French leave from his French master" and had arrived safely "in the glorious land of Freedom." James Connor's escapade shows just how far a slave from Pointe Coupée had to go to make his way to freedom, and how much strength, guile, and help he needed to get there.[34]

A second story from the 1850s, this one drawn from Louisiana court records, shows that the specter of enslavement shadowed even free people of color in Pointe Coupée. Eulalie had been the slave of Simon Porche, a False River planter, who allowed her to marry his wife's half-brother, a free man of color named Henri Oliveau. For forty-five years, Eulalie Oliveau lived as a freewoman with her husband and their growing family in the isolated "island" of False River. Although neither Porche nor his widow ever formally emancipated her, numerous neighbors testified that she and her family had enjoyed their freedom as long as they had known them. Refuting allegations that the family had been "impudent and troublesome" to its neighbors, one witness swore that they never did anything wrong. The children behaved themselves and "were very polite towards white people." This humble demeanor, along with the protection of white kin and tolerant neighbors, was the recipe for getting along as free people of color in Pointe Coupée's creole plantation society.[35]

But late in 1852, Eulalie Oliveau—along with her seven children and ten grandchildren—were "forcibly taken" and sold into slavery. The trial testimony suggests a conspiracy to enslave them. A Mr. Genault (or Hino), who may have been the Widow Porche's heir, authorized their sale to an Albert G. Loftin, who in turn sold them to Daniel Long and Zachariah Mabry, who shipped them out of the parish on a steamboat. The captain of the boat testified that there had been nothing unusual about their embarkation. They boarded publicly in daylight, without violence or restraint, and their apparent owners treated them "as masters usually treat slaves, that is, humanely."[36] Another passenger on the boat agreed that their treatment was "humane," but also observed that she and her family "openly declared that they were free, and were determined to institute an action against [Long and Mabry] for their freedom."[37] The testimony in the case hints at the split between the creole and "Anglo" communities in Pointe Coupée. Although most of the witnesses who testified for the plaintiffs were, like them, long-standing French-speaking residents of the parish, those who testified for Long and Mabry were relative newcomers who spoke English.[38]

Though kidnapped and whisked away to the slave pens of New Orleans and Mobile, Eulalie Oliveau and her children managed to sue Long and Mabry to regain their freedom—a not-unheard-of gambit in Louisiana.[39] The case bounced around Louisiana's courts for three years until it was finally resolved in favor of the plaintiffs on the grounds of a rule known as "prescription." According to Article 3510 of Louisiana's Civil Code, any owner who allowed his slave to "enjoy his liberty" for ten years (or twenty, if the owner was absent from the state) lost his right to recover possession of the slave.[40] The benign neglect of her owners meant that Eulalie Oliveau and her family were free, and when that de facto freedom was snatched away by a gang of slavers, she and her children appealed to the state's judiciary system for protection. It took a while, but they got their freedom back. The outcome reveals that even slave societies have rules, codified in law and honored by custom. In Louisiana, one of these rules was that free people should not be enslaved. Nonetheless, as kidnapping victim Solomon Northup wrote in his 1853 memoir of captivity in Louisiana, "Hundreds of free citizens have been kidnapped and sold into slavery, and are at this moment wearing out their lives on plantations in Texas and Louisiana."[41]

It is not far-fetched to speculate that Rose may have known Eulalie Oliveau or heard of her kidnapping. The two women did not live that far from each other in Pointe Coupée in the early 1850s. Both ended up in New Orleans. Eulalie Oliveau's frightful story could well have been transmitted through the slave quarters' "grapevine telegraph," and if she heard it, Rose would not have forgotten its lessons when her own children were abducted a decade later. Freedom could be taken away, but it might be regained through the law.[42]

2

New Orleans

A PETITION THAT Rose Herera submitted to the government in March 1865 asserted that she "was brought to New Orleans some twelve years ago." The timing means that she arrived in the city in 1853, quite possibly the worst year in the history of New Orleans—even worse, in terms of human lives, than 2005, the year Hurricane Katrina wrecked the city. Yellow fever had claimed its first victims in late May, and by August, wrote one observer, "the whole city was a hospital." Before the first frost ended the epidemic in late October, one in every twelve New Orleanians—about ten thousand people—had died.[1] The story of how Rose Herera got to this place, and the life she lived there, reveals the power of slaveowners to disrupt and direct the settled lives of their human property, yet it also demonstrates the resilience of enslaved people in the face of wrenching changes. Saddled by debt, Octave Leblanc sold his plantation and moved to New Orleans, where he went into business with his son. The move thrust Rose (who had not yet acquired her future husband's last name) into one of America's great urban settings, a "global city" that served as the financial center of a dynamic slave-based economy, an anchor of the transatlantic cotton trade, and a way station for free and enslaved migrants. Like so many other enslaved people in New Orleans, Rose found herself bought and sold; these transactions can be precisely traced through the city's notarial records, a paper trail of tears. Yet even as the legal rights to Rose's labor and progeny passed from owner to owner, she forged a new life for herself off the books.

Slaves were people held as property by someone else. They lacked the crucial rights attached to self-possession, and their status as property was regulated by law. In most states, slaves were legally defined as movable property, but Louisiana law defined them as real estate or "immoveables," more like a house than a sack of corn. That classification had some legal consequences, such as a requirement that slave sales be notarized, but it made little difference to most slaves' daily lives. Slaves could not make civil contracts, enter into legal marriages, or own property of their own. Slaves had market value. They were bought and sold. They counted as wealth. They were mortgaged, seized to pay debts, and passed on to heirs. They were movable "immoveables." A slave's market value depended upon the perceived value of the slave's labor and progeny, which in turn depended on both the overall condition of the market and the individual appearance, demeanor, and reputation of the slave. Slave prices rose steadily from the early 1840s to the Civil War, but fluctuated seasonally and varied with age, sex, health, and skill. Slaves lived with a price on their heads.[2]

At the same time, slaves lived within an intricate web of other social relations. Slaves had to work long and hard; they were scarred by whips and shackles; they were vulnerable to sale and sudden moves that shredded their communities. Yet despite these hardships, they had families and friendships. Field slaves worked with one another in teams and gangs, supervised by drivers, overseers, and owners. Many slaves bartered and traded with neighbors and strangers. They worshipped together under the watchful eyes of masters and priests, and in secret congregations in the woods and swamps. They loved and fought, celebrated and mourned, conspired and betrayed, ran away and returned home. This web of relationships was spun over generations and anchored to local landscapes like the Leblanc plantation where Rose and her fellow slaves lived and died. Historians of slavery have traced many dimensions of the "slave community," especially work, family, and religion. They have identified the different shapes that slave communities took on plantations, small farms, and urban settings. But historians have only begun to rise to the challenge of reconstructing the social webs of particular slave communities and the lives of individuals within them.[3]

Rose Herera's life shows just how fragile these webs were and how easily they could be swept away. In 1853, when Rose was eighteen years old, Octave Leblanc got out of sugar. He and his son, Martin Octave Leblanc, who had inherited half the plantation after the death of Leblanc's wife, sold their plantation with thirty slaves to one Joseph Stinson for $57,000. Stinson paid $10,000 up front and pledged to pay the rest in five annual installments of $9,400, plus interest. Stinson mortgaged his newly purchased property and eight additional slaves to secure his obligation to the Leblancs. Mortgaging slaves was a common practice; in essence, slaves financed their own sales.[4] The Leblancs' sale was part of a realignment of sugar planting in the parish in the 1850s, as creoles on the "coast" sold out to Anglo newcomers. These transactions had consequences for the Leblanc slaves. Their community was divided. Although most remained on the plantation under their new owner, several others, including Rose, were taken to New Orleans by Octave and Martin. The bill of sale that indicates the names, ages, and values of the slaves sold to Stinson does not indicate their occupations, but it seems plausible (and later evidence will suggest) that the Leblancs sold the field workers and hung on to their "domestics" for city living. With the capital earned from the sale, Octave and Martin Leblanc went into business together as commission merchants in the city under the sign of O. Leblanc & Son at 14 Carondelet Street on the uptown side of Canal Street. Their arrival in the city was acknowledged by an agent for the credit reporting company of R. G. Dun in April 1856, who noted that the father and son were respectable "Creoles" and well-known gentlemen of good character and habits.[5]

New Orleans is only one hundred and fifty miles from Pointe Coupée, but the bustling, clamorous, and stinking city was a different world. There Rose would have found more than a hundred thousand people, most of them free, arrayed in close quarters along the Mississippi. Three in four were white. Many of the free people of color appeared to be white. Nearly half of the white inhabitants were foreign-born, as German, Irish, and French immigrants enriched the city's diversity. The city was growing and changing. It stretched up and down the river from the French Quarter into gridded suburbs (known as *faubourgs*, or "false cities," in New Orleans) carved from outlying plantations. Canal Street came to signify the permeable boundary between the old creole neighborhoods of the First and Third Municipalities (the French Quarter and Faubourg Marigny), and the new "American" ones of the Second Municipality (Faubourg St. Mary). Meanwhile settlement crept away from the river into the low and muddy "back o'town," assisted by the Pontchartrain Railroad and New Basin Canal, which connected the city with the lake to the north. "Like a body approaching adolescence," panted one newspaper editorial, New Orleans "is rapidly filling out in all directions into proportions of beauty and vigor, and we have now some little promise of the greatness which is to be."[6]

Cotton was king of the South, and New Orleans was its throne. Steamboats carried the cotton crop of the lower Mississippi valley down the river every fall and winter to the New Orleans levee, where the city's merchants orchestrated the work of unloading, warehousing, and shipping it off to New York and Liverpool. Propelled by the booming cotton trade, the value of the city's exports nearly doubled in the 1850s, reaching nearly $185 million by the end of the decade. Despite the city's success, some of the city's leading men saw worrisome trends. They resented New York's dominance over the cotton trade and fretted about New Orleans' imbalance between exports and imports. Although most New Orleans merchants believed that the Mississippi River gave their city a natural advantage in trade, some began to promote railroads to expand the city's hinterland into Texas and connect it with Pacific markets, and steamship lines to cut out the Northern middlemen who had captured the transatlantic shipping of cotton. And as the sectional crisis between North and South intensified, New Orleans became a locus of proslavery schemes for the annexation of Cuba and the reopening of the Atlantic slave trade. Little of this agenda was realized before the Civil War, but it advanced a vision of New Orleans as the capital of a modern, commercial society rooted in slavery.[7]

New Orleans was a slave city in flux. Although its fortunes rested on slavery in the hinterlands, and the city's slave markets thrived, the city itself was stealthily emptying of slaves. Thirteen thousand slaves—not a small number—lived in New Orleans on the eve of the Civil War, but their importance to life and labor within the city had been shrinking for decades. More than one in three city dwellers was a slave in 1820, but fewer than one in ten by 1860. In contrast to plantation districts where a majority of households included slaves, only one in every eight New Orleans households included slaves in 1860, and three-quarters of these had fewer than five slaves. New Orleans was not the only Southern city where slavery appeared to be on the decline. The proportion of slaves in the population of every major Southern city declined from 1840 to 1860; slavery almost completely disappeared from the border South cities of Baltimore and St. Louis. Nor was this pattern unique to the United States. After the closing of the slave trade to Brazil in 1850, for instance, cities in that country gradually emptied of slaves as well. Rose's move to New Orleans defied the usual trajectory of urban slaves being shipped out to rural planters who paid higher prices for them.[8]

The apparent erosion of slavery in cities such as New Orleans troubled slavery's defenders in the mid-nineteenth century and has puzzled historians ever since.[9] The pattern in New Orleans resulted from its proximity to a dynamic plantation economy and its function as a gateway for immigrants. Cotton and sugar planters siphoned slaves out of New Orleans while free people of color and poor Irish and German newcomers did much of the work the slaves used to do. The astute Northern journalist Frederick Law Olmsted noticed the trend. "It is obvious that free men have very much gained the field of labour in New Orleans to themselves," he observed in the mid-1850s. "The majority of cartmen, hackney-coach men, porters, railroad hands, public waiters, and common labourers, as well as of skilled mechanics, appear to be white men; and of the negroes employed in these avocations a considerable proportion are free."[10] Yet Olmsted overlooked one sector of the urban labor market in which slaves remained in high demand: domestic service. Perhaps he overlooked it because most domestic servants were women and thus not recognized as part of Olmsted's masculine "field of labor." One survey of estate inventories in New Orleans found that three-quarters of the slaves recorded in those documents were employed as domestic servants, and although men, women, and children all performed domestic service, women predominated. The centrality of women in domestic service explains why more than 60 percent of the adult slaves living in New Orleans in 1860 were women. It is not surprising, then, that Rose worked in the city as a "domestic servant."[11]

One myth of domestic or "house" slaves is that owners favored them over other slaves, and they were always faithful to their owners. Fidelity was occasionally a selling point in the city's slave markets. An 1856 newspaper ad touted a slave named Aimee as "a negro woman aged about 47 years, a good cook, washer and ironer, faithful servant."[12] Another described Mary Louise as "a dark griffe, creole, aged about 25 years, a cook, washer and ironer, and general house servant, faithful and trustworthy." (Mary Louise was accompanied by her eight-year-old and six-year-old sons, Onesime and Alexander.)[13] Then there was Ellen, "about 43 years old, an excellent cook, washer and ironer; has sometimes a slight rheumatism in her hip; a very good and faithful servant, and her children—Frances, about 22 years old, a No. 1 lady's maid, seamstress, hair dresser and washer and ironer. Fielding, about 16 years old, drives a buggy handy, and a good house boy and good with horses."[14] These are unusual. Surprisingly few ads explicitly proffered domestic slaves as faithful or loyal. Far more common was praise for their skill as workers, as in the phrases "good cook," "excellent cook," "No. 1 lady's maid," and "good with horses" from the ads just mentioned. This sort of language suggests that household labor should not be mistaken for unskilled work. Plenty of skill was involved in satisfying masters' and mistresses' particular tastes in food, hygiene, dress, and social etiquette, and hence sellers graded domestic slaves along a spectrum of skill and talent from "excellent" to "good" to merely "tolerable."[15]

Domestics were hardly immune to the traumas of slavery. Many were exposed to hard work, suffocating oversight, cruel treatment, rape, family separation, and sale. They lived and worked right under their masters' and mistresses' noses; some even slept at the foot of their owners' beds. The intimacy of urban dwellings provided less breathing room for slaves and allowed for more surveillance over them at home. They rose early and performed an exhausting routine of household chores until the day was done. These chores may not have been as physically demanding as cutting sugar cane, but they could be physically and mentally taxing. Domestic slaves performed a variety of jobs. Judging from the occupational categories invoked by newspaper advertisements of slave sales, men served primarily as valets, waiters, cooks, and carriage drivers. Women served primarily as maids, cooks, nurses, seamstresses, and hairdressers. Some could do it all: a "valuable woman" named Susan, advertised for sale in the *Daily Picayune* in March 1856 by the auctioneer Gardner Smith, was described as "mulatto, aged 18 years, seamstress, house servant, lady's maid and fair hair dresser; fully guaranteed and sold for no fault." ("Fully guaranteed and sold for no fault" was a standard formula in advertisements for slave sales. "Fully guaranteed" meant that the slave did not possess any of the bad qualities of body and character that legally had to be disclosed to purchasers. "No fault" meant that the slave was not being sold because of any defect or misbehavior.)[16]

Urban slavery seethed with violence and the threat of violence, not just in the streets and slave marts and jails, but in people's homes. Much of the day-to-day supervision of slaves' household labor fell to white and free colored women, who could be physically and psychologically abusive.[17] Marie Delphine Lalaurie, for example, was a rich and charming creole woman who lived in a grand house on Royal Street in the French Quarter with her third husband and ten slaves. She was widely suspected of abusing her slaves. A neighbor saw her chase a young girl up to the roof; the girl fell, or jumped, and died. Madame Lalaurie's slaves were once even removed by the city and sold for their protection, but she managed to get them back. In 1834, her cook, who was chained to the floor of the kitchen, set fire to the house in a desperate bid for rescue or vengeance. A crowd rushed to douse the fire and save the house. Neighbors inquired as to the whereabouts of the slaves, but Madame Lalaurie was evasive. After a frantic search through the smoke and flames, the samaritans discovered a horrific scene of abuse: seven Lalaurie slaves were found in their garrets starved, whipped, bloodied, and chained in agonizing poses held for so long that they had been crippled. Two skeletons were recovered from the premises. Later that evening, Lalaurie fled the city with the aid of her everfaithful slave coachman, and an outraged mob of citizens lashed out by ransacking the abandoned mansion. Still moved by pangs of conscience, the mob threatened to fan out through the city to investigate other suspected cases of the abuse of slaves, but city authorities were fearful of the prospect of a slave revolt and put a stop to any further vigilantism. They organized patrols to protect slaveowners from the mob's unwanted scrutiny.[18]

The radical English author Harriet Martineau learned about the Lalaurie scandal from acquaintances in New Orleans whom she visited in the 1830s. Not surprisingly, they asked her not to publish it as a "fair specimen" of slavery, and although the antislavery Martineau agreed that "no one could suppose it to be so," she insisted that the Lalaurie scandal was "a revelation of what may happen in a slave-holding country, and can happen nowhere else." She noted that although Madame Lalaurie was exceptionally fiendish, similar offenses could very well go on all the time as long as the perpetrators "manage to preserve that secrecy which was put an end to by accident in her case." Martineau offered several other examples of more routine cruelty toward slaves among her own acquaintances, including the story of one girl who was "so white, with blue eyes and light hair, that it never occurred to me that she could be a slave." But a slave she was. The girl's father had been sold apart from his family, while she, her mother, and three siblings had been purchased together. Her mother, "a good cook and house servant," was then sold because her owners worried she would kill her children in a fit of rage. Now the owners wanted to sell off the girl for being a "depraved hussey." In fact, the girl's gravest offense was insolence, not promiscuity. "When detected in some infamous practices," Martineau explained, "this young creature put on an air of prudery, and declared that it gave her great pain to be thought immodest: that so far from her being what she thought, she had no wish to have any other lover than her master." Her offended master punished the girl by strapping her to a post and flogging her.[19]

As Martineau understood, household slaves like Rose Herera lived in fear of the auction block. This was particularly true in New Orleans, the great slave market of the South. A brisk trade in household slaves thrived in New Orleans and other Southern towns and cities where slavery persisted. Whatever privileges domestic slaves enjoyed did not shield them from being bought and sold, although the rhetoric of paternalism cropped up in the slave market from time to time. Husbands and wives were rarely listed for sale together. Slave dealer Thomas Foster's 1856 advertisement for "A Valuable Family of Slaves" consisting of "A No. 1 Brick Mason, plasterer, and ornamental finisher, about 30 years old, with his wife, a plain cook, first rate washer and ironer and general house servant, about 20 years old, with her infant six months old; good subjects fully guaranteed" was the exception, not the rule.[20] Women were often listed for sale with their children, in accordance with Louisiana's civil law, which prohibited children under the age of ten from being sold apart from their mothers. Some ads offered children older than ten for sale with their mothers, whereas others presented young children to be sold by themselves as orphans. Whether they actually were orphans is another story. Some ads explained that the slaves were being sold because their owners were moving away; others indicated that the sale was the result of ordinary legal proceedings, such as judgment in a lawsuit or a succession, which implied that the slaves were not being sold for any fault of their own.[21]

The Swedish reformer Fredrika Bremer witnessed a slave auction in New Orleans when she visited in the winter of 1850–51. It turned out to be a dingy affair, held in the cold and dirty basement of a house. Twenty "gentlemenlike" men gathered around a platform, while the slaves stood to the side "silent and serious." An auctioneer entered the room, took his hammer in hand, and announced in an English accent that the slaves were "a few home-slaves, all the property of one master." He explained that the master had given bond for a friend who became bankrupt and was now obliged to sell the slaves to pay his debt: "They are all faithful and excellent servants, and nothing but hard necessity would have compelled their master to part with them." In one stroke, the auctioneer covered for the moral character of owner and slaves, and thus fetched a higher price. Bremer watched as an elegant mulatto woman holding a sleeping child was bid up to $700 and sold to one of the crowd. "Who he was; whether he was good or bad; whether he would lead her into tolerable or intolerable slavery—of all this, the bought and sold woman and mother knew as little as I did, neither to what part of the world he would take her. And the father of the child—where was he?" Bremer wondered. Her rhetorical question punctuated the unspoken absence of the child's father. Other questions follow. Who was he? What had happened to him? In Bremer's *Homes of the New World,* the slave auction in New Orleans stood out as a perversion of domesticity not just because families were sold, but because the families that were sold usually lacked husbands and fathers.[22]

People who could not afford to buy a slave could rent one. A secondary market in slave hiring diffused the benefits of slave labor to nonslaveowners who could pay the going monthly or yearly rate. "Wanted" notices in the city newspapers testified to the demand: "Wanted to hire—A Colored Woman to do the housework and, washing for a small family"; "Wanted—A good Cook; one that also understands washing and ironing. The highest wages will be paid"; "Wanted—A good House Servant and Child's Nurse. Those coming well recommended will hear of good situations by applying at this office."[23] One cannot assume the subscribers were looking to rent slaves; some would have been satisfied to hire free people of color, and ads explicitly seeking white servants were not unusual. More common, though, were wanted ads like the first one that stated a matter-of-fact preference for "colored" servants: "Wanted—A young and healthy colored woman to do the washing and ironing of a small family and to take care of children. None need apply that are not fully capable"; and "Wanted to hire—A colored girl to wash and iron and do general housework." Hirers' preference for "colored" servants as opposed to white or black implies that those who employed domestic servants did so for reasons of prestige as well as comfort. Thus Rose's description as a mulatto might have increased her value as a domestic servant.[24]

Joseph Copes, a doctor and businessman in New Orleans, catered to his clients' need for domestic servants by brokering sales and hiring out his own slaves. His correspondence is filled with requests for domestics, negotiations over the terms, and complaints about their behavior. One man who owed Copes money offered him a slave as compensation. "I have a valuable mulatto man aged about 24 years, which I could let you have if you desire—He is the same we had in N.O. He is an accomplished house servant or dining room Servt & a very good cook—I am not anxious to part with him, yet would let you have him, as I am anxious to pay you with as little delay as possible." A Mrs. Harris complained that she could not live with a servant named Chloe without punishing her: "For the last week she has been particularly negligent—it is now nearly dinner time and she has not been seen since twelve o'clock—of course her work remains undone." Another employer complained about a slave named Mary who had not been cured by a stint in jail: "She has behaved much worse than previously and it is absolutely impossible for us to get along with her—during the time she has been with us she has burnt in ironing and therefore destroyed more than a year's wages would pay for." A slave woman named Hester was "useless" because she did not want to be apart from her husband. "She complains & lays up so much that she costs us the price of two servants," her mistress fumed.[25] Complaints about Copes's slaves should not be seen merely as an illustration of the special difficulties of managing hired slaves; domestic slaves and their owners frequently clashed.

Even house slaves ran away. Susan, a forty-year-old woman who was "many years house servant and nurse to the late Wm. McCauley, Esq.," ran away in February 1852. The notice in the newspaper did not explain her motives or her timing. "Tall and good looking," the seamstress and house servant Mildred Ann Jackson ran away in early May 1854. "She is supposed to be harbored in the upper part of the First District," the ad ventured, adding that "she has been in the First District about six years and is well known." A house servant named Elizabeth, "of English rearing but speaking French," ran away later that year; her owner requested that she be delivered to the corner of History and Love streets. A "cook and washer" named Sarah ran away from her owner in the city's Fourth District in 1857; like Mildred Ann Jackson, "it is supposed that she is harbored."[26] "Well-known" and "harbored": common words and phrases in the runaway ads provide clues to domestic slaves' social world outside their masters' homes. Daily routines of work took domestic slaves like Rose Herera into the city streets and shops, gave them the chance to socialize with friends and family, mingle with other slaves and free people of color, gain exposure to the full diversity of the city, and find refuge in hideaways outside their masters' gaze. Their skills as laborers and their networks of kinship and community would aid them when the Union army arrived and broke their masters' power.

In the meantime, though, Rose Herera coped with the anguish of life as a commodity. In September 1857, Octave Leblanc sold her along with a one-year-old child, Rose's mother Leocadie, and five other slaves named Henry, Mary Louise, Lewis, Nancy, and Alexandre. They were sold together to Valerian Allain for $7,415.[27] The notarized acts of sale in which these and subsequent transactions were recorded present a biography of the slaves' commodity-lives, their individual histories of being owned, priced, sold, and mortgaged. To read these acts is to witness the liquidation of Leblanc's slaveholdings and the dispersal of his slave property to multiple owners through the local slave market. Such local sales are less famous than the interstate and transatlantic slave trades, but may have involved more transactions over time. Except for acknowledging Rose's child, the notarial record neglects to mention whatever family relationships these slaves might have had. It does not reveal that Leocadie was Rose's mother, nor does it identify the name of the father of Rose's child. He had no legal rights to the infant anyway.[28]

Rose later recalled that Leblanc sold her because he was "in debt."[29] Precisely why and to whom Leblanc owed money is unknown. R. G. Dun credit reports show O. Leblanc & Son as having "good" to "fair" credit until July 1858 when the business failed.[30] It is possible that the same debts that may have forced Leblanc to sell his plantation in Pointe Coupée finally caught up with him in New Orleans. It is also possible that the onset of the Panic of 1857 squeezed Leblanc to the point where he had to sell his slaves. It could be a mere coincidence that the sale followed on the heels of the failure of the Ohio Life Insurance and Trust Company in late summer that launched the panic. In any event, Leblanc's sale of his slaves to satisfy his creditors was hardly unusual. The lines of credit that connected Southern planters and merchants to their sources of money were tethered down by slaves—the original form of "human capital." If a slaveowner needed money, he could sell some of his slaves and blame the hard hand of "necessity." Slaves and their families suffered the consequences.[31]

Rose Herera's new owner was a commission merchant named Valerian Allain, Leblanc's cousin. His offices were located in the French Quarter at 18 Conti St, on the block between Chartres and Decatur. The following March, Allain put the lot up for sale again. An advertisement placed in the "Auction Sales" column of the classified section of the March 13, 1858 *Daily Picayune* presented them to the public. Rose appears to have had another child, for the ad described her as a "good washer and ironer, with her two children, age 3 and 18 months." She was to be sold with the same six men and women that Leblanc had sold to Allain, all described as "valuable house servants." The ad offers a good example of the rhetorical reduction of human beings for sale in the New Orleans slave market.[32]

Allain entrusted their sale to Alfred Bouligny, a professional auctioneer located at 86 Gravier Street (in today's Central Business District), who intended to auction them off in the grand rotunda of the St. Louis Hotel in the heart of the French Quarter. The rotunda was a "gloomy looking place" that for many Northern and foreign visitors symbolized the crass and brutal commercialism of the domestic slave trade in America. It was adorned with portraits of heroes of the American Revolution, which

> **Good House Servants for Sale.**
> BY ALFRED BOULIGNY, Auctioneer—Office, No. 28 Gravier street—Will be sold at auction on SATURDAY, the 20th inst., at 12 o'clock, at the St. Louis Exchange, the following valuable house servants, to-wit—
> LEOCADIE, aged about 40 years, good cook, washer and ironer.
> ROSE, aged about 20 years, good washer and ironer, with her two children, aged 3 and 18 months.
> HENRY, aged about 40, good cook.
> MARIE, aged about 20, good cook and house servant.
> LOUIS, aged about 12, good house servant.
> NANCY, aged 40, good cook, washer and ironer.
> ALEXANDER, aged 14, good house servant and ostler.
> Conditions—One-half cash; balance for notes with 8 per cent. interest, bearing mortgage on the slaves, endorsed to the satisfaction of the vendors.
> Acts of sale before Felix Grima, notary public.   mh7

Advertisement for the sale of Rose and other slaves previously owned by Octave Leblanc.
From the New Orleans Daily Picayune, *13 March 1858.*

sharpened the appearance of hypocrisy in the eyes of some critics. "The privilege of beholding their benevolent countenances," Matilda Houstoun sarcastically observed, "was, doubtless, duly valued by the slaves who had the *good fortune* to be sold in the Rotunda."[33]

Allain sold off four of the Leblanc slaves to different buyers in March 1858. He sold Lewis to George Washington Dunbar for $1,000 cash, Leocadie to a Mistress C. Jarreau also for $1,000 cash, Marie Louise to Hypolite Escousse for $1,375 cash, and Nancy to Julia Ann Yager for $750 cash. According to the notarial acts of sale, only Mary Louise was sold at a public auction; the others were sold in private sales. Allain sold Henry two months later to Alexandre Lecourt for $900. Then in October, Valerian Allain transferred Rose with her two children to his uncle, the West Baton Rouge planter Sosthene Allain, for $1,158. The notarial act indicated that Valerian had purchased Rose and her children from Leblanc "on behalf" of Sosthene. The dispersal of Leblanc's slave property that had begun five years earlier with the sale of the plantation in Pointe Coupée was now completed.[34]

New links were added to the chain of title for Rose in April 1860. Sosthene Allain sold Rose and her two children, Ernest and Marie, to one of the richest men in America, the New Orleans doctor William Newton Mercer. The doctor lived in a magnificent residence on Canal Street that later became the headquarters of the elite Boston Club. He owned several plantations in Mississippi and hundreds of slaves. Much of his fortune he donated to New Orleans charities. One nineteenth-century chronicler described him as "the model of the Southern gentleman, patriot, philanthropist and Christian."[35] Mercer purchased Rose and her children on behalf of a dentist named James Andrew De Hart, who lived around the corner from him. He may have brokered the sale as a favor because De Hart did not have the cash to pay for the slaves up front. Mercer paid Allain, and De Hart promised to pay Mercer back in two installments. De Hart took responsibility for the slaves, but if he defaulted on his debt to Mercer, the doctor would possess them. Mercer recorded the "understanding" hammered out between the two men in his diary and formalized it with a local notary. "Have agreed to advance De Hart $1000 for the purchase of a negress, to be repaid in six mths.," he scribbled on April 5, 1860. Then a follow-up on April 17: "Gave cheque of $1000 to F. Grima for the purchase of three slaves in my name to oblige De Hart who pays $500, & gives his notes for $500 in three months and ano N pay^{be} 1 Dec with 5% Int. The understanding is that upon punctual payment I renounce my title but in default on his part, that the property vests in me. He assumes moreover all responsibility in regard to the slaves. The act is lodged with Grima, Not. pub."[36] Mercer's terse entries never refer to Rose and her children by name, only as "a negress," "three slaves," "the property," and "the slaves." She was significant to him merely as a neighborly business deal and nothing more. De Hart lived up to his part of the bargain. He paid Mercer back, and on January 23, 1861, the doctor transferred Rose, her four-year-old son Ernest, and two-year-old daughter Marie to him. Three days later, Louisiana seceded from the Union.[37]

Rose was sold four times from September 1857 to January 1861. She passed from Leblanc to Valerian Allain, from Valerian Allain to Sosthene Allain, from Sosthene Allain to William Newton Mercer, and from William Newton Mercer to James Andrew De Hart. Neither the Allains nor Mercer were among the eighteen "Slave Dealers" listed in the city's business directory for 1861. Valerian and Sosthene Allain were more famous for their grand hospitality and "Parisian dinners" than for buying and selling slaves. Mercer was known as a doctor and philanthropist, not a slave trader. Nevertheless, buying and selling slaves was a routine part of their everyday business.[38] The city's recognized slave dealers captured the attention of critics of slavery and subsequent historians, but the transactions between family, friends, and neighbors that bypassed their services, like the sale of Rose and her children, were no less important to the everyday functioning of slavery as a commercial system.

The existence of a class of slave dealers who could be scapegoated for the commercial aspect of slavery deflected attention from the reality that people who were not slave dealers also dealt in slaves—not as their vocation, perhaps, but neither as a hobby nor an accident.³⁹

Rose had her own perception of the chain of title to her. Under cross-examination in court in 1865, Rose testified that "I was bought of Leblanc by De Hart. I did not belong to Allain. Allain sold me for Leblanc."⁴⁰ In her recollection, Leblanc sold her to De Hart. Allain acted as the broker, and Mercer was invisible. Rose's notarized commodity-life did not match her subjective experience of being sold, but the result was the same. She and her children found themselves owned by James Andrew De Hart. If there was any consolation for the trauma of being sold, it may have been that Rose was not sold out of the city. She stayed in the vicinity of her former owner. Her mother, Leocadie, was still nearby.⁴¹ Her social life in New Orleans remained intact despite the constant flux in her commodity-life, yet becoming the property of the De Harts would have profound and unexpected consequences.

James De Hart and his wife Mary were a microcosm of antebellum New Orleans. He was an immigrant; she was a creole. An 1876 passport application indicates that De Hart was born in Amsterdam on November 27, 1819. It describes him as 5′4″ with dark hair and hazel eyes. According to his obituary published in a local newspaper in 1890, De Hart migrated to the United States "when quite young" and somehow found his way to New Orleans, where he became a naturalized citizen on September 23, 1868. That timing is historically significant because the

BUSINESS

Slave Dealers.

Andrius Henry, 195 Gravier
Boazman J. W. 166 Gravier
Bruin Joseph, Esplanade c. Chartres
Campbell Walter L. 54 Baronne
Elam R. H. 58 Baronne
Foster Thomas, 76 and 78 Baronne
Hatcher Charles F. 195 Gravier
Johnston Theodore, 8 Moreau
Lilly A. 48 Baronne
Long R. W. 161 Gravier
Loftin E. 169 Gravier
Matthews Thos. E., Esplanade c. Chartres
Peterson H. F. 8 late 15 Perdido
Poindexter & Little, 48 Baronne
Rutherford C. M. 68 Baronne
Smith John B. 90 Baronne
Weisemann A. 177 Gravier
Wilson J. M., Gravier c. Baronne

Soap Manufactories.

Allerbush D., Liberty n. Josephine
Billaud Andrew, Elysian Fields n. Celestine
Ellebush J., Liberty n. Jackson
Fisk F. M., New Levee n. Notre Dame
Hare P., Second c. Liberty
Keller John H., St. Andrew c. Howard
Kirchberg C., Third n. Howard

New Orleans slave dealers.
From Gardner's New Orleans Directory for 1861 *(New Orleans: Charles Gardner, 1861), 489.*

question of De Hart's loyalty would arise during the legal battle over custody of the Herera children. More broadly, the loyalty of immigrants to their new country was one of the great political and cultural issues of the nineteenth century, and it took a distinctive shape in the antebellum South, where immigration was saddled with the all-important question of slavery.[42]

As an immigrant in antebellum New Orleans, De Hart was not alone. The city was full of them. "If there is ever to be a Congress of nations," wrote a tourist in 1851, "let it be held in New Orleans; there will be no mileage for delegates."[43] New Orleans trailed only New York (distantly, to be sure) as a port of entry for immigrants to the United States before the Civil War. More than half a million foreigners arrived in New Orleans between 1820 and 1860, roughly 10 percent of all foreigners who entered the United States through its seaports. The number of arrivals steadily increased from 12,000 in the 1820s, to more than 50,000 in the 1830s, to more than 160,000 in the 1840s, to almost 300,000 in the 1850s. Most of the immigrants arriving in New Orleans headed upriver to St. Louis and the upper Mississippi, but enough stayed in the city and survived its fevers to give New Orleans a heavy foreign presence. The 1860 census enumerated more than 64,000 free, foreign-born persons in New Orleans, making up almost 40 percent of the city's population. Not all foreigners in the city were immigrants. Some were temporarily there for business, others for pleasure. They filled the city's hotels and exchanges, taverns and brothels. The city's vaunted diversity was not merely a colonial hangover, but an effect of ongoing patterns of transatlantic circulation that brought new blood to New Orleans.[44]

Immigrants scattered across the city, with distinct enclaves forming in fuzzily defined neighborhoods. Germans gathered in "Little Saxony" below Esplanade Avenue and in the uptown suburb of Lafayette. Many Irish immigrants settled into a swath of the city upriver from the French Quarter close to the wharves and docks where they labored. Later dubbed the "Irish Channel," it was never exclusively Irish. A common language drew French immigrants into the First Municipality, the old heart of the city below Canal Street where the creoles (including refugees from St. Domingue and their descendants) still held sway. Even in the insular French Quarter, more than half of the free people were foreign-born. Spaniards and Italians mixed with new immigrants from France. De Hart settled down at the edge of the Second Municipality, near William Newton Mercer and Octave Leblanc. The neighborhood where they all lived was a meeting ground for creoles, Anglo-Americans, immigrants, and people of African descent.[45]

Many immigrants lived in New Orleans, but few of them were Dutch like De Hart. The common ethnonym "Dutch," an Americanization of the German word *Deutsch*, usually referred to the far more numerous Germans. An oft-quoted observer in 1843 lumped the "natives of Holland, Prussia, and all the German States" together as "Dutch" and added to the confusion by declaring that part of the French Quarter was "so thoroughly Dutch that the very pigs grunt in that language; you may well imagine yourself to be on the precincts of Amsterdam."[46] However, the Dutch did not emigrate to America in big numbers before the Civil War. Out of roughly 30,000 who did, only about one in twenty entered through New Orleans, and most of them headed up the Mississippi to the Midwest.[47] One Dutch immigrant who passed through the port on his way to St. Louis in 1846 caught a glimpse of its energy: "Everything seems to be but just begun, and one sees hundreds of houses rising up everywhere; all is bustle." He warned friends and family back home to be wary of the translators who buzzed around new arrivals—"some of them are grafters." Reflecting on the pressures of a new country on old habits, he cautioned that "not everyone must expect to be able to remain a Hollander if he comes to live in America."[48] That would have been especially true of De Hart. Without a sizable community of his own countrymen around him, De Hart must have felt pressure to assimilate to the city's local culture—but which one? New Orleans offered many cultures to choose from. One important step was his marriage in 1854 to Amelie Valcour, a creole woman who became known after her marriage as Mary De Hart. At the same time, he integrated into a community of medical professionals who were mostly Anglos and immigrants. Perhaps the cosmopolitan De Hart moved at will within New Orleans' "world in miniature."[49]

The earliest record placing James De Hart in New Orleans dates to November 1852, when a local newspaper printed a toothsome ad for his services.[50] De Hart and a partner offered their "professional services to the ladies and gentlemen of New Orleans and vicinity." They touted their office on Canal between Bourbon and Dauphin as "having all the late improvements," boasted that "their rooms and accomodations are surpassed by none," and promised a money-back guarantee of satisfaction.[51] Toward the end of the decade, De Hart teamed up with a new partner at 17 Baronne Street between Canal and Common to

> W. H. DAVIDSON, D. D. S, and DR.
> J. A. DE HART, Dentists—Tender their professional services to the ladies and gentlemen of New Orleans and vicinity, being permanently located, and having all the late improvements. Their rooms and accomodations are surpassed by none. Those favoring them with their patronage may rest assured that all operations will be satisfactory, or no pay. Office and residence, 120 Canal street, between Bourbon and Dauphin, two doors from Holmes's store.
> n20—6m

Advertisement for Davidson and De Hart, Dentists. *From the* New Orleans Daily Picayune, *23 November 1852.*

offer "cheap and durable SETS OF TEETH."[52] By then De Hart had established himself in Southern dentistry. He showed up at a state fair in Mississippi to show off his "amber" teeth, an invention one newspaper lauded as "a valuable acquisition to the dentist's profession."[53] Nevertheless, his credit rating was poor. "He is a man of not much popularity either as a dentist or a gentleman," reported R. G. Dun's agent in New Orleans in 1859, "his practice is small & his [credit] very small. He is already indebted to a good many other dental gentlemen & also the Dental Depot."[54]

The whole idea that dentists were professionals and gentlemen was quite new to the United States. The country's first school (Baltimore College of Dental Surgery), journal *(American Journal of Dental Science),* and association (Society of Surgeon Dentists of the City and State of New York) sprang up at the end of the 1830s on the Eastern Seaboard. These institutions campaigned to improve the quality and reputation of dentistry as a profession. Although New Orleans' dentists lagged behind their eastern counterparts, they organized themselves just before the Civil War, founding a dental school in the city in 1861 (De Hart was not on the faculty).⁵⁵ The city's dentists, including De Hart, congregated near the University of Louisiana at Common and Baronne streets in the Third Ward, a commercial neighborhood on the "American" side of Canal Street that was also home to several slave dealerships. An 1861 city directory listed forty-two dentists. They formed a professional community even as they vied against each other for clients. Most came from outside Louisiana: only four out of twenty-six whose nativities can be identified in the 1860 census had been born in the state. Sixteen had been born elsewhere in the United States, including seven from New York, and six more were immigrants. New Orleans imported its professional talent.⁵⁶

One of De Hart's neighboring dentists was a New Yorker named A. P. Dostie, who lived directly across Baronne Street from De Hart. Dostie arrived in New Orleans around the same time as De Hart in 1852 and became known as a "popular dentist, and a gentleman of refinement."⁵⁷ One of his patients, the young diarist Clara Solomon, attested to his effective bedside manner. "Dr. D. is so kind," she mused in July 1861. "He said my teeth were in a very bad condition—I appreciate highly his kindness—I asked him to call. He said he would if I promised not to talk politics." It's no wonder Dostie didn't want to talk politics. A staunch and outspoken unionist, he had already lost many friends during the secession crisis, and less than a month later, he would flee New Orleans after refusing to take an oath of allegiance to the Confederacy. For proslavery ideologues,

Dostie epitomized the South's city problem. Alien and potentially hostile to slavery, the urban working and professional classes were sometimes regarded with suspicion and even contempt by many Southern-born white people. Nevertheless, Solomon liked and heeded Dostie. "I have vowed faithfully to perform my duty to my teeth. God aid me in it."[58]

Slaves trained in dentistry were not unheard of in the United States. Roderick Badger learned the art from his owner, who was also his father, and then hired his own time as a dentist in Atlanta before the Civil War. The town's white dentists felt "aggrieved" by his presence but he soldered on, eventually becoming a leader of Atlanta's small cadre of black professionals in the era of the New South.[59] Even more remarkable was Sam Nixon, the slave of a prominent dentist in Norfolk who taught him "dentistry in all its branches" and trusted him to tend to patients. Nixon learned to read and write, and moonlighted as an agent of the Underground Railroad in Norfolk. In 1855, he escaped by schooner to New Jersey, leaving his wife and daughter—also slaves—behind. He boasted to a skeptical Quaker activist who harbored him that "nobody can make a better set of teeth" than he could. Nixon made his way to Philadelphia to rendezvous with William Still, who sent him on to New Bedford (the same Massachusetts town where Frederick Douglass had found refuge after his escape from slavery). There Nixon adopted the new name of Thomas Bayne and hung out his own shingle. As his dental practice flourished, Bayne became a respected member of the town's sizable black community and a dedicated abolitionist. He returned to Norfolk after the Civil War and plunged into Reconstruction politics. An outspoken delegate to Virginia's constitutional convention in 1867–68, he supported equal suffrage and integrated schools.[60]

No slaves became famous for dentistry in New Orleans, but the city did have one free black dentist, Thomas Jinnings Jr. He was listed in an 1861 city directory as the proprietor of the New Orleans Dental Depot ("dealer in Mineral Teeth, Gold Foil, Plate and Dental Materials") at 53 St. Charles St., just a couple of blocks from De Hart. The directory was polite enough not to mention his race, but the 1860 census recorded his color as M for mulatto, noting as well that he was a New Yorker and possessed a personal estate worth a hefty $5,000. He appears to have been the son of Thomas Jennings, one of New York's more illustrious African-American businessmen and civil rights activists, who is credited with receiving the first patent earned by a black person in the United States.[61]

Being purchased by De Hart did not put Rose on the path to dental school. A "good washer and ironer," she was destined by gender conventions for domestic chores. De Hart's motives probably resembled his fellow dentist James Knapp's, who professed an interest in hiring "a good Servant Woman" from Joseph Copes "to care for my house in the city, cook for me, & do washing for me & my office &c."[62] For many of the city's professional men, acquiring a domestic slave or two was more than a convenience. The transaction boosted their prestige by elevating them into the ranks of masters, with all that position entailed for their families. As New Orleans' proslavery propagandist J. D. B. DeBow argued, "The non-slaveholder knows that as soon as his savings will admit, he can become a slaveholder, and thus relieve his wife from the necessities of the kitchen and the laundry, and his children from the labors of the field." DeBow contended that nonslaveowning men desired slaves for the sake of their own wives and children, thus shoring up their own standing as benevolent patriarchs. Wives, in turn, pressured their husbands for "help" and then assumed primary responsibility for managing their domestics' daily regimen. In the absence of direct evidence of his motives, one may reasonably guess that De Hart bought Rose and her children as a maid for his wife Mary and a nanny to their ten-year-old son, Edward. Rose herself testified that she worked "as a domestic servant" in the De Hart household. Her children were still too young to be of any immediate use to De Hart, so he probably calculated that they would profit him as they grew up. If a purchaser bought a woman, DeBow noted, "her children become heir-looms and make the nucleus of an estate."[63]

Rose might have had reason to be worried about being sold to James De Hart. In August 1858, the dentist was required "to answer to a charge of having beaten and seriously injured a slave woman belonging to Mrs. A. G. Blanchard." Mrs. A. G. Blanchard was probably the wife of Albert G. Blanchard, secretary of the New Orleans & Carrolton Railroad Company, whose office was located on the same block as De Hart's.[64] Two weeks later, witnesses testified that the dentist had caned the woman because she was "extremely saucy," which presumably excused the violence in the eyes of the community, if not the law.[65] A frequent complaint against slaves, sauciness or insolence was an offense of speech and demeanor, like a rude gesture or insult. Almost anything had the potential to offend. Frederick

Douglass captured the ominous indeterminacy of insolence, which could be discerned "in the tone of an answer, in answering at all; in not answering."⁶⁶ The slave woman offended De Hart in some way or another, and rather than seeking redress from the woman's owner or nearby authorities, he asserted the power to punish her himself—not simply to punish her but by caning, to demean her. If he had owned her, this power would not have been disputed, but because she was another person's property, he had to answer for the damage in court.⁶⁷ The question for Rose and her children was whether he would abuse his own slaves.

The bills of sale that attested to Rose's growing family gave no account of her children's paternity. She had one child when Octave Leblanc sold her to Valerian Allain in 1857. The following year, when Valerian Allain sold her to Sosthene Allain, she had two small children. By the time De Hart acquired them in 1861, Rose's son Ernest was four years old, and her daughter Marie was two. Louisiana law prohibited a mother from being sold apart from her children until they were ten years old, so for now they conveyed with her. Soon after her sale to De Hart, Rose gave birth to a girl named Josephine, who also became his property.⁶⁸ The children just magically appear in the notarial acts as if by spontaneous generation, a cousin to the fiction of "natural increase." Their father is conspicuously absent in the records that document their lives as commodities. Yet other sources reveal his identity, so it is not necessary to guess who he was. His name was George Herera, and he was a free man of color.⁶⁹

George Herera appears in the historical record with various spellings of his name, including "Herrera," "Elyra," and "Elera."

The 1860 census lists him as "Airera." According to that census, he was twenty-three years old and black. He was living in New Orleans' Fifth Ward (which includes part of the French Quarter and Tremé) in a household that included an older black man identified as John Arear who was probably his father. The two men were both identified as natives of the city and as painters.[70] The census data is corroborated by a city directory published in 1861 that listed a "Herrera J. f.m.c. painter" at 208 St. Philip Street.[71] As one of the city's newspapers grudgingly recognized in 1859, free people of color "form the great majority of our regular settled masons, brick layers, builders, carpenters, tailors, shoe makers etc."[72] Much of the beauty in the houses of New Orleans is the handiwork of tradesmen such as George Herera, who passed their artisanal skills down to their sons for generations.[73]

The story of how Rose met George Herera, their courtship and romance (if there was any), and what their life as a couple was like is unrecorded. They might have jostled past each other on the street, drank and danced together in a bar, or prayed next to each other in church. They might have seen each other every day or every now and then. They lived in different houses about ten blocks apart—she with her owners, he with his father. Despite the circumstances, Rose and George Herera had five children together between 1857 and 1864. According to Rose, they were married by Father Coste at the Cathedral in New Orleans after the birth of their second child, sometime in 1859 or 1860, but church records do not confirm her assertion. No marriages involving slaves were recorded at all.[74] It must have been galling to George Herera that his marriage was not legal and that De

Hart owned his wife and children. Though he was free, he was still held down by slavery.

Free people of color such as George Herera were of great significance to the history of New Orleans. Their roots reached back to the previous century, when their ancestors in French and Spanish Louisiana gained their freedom through military service, self-purchase, or the largesse of a white patron or father. George Herera's last name suggests that his family had a Spanish lineage; the largest growth in the free colored population took place in the era of Spanish rule. Free people of color often had white ancestry, which is why so many were described as mulatto. Some appeared to be white yet identified with people of color, and more than a few "passed" into whiteness. A few were wealthy. Many owned slaves themselves. They were well educated and cosmopolitan. Their numbers included inventors, artists, poets, and musicians, as well as tradesmen like George Herera. They preferred to speak French. The elite intermarried among themselves, formed influential clans, and developed a sense of community. They were mainstays of the Catholic Church, but they also built independent and secular mutual aid, self-help, and cultural institutions to elevate themselves. They were proud and resentful of the stamp of inferiority placed upon them by law and custom, but did not loudly agitate for change until the Civil War changed the whole calculus of politics. They had too much property and status to lose by incurring popular wrath. Yet their standing in New Orleans had been slowly eroding over the half century since the Louisiana Purchase in 1803, and by the end of the 1850s, it threatened to dissolve completely under the pressure of what their earliest historian called a "new despotism."[75]

The city's free colored population grew much more slowly than its white population during the great slave boom of the nineteenth century. After an influx from St. Domingue and Cuba in the first decade of the century, immigration of free people of color slowed to a trickle. New laws staunched manumission, and some free people of color left. They had composed nearly 20 percent of the city's population in the early 1800s, but only 6 percent in 1860.[76] Weakened by this relative decline, the city's eleven thousand free people of color (along with another eight thousand or so in the rest of Louisiana) found themselves buffeted by stiffening political winds. Free people of color were anathema to proslavery dogma, which held that all people of African descent should be slaves, all free people should be white, and all white people should be free. Putting this dogma into practice was part of the proslavery agenda before the Civil War, along with such causes as annexing Cuba and reopening slave importation. As they imagined a tropical empire for American slavery, proslavery demagogues tried to tighten the screws on free people of color at home, clamping down on their legal rights and customary privileges, and pushing them into enslavement or exile.[77]

"A plague and a pest in the community," "elements of mischief to the slave population," "a worthless population"—these were some of the insults hurled against free people of color as the assault intensified in the mid-1850s.[78] Throughout the decade came new laws from Louisiana's legislature regulating the movements of free people of color on vessels and steamboats, beefing up the policing of fugitives, requiring that newly freed people emigrate to Liberia unless provided with a special exemption from the state, and restricting their freedom of speech and worship. In 1858 New Orleans authorities shuttered the city's African Methodist Episcopal Church under a new ordinance that subjected free people of color to the "discipline and management" of white religious authority. The AME sued, but the Louisiana Supreme Court upheld the ordinance on the grounds that the "African race are strangers to our Constitution, and are the subjects of special and exceptional legislation."[79] Then came the sham kindness of 1859's Act to Permit Free Persons of African Descent to Select Their Masters and Become Slaves for Life, which allowed free people of color to *voluntarily* opt into slavery under a master of their own choosing. The historian Judith Kelleher Schafer has found seventeen cases of free people of color in New Orleans availing themselves of the law, mostly, it appears, to avoid being deported.[80] Proslavery advocates milked cases of self-enslavement for propaganda, but nobody could fail to notice that most free people of color preferred to be free, or that the gate only swung one way. Free people could now choose to be slaves, but slaves could not choose to be free.

As in Pointe Coupée, the city's most vulnerable free people of color faced a real danger of being enslaved. Unlike mulattoes, those with darker complexions faced greater danger because people classified as "Negroes" were presumed by law to be slaves unless they could prove otherwise. Black people in New Orleans were regularly thrown in jail as suspected runaways, vagrants, and criminals and required to prove their freedom or be sold.[81] A victim of mistaken identity, Constance Bique Perrine sued the city jailer in 1858 for whipping her "as a slave." She had been arrested for public drunkenness and disturbing the peace, but the jailer confused her with a runaway slave whose master had authorized a whipping. Perrine was tied down, stripped naked, and whipped "ten lashes with a heavy whip." Soon after, she suffered a miscarriage.[82] Early the following year, two free women of color, Euphémie and Andrinette, charged that they were victims of a conspiracy by Juliette Maran and Jordan Noble (also free people of color) to enslave them and their children. The children had been taken by "force and violence," penned in J. A. Beard's "negro trader yard," and advertised for sale. Naturally the defendants told a different story, contending that the plaintiffs had been the lawful property of Juliette Maran's dead brother. Slavery was already toppled by the time the state Supreme Court ruled in Euphémie and Andrinette's favor in 1865.[83] Cases such as these, as well as that of Eulalie and her children described in Chapter 1, reveal the slipperiness of the slope from freedom to slavery, but they also indicate that the courts did hear petitions and suits for freedom from people held as slaves. On rare occasions, the law came to their rescue.

The marriage of George and Rose Herera points to intimate ties of family and community among free and enslaved people of color. George Herera was free, but his wife and children were slaves. Families like the Hereras who straddled the line between slavery and freedom have been lost to the myths of "plaçage" (black women monopolized by white men) and caste (exclusive intermarriage among free people of color). There was not much George Herera could do to free his family. He might try to buy them himself, but that would cost more money than he could dream of making as a painter. He might appeal to their owner to free them, but even if De Hart had been willing (an unlikely prospect since he had just bought them), the law put up daunting roadblocks. He might try to take them away, but the penalty for stealing slaves was harsh and a safe destination was out of reach. Some free people of color thought about emigrating en masse to Mexico and Haiti in the late 1850s. Too expensive and filled with uncertainty, these projects fizzled out. A boatload of New Orleanians, liberated by the controversial will of the late philanthropist John McDonough, sailed to Liberia in 1859 on the *Rebecca;* the ship delivered a cargo of Congo slaves to Cuba on the voyage back.[84] Prudently, George Herera stayed in the city and eked out a living as a painter while Rose and their children lived under her master's roof on the other side of Canal Street. Neither the Hereras nor the De Harts could have foreseen that their world was about to change.

3

War

TOURING THE United States for the London *Times,* war correspondent William Howard Russell reached New Orleans late in May 1861, where he discovered a city all ablaze. Confederate flags flew from the public buildings and private homes. Uniformed soldiers paraded through the streets in smart columns of dash and pomp. Gentlemen at the St. Charles Hotel pored over the latest papers for news of the dawning war. The police were rounding up suspected abolitionists, and every night mysterious fires flared up around the city—set, it was rumored, by the slaves. After hobnobbing with politicians, planters, and merchants in New Orleans, Russell observed that the Confederate elite "believe themselves, in fact, to be masters of the destiny of the world."[1] They would soon discover that they were not even masters of their own homes. Secession was followed by war, and the war reached the New Orleans levee in the spring of 1862 in the form of Union gunships. The Federals came to restore Louisiana to the Union, not to liberate the slaves, but slavery began to fray anyway from what Abraham Lincoln called the "friction and abrasion" of war. New Orleans and its environs became an arena of chaotic struggle between slaves, masters, and Union authorities. It was in the heat of this moment that the De Harts fled to Cuba with three of Rose Herera's children. Piecing together the puzzle of why and how they did so reveals the intimate battles that took place inside slaveholding households, the shifting balance of power in the city, and the lengths that masters would go to keep hold of their precious chattels.[2]

New Orleanians fought bitterly over secession. Voters in the city overwhelmingly preferred the unionist candidates John Bell and Stephen Douglas to the Southern-rights Democrat John Breckenridge in the election in 1860, but the hope of reconciliation with the North faded after Lincoln won the presidency without a single electoral vote from a slave state.[3] Most white Southerners viewed the Republicans as a purely Northern antislavery party, and they regarded Lincoln's election as an existential threat to slavery. Secessionists rallied for immediate separation whereas more cautious men like William Newton Mercer stalled for time. Mercer, who owned Rose and her children during the critical months before secession, was no mere bystander in the crisis. He had been a firm Whig and staunch unionist in the 1850s, but Lincoln's election in 1860 pushed him to the edge. "However dreadful the alternative, I agree cordially with those who insist that we must maintain our rights as best we can, if not in the Union, then out of the Union," he wrote to a business associate in New York in late November 1860; "In the North it is a question of abstract philanthropy, or at most of political power, with its advantages. With us, of life and death." Mercer assured his northern friend that his conversion to a hesitant secessionism was painful: "You know my temperate & conservative sentiments, how ardently I love our glorious country, & what anguish I must feel to speak as I have done."[4] Mercer opposed the Southern hotspurs who agitated for immediate secession. He preferred a "more temperate and deliberate course," but by early December feared that the "extremists" would succeed. Time for "conciliation" was running out.[5]

After the proponents of immediate secession narrowly won a majority of the vote for delegates to a special state convention in early January, Mercer still refused to submit to "the gross infraction of our rights, perpetrated & menaced by the Republican party," but he regretted "the boast & bluster and threats in which we indulged, that not only increased the violence of the Republicans, but have estranged from us, honest & intelligent men, friends of justice & the Union, & therefore friends of the rights of the South."[6] Mercer was both relieved and fearful when the convention voted for secession at the end of January and Louisiana left the Union. "We have at least one advantage now—our suspense is over, and we know where we are now: But God only knows where we shall be a year hence; or what will have become of our Country. My heart bleeds at the prospect."[7] By the middle of 1861, a desperate Mercer could not believe that the North would try to force the South back into the Union. "To subjugate a brave & high spirited people, scattered over a large extent of country, favored by climate, and contending for all that is dearest, never had been & never can be accomplished," he warned his Northern associate, "but if we were subdued, the country itself deprived of its peasantry, and desolated by war, would be a vast desert."[8] Mercer's letters display the political impotence of the South's conservative unionist elite on the eve of the Civil War. Despite great wealth and prestige, he could not slow down his state's secession or stave off a ruinous war.[9]

Mercer was drowned out by New Orleans' powerful secessionist voices. Most influential was Benjamin Morgan Palmer, leader of the city's First Presbyterian Church. Palmer's Thanksgiving Day sermon on November 29, 1860, electrified the whole secessionist movement. Southerners, he told his congregation, had a God-given duty *"to ourselves, to our slaves, to the world, and to almighty God . . . to preserve and transmit our existing system of domestic servitude with the right, unchanged by man, to go and root itself wherever Providence and nature may carry it."* The secessionist press circulated thousands of copies of Bishop Palmer's call for Southerners to "take all the necessary steps looking to separate and independent existence, and initiate measures for framing a new and homogeneous confederacy."[10] In January, voters statewide narrowly elected a secessionist majority to Louisiana's convention to decide whether to stay or to go. New Orleans jumped on the bandwagon: twenty of Orleans Parish's twenty-five delegates supported secession. Rose Herera's former owner Octave Leblanc was elected as a delegate for Orleans Parish on the "cooperationist" ticket, which preferred that Louisiana coordinate with other Southern states instead of seceding on its own. One of the also-rans was Thomas Jefferson Durant, also a cooperationist, who will soon appear as a major figure in Rose Herera's story. Secessionists controlled the convention, overriding calls for coordination with other Southern states and a popular referendum. With South Carolina and four other cotton states already gone, the Louisianians did not want to appear laggard.

On January 26, 1861, the convention's delegates hustled Louisiana out of the Union by an overwhelming 113–17 vote. "Troublous times of tempest, and political storms," mused a New Orleans architect.[11]

Louisiana seceded to protect slavery. That is what Mercer wrote to Northern business associates. That is what Bishop Palmer told his congregants. That is what the delegates to the convention declared in no uncertain terms. One delegate's preamble to a proposed resolution of secession warned that Lincoln "will keep the promises he has made to the Abolitionists of the North" and if kept, "will inevitably lead to the emancipation and misfortune of the slaves of the South, their equality, with a superior race, ere long, to the irreparable ruin of this mighty Republic, the degradation of the American name, and corruption of the American blood." The preamble to a unionist proposal calling for a convention of slaveholding states "to finally settle and adjust all questions relating to the subject of slavery" conceded little. Its bill of charges drew attention to the clamor of antislavery opinion in the North, John Brown's raid on Harpers Ferry, the "Black" Republicans' efforts to stop the expansion of slavery, and the obstruction of the Fugitive Slave Law, concluding that "the rights of the South have been invaded, their opinions outraged, and our institutions imperilled by the triumph and attitude of a sectional party." Still another version alleged that "a sectional party known as the Black Republicans, has recently elected Abraham Lincoln and Hannibal Hamlin to the Presidency and Vice Presidency of the United States, upon the avowed principles that the Constitution of the United States does not recognize property in slaves, that the Government should prevent the extension of slavery in to the common territory, and that all the powers of the Government should be so exercised as in time to abolish this institution wherever it exists."[12] The delegates agreed that Lincoln's victory posed a mortal threat to slavery. The question was whether by inviting war, secession would wreck the very thing it was supposed to save. Most did not foresee that outcome, but a New Orleans schoolteacher whose family had fled a slave insurrection on the Caribbean island of St. Croix saw the coming disaster. She confessed her fears to her journal in December 1860: "If the South goes to war for slavery, slavery is doomed in this country. To say so is like opposing one drop to a roaring torrent."[13]

The roaring torrent swept many New Orleanians off to war. "The streets are full of Turcos, Zouaves, Chasseurs," observed Russell, comparing soldiers in New Orleans to multinational units of the French army. "The walls are covered with placards of volunteer companies; there are Pickwick rifles, La Fayette, Beauregard, MacMahon guards, Irish, German, Italian and Spanish and native volunteers." The city's tailors and seamstresses were too busy sewing uniforms and flags for the volunteers to make him a shirt.[14] Hundreds of New Orleans men rushed off to Virginia, where they gained a name for themselves as notorious brawlers and fierce soldiers. Many had martial experience as filibusters, men who participated in private, illegal military expeditions to Cuba and Nicaragua in the 1850s, and they were itching for new battles.[15] The spectacle of "600 Louisiana Zouaves" marching through Petersburg, Virginia, astounded one witness in June 1861. They seemed like a different race of people altogether. Two months' training in Pensacola had turned the men "browner than I ever saw a white man." Their colorful Zouave uniforms, dark complexions, and rough demeanors created an outlandish appearance. The soldiers "were the most savage-looking crowd I ever saw."[16] Though part of the Confederacy, Louisiana still seemed exotic to other Southerners.

The city's ethnonational diversity complicated wartime allegiances. Although ethnic regiments like the Irish Tigers proudly announced their fusion of Old World nationalities and new Confederate allegiance, some immigrants—especially German New Orleanians—grudgingly joined under fierce social and political pressure to adhere to the Confederacy. Their loyalty to the Confederacy collapsed on the first appearance of Union gunships, and they became the bedrock of the white unionist community in the city. Other foreign men walked the tightrope of neutrality. They mustered into a European Guard, composed mostly of British and French citizens, with the sole purpose of protecting life and property in their city of residence. A few men, like the Northern-born dentist A. P. Dostie, refused to swear allegiance to the Confederacy and fled the city altogether. (Another dentist, a Dr. Metcalf, was arrested for saying "Lincoln is a second Jackson, and that, were he in Lincoln's place, he would lay Charleston in ashes, and have the levees cut in this state.") Despite white Louisianians' concerns about the loyalty of free people of color, a regiment of free men of color joined the Louisiana militia as the Native Guards. They were treated poorly by Confederate authorities and would switch sides when the Federals arrived. Unlike many of New Orleans' free men of color, George Herera did not serve as a soldier in the Civil War.[17]

Like many immigrants in the South, in contrast, James De Hart went into the Confederate service. He was not among the first wave of enthusiastic volunteers. His responsibilities to support his family and slaves may have loomed large in his decision not to rush into service. Perhaps his wife and son could not afford to lose him. But De Hart eventually signed up. He became a captain of the Carondelet Light Infantry in the Beauregard Regiment of the Louisiana militia's Second Brigade. The company was formed late in 1861 and was made up of men from De Hart's immediate neighborhood. In late September 1861 many of the home guards were incorporated into the Louisiana state militia, and then early in 1862, Louisiana's Governor Moore transferred them into the Confederate service under General Mansfield Lovell, who was responsible for the defense of New Orleans. De Hart's company was stationed at Camp Chalmette below New Orleans when the Federals took the city and disbanded shortly after. De Hart never saw combat.[18]

"If affairs continue as they are much longer," salesman Natty Palmer wrote to his father from New Orleans in late April, "there will be no men in the country to attend to domestic affairs for all are joining volunteer Companys, & offering their services to Pres Davis." Despite their bravado concerning the loyalty of their slaves, local authorities fully understood that the absence of so many able-bodied white men from their households demanded additional public measures to preserve order in a city full of slaves and free people of color. In previous crises, including the British invasion of 1814 and the 1853 yellow fever epidemic, local authorities had ratcheted up their vigilance over the black population.[19] Now men who stayed in the city mustered into "home guards" to defend against Northern invaders and internal unrest. "Soon the City will be under a military controll (I understand today) to look out for dangerous persons & the Negroes," predicted Natty.[20] Another diarist heard a "rumor of rising of negroes precaution taken," and early May brought "continued arrests for abolitionism."[21] False rumors of a slave insurrection caused a "great commotion" on the Fourth of July, reported Clara Solomon in her diary.[22] After a suspicious fire at a drugstore on Tchoupitoulas Street in late July, thought to be the work of a "fiendish incendiary," the *Daily Picayune* urged police to keep a strict watch. "In these war times, the safety of the city demands the utmost vigilance."[23] The next day, the newspaper reported the arrest of one Stephen A. Marshall on charges of "using incendiary language and being an open enemy to the Southern Confederacy."[24] White southerners were not just being hyperbolic when they attacked abolitionists as "incendiary." They thought that abolitionists were quite literally setting fire to the South.[25]

The first year of the war was particularly rough on black people in New Orleans. The black dentist Thomas Jinnings and his wife were arrested for attending a charity fair for the Children's Home of the Protestant Episcopal Church in late May 1861. He was accused of "having intruded himself among the white congregation . . . and conducting himself in a manner unbecoming the free colored people of this city, and in a manner to create insubordination among the servile population of this State."[26] All the way at the other end of the spectrum of black society, an Afro-British sailor on his way from Mobile to Halifax appealed to the British consul for aid a few days later. Russell noted that the poor fellow "was in much terror lest police shd. arrest him if found in City." Terror was the correct word. A black sailor made an easy target for police on the lookout for suspicious strangers. "It is too bad," Russell judged, "This state of things ought not to be tolerated at all."[27] Having a wife and children with no prospect of freedom in an independent Confederacy, George Herera probably hoped the Federals offered something better than a reign of terror.

Rose Herera, too, must have been aware of her owner's activities and the prospect of war. She did not need her husband to keep her in the loop. Slaves were neither blind nor deaf to the tumult in the city. They watched the parades and presentations of flags. They read the newspapers or gleaned the information secondhand. They saw the young men march off to wage a distant war to keep them from tasting freedom. The perceptive Russell was not convinced by his hosts' insistence that the slaves were happy. He thought many appeared "morose, ill-clad, and discontented" and noted that the patrols had been strengthened.[28] Dora Richards's house crackled with conversations about politics stoked by the latest rumors to appear in the newspapers. She marveled at how "the black servants move about quietly never seeming to notice that this is all about them" and asked, "How can you speak so plainly before them?" She received a brutally honest answer: "Why, what matter? They know that we shall keep the whip-handle."[29] But if slaves understood that lesson, they also learned more than their masters wanted to convey.

All their masters' loose talk about the Black Republicans and abolitionism created an expectation among slaves that the coming of the Federal troops would break their chains. Small wonder, then, that slaves working on the levees along the Mississippi saluted the Union gunboats steaming upriver to New Orleans in late April 1862.[30] "Thousands of negroes welcome us with various demonstrations of pleasure," noted Rufus Kinsley of the 8th Vermont in his diary as he came up the Mississippi.[31] John De Forest of the 12th Connecticut wrote that the black people along the river "gathered to stare at us, and when there were no whites near, they gave enthusiastic evidence of good will, dancing at us, waving hats or branches and shouting welcome." He was close enough to shore to hear an old woman's joyful outburst: "Bress de Lawd! I knows dat ar flag. I knew it would come. Praise de Lawd!" De Forest viewed the scene as funny and accentuated its comedy by transcribing the woman's words in a demeaning way. After several weeks among New Orleans' resentful white Confederates, he would come to appreciate the black inhabitants' unionism: "As to the Negroes, they are all on our side."[32] The real question was whether the Union was on the Negroes' side.

On April 24, 1862, a fleet of Federal warships commanded by Admiral David G. Farragut battled past the forts guarding the river below New Orleans. The city's lackluster defenses were no match for Farragut's mortars. The garrison at Fort Jackson mutinied, and Confederate troops abandoned the city. The mayor quickly surrendered. While Farragut's fleet continued up the river to seize Baton Rouge and Natchez, General Benjamin Butler took control of New Orleans with fifteen thousand soldiers, declaring martial law on May 1. The Union would retain—or "occupy"—the city for the duration of the war.[33] As the historian Michael Pierson points out, when historians choose to describe the era of Union military government in New

Orleans as an occupation, we are using a loaded word. The word "occupy" implies that the Union was a foreign power ruling a hostile population, which reflects a Confederate point of view. Rather than say that Admiral Farragut captured New Orleans, one might say that he recovered it. Rather than say that General Butler occupied New Orleans, one might simply say that he governed it. The dilemmas of language are compounded by the fact that what felt like an occupation to some people was closer to a liberation for others.[34] Even "liberation" is not a perfect word to describe the gnarled process of emancipation that took place in New Orleans during the Civil War. Contrary to the slaves' own hopes, freedom did not arrive with Admiral Farragut's warships in May 1862. The Union was not yet committed to a policy of wholesale emancipation at that juncture in the war. Strong political headwinds—the demands of the Union slave states, opposition from Northern Democrats, constraints imposed by the Constitution—slowed antislavery Republicans and frustrated Northern abolitionists. Progress toward emancipation was ad hoc and incremental, and it was pushed forward by slaves and free people of color who pressed for change. The arrival of Union troops marked the beginning of the end of slavery in New Orleans, but the end of slavery in New Orleans was not a foregone conclusion.[35]

Union authorities clashed with each other over the problem of slavery. General Benjamin Butler was no abolitionist. He was a Massachusetts Democrat who had curried favor with the Southern wing of his party in the late 1850s. Secession turned him against the South, and once the war started, he grasped that slavery was a key to Confederate power. While commander of

Fortress Monroe in Virginia in 1861, Butler cleverly classified runaway slaves coming from Confederate installations as "contraband of war." Classifying slaves as contraband made them liable to seizure just like other articles of enemy property used for military purposes. Butler's gambit was eventually codified in the Confiscation Act of August 1861 and afforded protection to a widening circle of slaves.[36] When he got to New Orleans, in contrast, Butler moved cautiously on the slave question. He wanted to cultivate the buried seeds of unionism among local white people and to preserve the economy, which depended on slave labor. "It is found that a large portion of property held here is in slaves," Butler explained to the Secretary of War in late May 1862. "They till the soil, raise the sugar, corn, and cotton; load and unload the ships; they perform every domestic office, and are permeated through every branch of industry and peaceful calling." But the arrival of the Federals loosened masters' hold of this portion of their property. Many slaves began to flee to the Union army. Butler found employment for some but turned others away. He could not take them all, he protested. "What would be the state of things if I allowed all the slaves from the plantations to quit their employment and come within the lines is not to be conceived by the imagination."[37]

Brigadier General John Wolcott Phelps, a patrician abolitionist from Vermont, thought differently. Upon arriving in New Orleans, Phelps established Camp Parapet just upriver from the city and made it known that he would welcome and protect slaves who managed to escape to his encampment. They came in droves, men and women, old and young, alone and in groups, on foot and by water. Some had been kicked out by their masters. Many arrived on their own. Others were brought in by Phelps' raiders. Several hundred escapees gathered under Phelps' protection by summertime. A Union officer whom Butler sent to Camp Parapet reported that the soldiers' influence was creating chaos on nearby plantations. The slaves refused to work "as they say they have only to go to the fort to be free, and are therefore very insolent to their masters."[38] Owners flooded Union authorities with protests, professions of loyalty, and demands for the return of their human property. Typical was the complaint of V. Kruttschnidt, the Prussian Consul in New Orleans: "I am informed that two of my slaves, viz: Nancy, a negress, about 35 or 40 years old, and Louisa, a dark griff about 40 or 45 years old, are at the camp of General Phelps above Carrolton." He requested that the two runaways be delivered to the police.[39]

Phelps not only harbored runaway slaves. Following passage of the Second Confiscation and Militia Acts in July 1862, he also began to arm and drill the black men who came into the camp. Phelps asserted that "the best way of preventing the African from being instrumental in a general state of anarchy is to enlist him in the cause of the Republic."[40] Butler denied that Phelps had any authority to do so and feared that arming the slaves would lead to a revolt. "We shall have a negro insurrection here I fancy," Butler confided to his wife in late July. "The negroes are getting saucy and troublesome, and who blames them?"[41] Butler pressed Phelps to stop arming slaves, return slaves to loyal masters, and set the others to work cutting wood, but the indignant Vermonter refused to play "slave-driver." He advised Butler that conditions outside Camp Parapet were treacherous:

> While I am writing, at 8:30 o'clock p.m, a colored man is brought in by one of the pickets, who has just been wounded in the side by a charge of a shot, which he says was fired at him by one of a party of three slave-hunters or guerrillas a mile or more from our line of sentinels. As it is some distance from camp to the lake, the party of wood-choppers which you have directed will probably need a considerable force to guard them against similar attacks.[42]

Rather than send black men and women back into slavery, Phelps resigned in protest and went home in early August. He had been ahead of the curve. Union policy soon caught up with the logic of events on the ground, and Butler himself welcomed slaves and free people of color into the Union army later in the year.

The recruitment of black soldiers crippled slavery in Louisiana. More than twenty-four thousand black men entered the Union service from Louisiana, more than any other state. Some came from the ranks of free men of color, but most had been slaves. Military service was their ticket to freedom and their chance, finally, to wage war against slavery. Black soldiers fought on multiple fronts. Not only did they fight against the Confederacy, but they fought for fairness within the Union army by demanding equal pay with white soldiers, the opportunity to see combat, and the chance to serve as officers. While vindicating the "manhood of the colored race," black military service had a powerful impact on the home front. Recruitment of able-bodied men left planters short of labor. The slaves who stayed behind pressed for better conditions. While black soldiers gained honor on the battlefield, black women waged their own battles in contraband camps and on the home front. Soldiers' families faced harassment and reprisals, but they also stood up for themselves. Women ran away. They talked back. They refused to be beaten. They reclaimed their children from owners. A "war within" slaveowning households in New Orleans tumbled out into public view in the streets and the courts of the city.[43]

For the first time, slave and freed women in New Orleans found powerful allies in the agents of the Union. They were unreliable allies to be sure. Many Union soldiers, officers, and officials were unsympathetic, if not downright hostile to their individual grievances and collective aspirations. Some mocked, abused, and exploited the "contrabands," a word that placed black people in a limbo between slavery and freedom.[44] Nevertheless, the presence of federal authority emboldened slaves and freedpeople, who constantly hammered home their loyalty to the Union, rather than to their masters. Black people finally had an arbiter who would listen to their side of the story. One might say that slaves and newly freed people "occupied" the attention of the government. They insisted on not being ignored, and as the true-blue unionists of New Orleans, they made claims to protection and rights that were often far in advance of what the Union was ready to grant.[45]

Despite Phelps's departure, Union soldiers in and around the city gave slaves courage to defy their owners. Many continued to run away, and even those who did not had a new spring in their step. Slaves bargained for better treatment, wages, and more time to themselves. That genie *insolence* escaped its bottle. Particularly shocking to slaveowners was the behavior of domestic slaves, who began to break out of the habit of subservience. As the teenaged Clara Solomon lamented in New Orleans late May 1862, "There are many instances in which house-servants, those who have been raised by people, have deserted them, though they have received the kindest treatment at their hands; but they imagine no sacrifice too great with which to purchase freedom."[46] To Confederates steeped in proslavery values, the desertion of the slaves they had presumed to be most loyal to them came as a psychic shock. They felt betrayed. They comforted themselves by blaming the Union soldiers for luring the slaves with false promises and robbing masters of their lawful property.[47]

Ann Wilkinson Penrose was one of those Confederate women in New Orleans whose privileged world fell apart when the Yankees arrived. She had a fine pedigree. Her grandfather was James Wilkinson, a famous general. Her husband, Clement Biddle Penrose, was a wealthy Philadelphian who moved to Louisiana and then died of yellow fever. One son died just before the war, and the other—grandly named Joseph Biddle Wilkinson Penrose—marched off to fight in the East, leaving his mother to look after her elderly father, three other "retired & quiet" women, and their slaves. In her spare time she kept a diary composed of unsent letters to her soldier son. She may have hoped he would read it someday, but its more immediate purpose was to let her vent her anxiety and frustration at living under Union misrule. From May 1862 to October 1863, she poured her heart onto the pages of that volume, commenting on everything from the weather and her health to the indignities of occupation and the unraveling of slavery. Though not a perfect substitute for a journal or memoir written by Mary De Hart herself, Ann Penrose's diary nevertheless sheds light on how the Civil War reverberated in the city's domestic chambers.[48]

Her life was full of woe. Penrose was sixty years old and hobbled around on crutches. She suffered from sore feet and anxious headaches. "I may say we never lay down to rest with an easy mind," she wrote after a sleepless night in August 1862.[49] She longed to know where Joseph was, how he was doing, how the war was really going. She fed off a steady diet of rumor. False news of glorious victories, recognition by foreign powers, and prospects for peace and independence raised her hopes and dashed them over and over. She reported incessant harassment by Union authorities. One day in June 1863, Penrose heard encouraging news that the Confederacy was plotting to retake New Orleans. "Oh! what happiness it will be to those here, if we can regain it," she fantasized, "& be once more surrounded by our own soldiers, instead of those detested Yankees, that insult & wrong us in every way they possibly can; thieves & robbers, that steal and appropriate our property continually."[50] The Confederacy never did regain New Orleans, but it is sobering to imagine what might have happened to the city's black people if Penrose's fantasy had come true.

Penrose felt almost trapped in New Orleans by her family's slaves. Her invalid father lived off the earnings of his slaves "hired about town." He couldn't remove them from New Orleans, and even if he could, "it would be very improbable that he could hire them out elsewhere, in the present state of the country." Moreover, Penrose took it upon herself to look after Joseph's interests. "Even if I were well," she told her absent son, "I think it would be better to remain to take care of yr property, and not abandon it, either serv^ts or places."⁵¹ Taking care of the property was easier to write about than to do. Penrose's mastery was undermined by the presence of the Union and the resistance of the slaves. Just weeks after the Federals arrived, Penrose began to hear of slaves running off in a "stampede" to Fort Jackson and other places. Some runaways had been put to work fixing a breach in the levee, and she hoped their new masters "will keep them hard at it."⁵² On May 27, a slave named James Guy ran off "very coolly and deliberately." He had been sent to the market and never came back, although he had the politeness—perhaps it was a jab—to send home the groceries and his streetcar ticket.⁵³

Things went downhill from there. At the end of May, Penrose's father was arrested by Yankee soldiers for plotting to have Butler assassinated. The allegation came from one of the family's slaves, a man named Ben Travis, who had been one of the first to run away. Penrose thought that Travis trumped up the charge "for the purpose of getting off Grace & his children." Travis arrived with the soldiers to arrest Wilkinson. He entered the house and "behaved in the most insolent manner to us, telling Grace to come up stairs, and talk to us, as she pleased, and not to be afraid, and if she was, to call to him & he would come and talk to us himself." None other than James Guy accompanied Travis, but he stayed outside. Penrose's reaction to this turn of events echoes Clara Solomon's lament about the desertion of faithful domestics. "If accusations of vindictive servants are to be taken, no one can feel safe," Penrose complained, "so indulged, I may almost say, petted, as those serv[ts] have been, and such confidence as we had in them; now, I have in none, if they could turn against us."[54]

Penrose's fear and rage at the crumbling of slavery mounted throughout the summer and fall of 1862. She complained of the "misrule & anarchy prevailing among a certain class, which is allowed by our masters, who always take part with them, and they do anything they please with impunity; no matter how insolent they are, or what provocation they give." If punished, the slaves appealed to the provost marshal, who would arrest their masters and impose a fine or throw them in prison.[55] Nerves tautened when "Proclamation Phelps" began to arm the black men flocking to Camp Parapet. "They say Phelps has 4000 of them at his camp just above, drilling them to be soldiers; bands of them continually arrive from below, without any hindrance from the Yankees who receive & shelter them; numbers too are daily arriving from above & joining Phelps camp. Our fears are, that should his camp, or the city be attacked, they may be let loose upon us." By wintertime, the whole society seemed upside down: "Our negroes run rioting about; in any jarring between those who stay at home & their owners, their part is invariably taken; masters have accusations laid against them by their slaves, & true or false are imprisoned or fined at their instigation. Regiments of negroes parade our streets, in short they are our masters."[56]

Penrose's grip on her own household loosened. "Our servants do pretty much as they please," she fumed in September.[57] Time and again Penrose complained of their insolence.

Feb 2 [1863]: Old Lyddy was here this morning, and very insolent indeed, telling Rebecca that she was free, and signifying she would do as she please, having previously used words to that effect, and even more insolent still to Kate.[58]

April 13: This morn. at breakfast, the bread was as usual intolerably bad, and as the flour is good it is the result of Becky, who is our cook at present; when the cakes came in they were also as bad as could be, heavy as lead, and like dough; I rose and went into the kitchen to speak to Becky; she was leaning down, with her back towards me as I entered, and I could not resist giving her a good hard slap on the shoulder, which bye the bye hurt my hand, I have no doubt, more than it did her, at the same time I asked her how she dared to send in such bread & cakes; she started up, looked furiously at me, and exclaimed, "don't you do that again, let it be the last time, or I'll just march out of this yard;" l made her some reply, to which she answered; finding I was getting the worst of it, I turned and went back to the dining room, but she went on in the most violent manner; . . . On her continuing, Rebecca sent her word if she did not hush, she send for a policeman, to which she replied, "she might send for whom she pleased she didn't care." What to do we knew not, for it was a bad example to the other servants to submit quietly to her violence & impertinence.[59]

May 6: This morn. we have had to endure Margarets insolence; they never do any thing after dinner but sit on the banquette before the door and have little enough to do in the mornings but yet if they are given a few more pieces to wash than they choose to do or if a word of remonstrance is said to them about the quantity of soap or flour it pleases them to take they fly out and are just as impudent as possible. . . . Margaret especially is a little ungrateful humpbacked wretch, who for wee-[ks] at a time has been laid up in her bed, with the D^r attending on her, & now repays us with her insolence.[60]

May 21: Clara had been most insolent and insubordinate to both yr aunts Vir. & Julia. Yr aunt V. took hold of her by her sleeve, I think, and attempted to slap her, whereupon she broke from her & ran screaming down the street, to a house about a square from this, which is the headquarters of some of the officers, and where there are always a number of negroe men in their service & uniform. There she laid a complaint, that she had been whipped with a cowskin, beat with a stick, and pitched down stairs. I was very uneasy knowing the consequences that have followed such reports, true or false, for they always take their side.[61]

Although Penrose fumed over their laziness, incompetence, and impudence, Lyddy, Becky, Margaret, and Clara refused to be scolded and slapped. They were not going to put up with their mistresses' verbal and physical abuse anymore. With no able-bodied white men at home, and black soldiers stationed nearby, the Penrose household collapsed into a private civil war.

Just as in the De Hart household, children were caught up in the fray. Jane Thompson, one of the Penrose "servants," disappeared in late December 1862, probably spurred by fears that Penrose was arranging to have her shipped to a plantation outside the city on the pretext of sending her to see her husband. "Where Jane Thomp. has gone to I cannot imagine," Penrose lamented in early January. A few days later Penrose heard that a desperate Thompson tried to hire herself out "saying she and her children were starving, that her mistress had gone into the Confed^{cy} and had left her to take care of herself." A rumor that Thompson's youngest child had died confirmed Penrose's belief that her slaves could not take care of themselves. In February, Thompson came to Penrose for a pass, which she refused to provide. Instead, Penrose found Thompson's two daughters, Mary and Emma, brought them back to her house, and sent a message for their mother to come home: "I knew very well she would do that as I had her children." When Thomson did not show up, Penrose began to suspect that "she was arranging about a place to go to, & then coming up to steal off her children." That Penrose imagined Jane Thompson's attempt to recover her own children as a form of theft is a perfect illustration of slaveowners' belief that their property rights took precedence over slaves' claims to their children. In the end, Penrose's ploy worked. Thompson came back and did not run off again. She cropped up in the diary one last time in August 1863, when Penrose reported Mary's death from diphtheria. "She was a fine child, and I am sorry for her death, we may get our rights some time or other, and she would in that case, have been valuable to you," she told her absent soldier son. Penrose still held on to the hope that slavery could be resuscitated.[62]

Penrose's diary unwittingly depicted slaves' family ties, community networks, and political connections. It shows that the war for freedom was waged by women cooking in kitchens as well as soldiers massing on battlefields. It shows, moreover, that slavery crumbled in New Orleans not from a single dramatic blow or stroke of a pen, but from the accumulated weight of resistance by slaves such as Lyddy, Margaret, Becky, and Clara once the Union army arrived. In October 1863, with "nothing to stay here for," Ann Wilkinson Penrose fled to the Confederate bastion of Mobile.[63] Her son Joseph probably never read her painful chronicle, since he was killed in battle just three days before Lee surrendered at Appomattox. If he had survived to make it back home, he would have scarcely recognized New Orleans.

While Joseph Penrose fought to the bitter end, James Andrew De Hart returned to civilian life when the Federals arrived. The new regime posed a challenge for those who had served the Confederacy. Butler's Proclamation on May 1, 1862 promised that anyone who laid down their arms, returned to peaceful occupations, kept the peace, and ceased giving "aid and comfort" to the Confederacy would "not be disturbed in their persons or property" unless "the exigencies of public service" made it necessary.[64] That was a big loophole. Confederate-leaning citizens of New Orleans found their homes and property confiscated by the Butler regime for the benefit of Union soldiers and, notoriously, Butler's own pocket. The following month, Butler issued orders requiring anybody doing business with the

Union to swear allegiance to the United States, and then in July, passage of the Second Confiscation Act intensified the pressure on Confederates' property by freeing slaves of rebels, blocking the return of runaway slaves, and authorizing the employment of black people by the United States. Dismissing a complaint from Thomas Jefferson Durant that the army was disrupting slavery in Louisiana, President Lincoln defended the stepped-up policy: "What would you do in my position? Would you drop the war where it is? Or, would you prosecute it in future with elder-stalk squirts, charged with rose water?"[65] Confederates such as Ann Penrose saw their slaves slip away from them, and even slaveowners who were loyal to the Union lost their grip on their human chattel.

As slavery tottered in New Orleans, the slave market still churned, and Rose Herera was sold one last time. On August 14, 1862, James De Hart transferred ownership of Herera and her now three children—Ernest (6), Marie (4), and Josephine (20 months)—to his wife's aunt, Carmelite Roland, who lived with the De Harts. A widow, Roland paid $900 for the four slaves, $400 cash and the remainder to be paid in two installments of $250 plus interest, to be paid at six and twelve months.[66] If legitimate, the sale was either an act of folly or an act of faith. Although substantially less than the $1,500 De Hart had paid Mercer less than two years earlier, $900 would have been a lot of money for a widow of no apparent means, especially at a time when slaves might not have any value at all in New Orleans in six to twelve months. Rose Herera's lawyers would later argue that the sale was a sham designed to protect De Hart from the seizure of his slaves. These transfers of property had become a common tactic in New Orleans. "All the property of New Orleans is changing hands into foreigners and women, to avoid the consequences of the confiscation acts," Butler observed in September.[67] Such shady deals were not new. Southern courts before the war had litigated countless suits in which debtors were accused of illegal manipulation of their human property to defraud creditors. Indeed, De Hart might have passed off Herera and her children to his aunt to avoid losing them to his landlord, who was breathing down his neck for rent money.[68]

The sale preceded a more dramatic move by De Hart. In October, he left New Orleans for Havana, leaving his wife and son, the widow Roland, and Herera and her children behind for the time being. Though he left without his family, he was not alone. Untold numbers of Confederates fled New Orleans in the aftermath of its capture by the Federals. A wave of refugees immediately rolled out of the city in May 1862. Others waited to see just how bad Union rule would be. Most escaped into northern Louisiana and Texas. Many shipped off to Mobile and points farther east in the Confederacy. Some fled to Mexico or Europe. De Hart was part of the exodus to Cuba. "A large number of persons are coming to this place from New Orleans," observed the Confederate agent in Havana, Charles Helm, in late October 1862.[69] The war, like all wars, shuffled people and dealt them out across the world. Reflecting on the carnival of refugees, including "many from New Orleans" who descended on Jackson, Mississippi, in July 1862, one diarist wrote that "conditions of time, space, locality, and estate were all loosened; everybody seemed floating he knew not whither, but determined to be jolly, and keep up an excitement."[70] A Northern songwriter used the language of blackface minstrelsy to mock slaveowners who fled at the sight of Union gunboats:

> De Massa run? ha! ha!
> De darkeys stay? ho! ho!
> It mus' be now de kingdom comin'
> An' de year Jubilo!

Black schoolchildren sang this song within earshot of a *New York Times* reporter in New Orleans in 1864.[71]

De Hart's departure coincided with a wave of New Orleanians who left to avoid the brunt of the previous summer's Confiscation Act. In late September, as the act's grace period ended, Butler issued General Order No. 76, which required all men and women who had ever been U.S. citizens and who had not taken the oath of allegiance by October 1 to register themselves as enemies of the United States and provide the authorities with a list of everything they owned. Confederate New Orleanians had to choose between the sin of swearing an oath they did not believe in or suffering the loss of their property. Thousands swore the oath, but some stalwarts accepted the status of registered enemy.[72] One of De Hart's neighbors would later testify that all the members of De Hart's militia company swore the oath of allegiance to the Union in September 1862, but he never actually testified that De Hart did so.[73] It is certainly possible that De Hart left to avoid having to swear the oath, or perhaps he swore the oath but expected to endure harassment and confiscation by Butler's regime if he stayed. He might have left for entirely different reasons having nothing to do with the oath.

Maybe business was slow, and he figured he would make more money pulling teeth somewhere else.[74]

Havana was a logical choice. It was close to New Orleans, and the cities had much in common. Both were urban centers of thriving plantation societies based on sugar and slaves. Cuba was the world's leading sugar producer in 1860. Favorable ecology, steam power and railroads, and massive illegal slave imports sustained its economy. As Louisiana's sugar planters struggled to keep up, they kept close watch on their Cuban rivals. A steady stream of news and information about sugar, politics, public health, and the "gay musical and theatrical world" passed between New Orleans and Havana. It took a steamship only three days to complete the 669-mile trip from one port to the other. Vessels heading to or coming from New Orleans often stopped at Havana to discharge and pick up passengers traveling for business, health, and pleasure. New Orleans merchants shipped bacon and corn to Havana; their counterparts shipped cigars and coffee back to New Orleans. (New Orleanians have always loved their coffee.) Seven-year-old Loreta Janeta Velazquez was sent from Havana to New Orleans to live with her aunt in 1849. She would later fight for the Confederacy disguised as a man. One of New Orleans' richest men, James Robb, held the contract to supply Havana with gaslight.[75]

New Orleanians had their eyes on Havana for some time. The city's merchants wanted to pry open the island's protected colonial market and stuff it with midwestern wheat, whereas proslavery ideologues wanted to annex Cuba, insulate it from British antislavery, and shore up the nation's Southern bloc. These interests made the city a haven for filibusters. The Venezuelan rebel Narciso López launched two ill-fated invasions of Cuba from

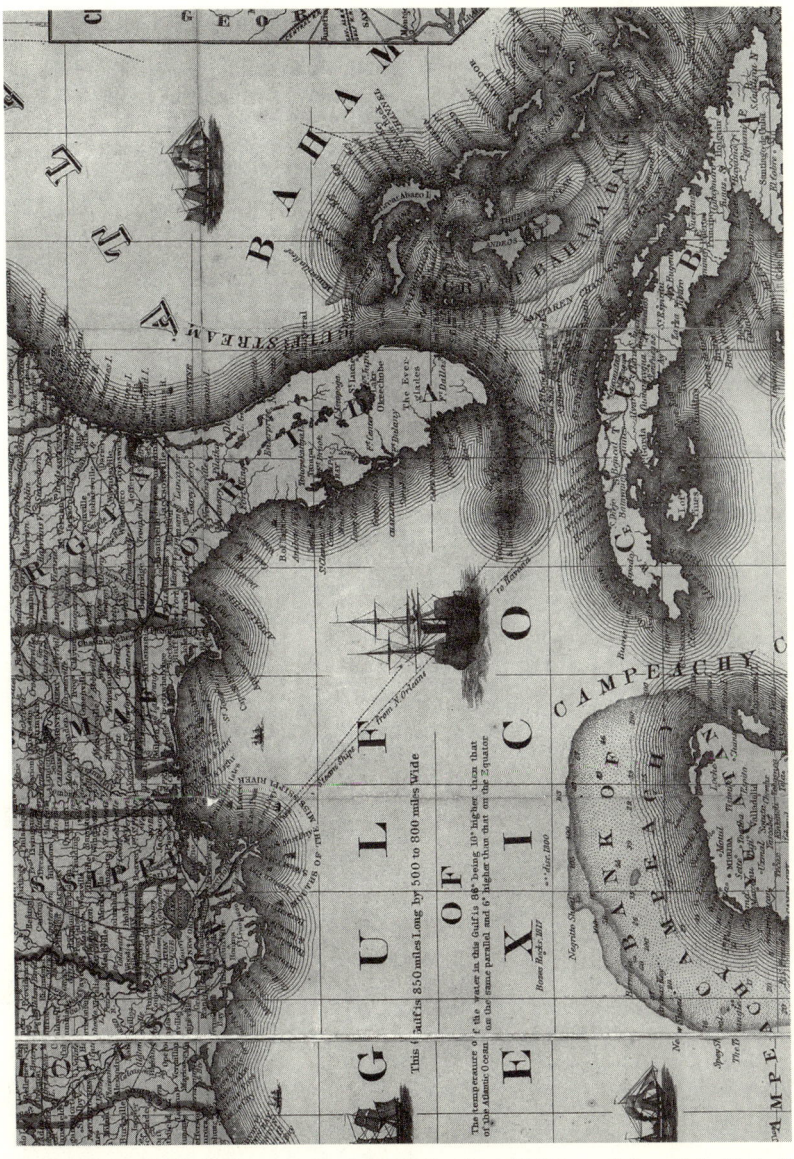

Detail from J. H. Colton, *Colton's Rail-Road and Military Map of the United States, Mexico, the West Indies, &c.* (New York, 1862), showing steamship connection between New Orleans and Havana.
Geography and Map Division, Library of Congress, Washington, D.C.

New Orleans in 1850 and 1851. The second ended with López garroted by the Cuban authorities and fifty-one of his American comrades shot by a firing squad. Vengeful New Orleanians attacked the city's Spanish community, wrecking fruit stands, cigar shops, and pro-Spanish newspapers, and fortifying the United States' international reputation for mobocracy. New Orleanians kept their sights on Havana even after the López debacle. One of the city's leading Democrats, Pierre Soulé, secured a plum position as minister to Spain in the Pierce administration. He coauthored the notorious Ostend Manifesto, which justified the seizure of Cuba by the United States if Spain refused to sell it. Fierce northern opposition scuttled that plan, but Southern Democrats like Soulé kept pressing for Cuba until secession changed the political map. If filibusterism created sparks between New Orleans and Havana, it also revealed the explosive potential of communication and collaboration among dissidents in the two cities.[76]

Less famous than the filibusters are the slavers. An illegal slave trade from Africa to Cuba thrived in the mid-nineteenth century. More than a hundred thousand captive Africans were smuggled into Cuba in the 1850s, and it was no secret that some New Orleanians were involved. The U.S. government refused to allow the British navy to stop and search vessels flying the American flag. As a result, many illegal slavers flew the stars and stripes to escape detection. The U.S. naval squadron deployed to suppress illegal slaving was too small to patrol the ocean effectively, at least until the late 1850s, when the Buchanan administration intensified its efforts to police illegal slaving by American vessels. As a consequence of the United States' insistence on its own sovereignty, vessels flying the U.S. flag carried more than half of the slaves transported to Cuba in the 1850s. Reliable information is scarce, so most of what is known about New Orleanians' stake in this traffic comes from the handful of vessels that were unlucky enough to be captured in the late 1850s, along with scraps of intelligence about other vessels that evaded capture. As many as thirty-one slavers from 1856 to 1860 can be linked to New Orleans. Ten of them are known to have landed Africans in Cuba—more than 5,000 Africans in all, mostly drawn from the slave markets of the Congo River. Thirteen hundred people perished as they crossed the graveless ocean in these ships. So conspicuous was New Orleans in this awful business that a British naval officer stationed off the African coast in 1859 condemned the city as "a port of slaving celebrity."[77]

The master of one captured slaver out of New Orleans, the *Jupiter*, spilled the secrets of his business to his British captors. Investors in Havana raised money for the voyage and sent an agent to New Orleans. The Cuban agent partnered with Goldenbow & Lesparré, shipping agents located at 75 Camp St. (between Poydras and Gravier), just a few blocks from where Rose lived with the De Harts. The shipping agents found a naturalized American citizen to act as master, and he received money to buy a ship and register it in his name. The shipping agents fitted out the ship with food, water, and equipment. Excess food was hidden in water casks. They hired a crew of Spanish and Portuguese sailors and gave them false American "protections," or identity papers. The Cuban agent, the real owner of the ship, accompanied the vessel as its supercargo, the person in charge of managing the ship's merchandise. Disguised by this fraudulent paperwork, the vessel cleared New Orleans and sailed to Tenerife in the Canary Islands, where it took on its "slave-coppers," special boilers used for cooking the captives' food. The vessel then continued on to the island of Annobon in the Bight of Biafra, where arrangements were made to pick up a cargo of captives at Lagos. The *Jupiter* was then supposed to deliver the Africans (dubbed *bozales*) to a rendezvous point off the southern coast of Cuba, but the slaver was seized at anchor on the African coast before it could cross the Atlantic. To avoid being handed over to the U.S. Navy and charged with piracy, the *Jupiter*'s master destroyed all evidence of the ship's nationality. This allowed him to get off scot-free as the British condemned the vessel, rescued its human cargo, and sent them to Sierra Leone to join thousands of other "liberated" Africans.[78]

The close ties between New Orleans and Havana were strained by the Civil War but not severed. Confederates gained sympathy in Havana among expatriates, planters who detested abolitionism, and liberals who admired the Southern struggle for national self-determination. "I find a large majority of the population of Havana zealously advocating our cause," boasted Confederate agent Charles Helm in October 1861.[79] Months later, the Louisiana politician John Slidell (who had been captured on board the British mail steamer *Trent* en route from Havana to England), told the Confederate secretary of state that there was "almost universal sympathy with our cause among the people of the island, as well European Spaniards as Creole."[80] Blockade runners from New Orleans slipped through the U.S. naval cordon and made their way to Havana, where the authorities allowed them to do business.[81] Money, cotton, and arms passed between the two ports. During the first year of the war, a U.S. official complained, blockade running between New Orleans and Havana provided the rebels with their "chief mode of communication."[82]

The Federals' capture of New Orleans drove blockade-running to other Gulf ports and normalized commerce between the two cities, yet new tensions swirled around the movement of goods and people between them. Upon arriving in New Orleans, Butler discovered evidence that Spanish merchants had been aiding the Confederacy. Puig Bros., he alleged, had carried on "the nefarious traffic of supplying the rebels with arms and munitions of War from Havana, and for that purpose one of the partners was a resident of Havana, to ship the contraband articles which the other received and distributed here." Similarly, the New Orleans–based firm of Avendaño Bros. had been "running cotton through the blockade, and importing arms and munitions of war." Butler's crackdown on these firms sparked protests from the Spanish consul.[83] Fearful of yellow fever, Butler ordered strict quarantine measures for vessels arriving from disease-ridden ports, including Havana. In early June a vessel from Havana, the *Cardenas,* carrying fruit and "rebels who had been in Havana buying arms and munitions of war for the Confederates" was detained at the quarantine station. The consul accused Butler of unjust discrimination and retaliated by refusing to clear an American vessel for Havana. The back-and-forth between the two officials dragged on for months as just one of many spats between Butler and the city's foreign consuls.[84]

In late September, a Spanish war steamer called the *Blasco de Garay* tried to leave New Orleans for Havana without clearance from Union officials. Suspicious that the vessel was carrying rebels and criminals, Butler demanded that detectives be allowed on board to examine the passengers. One of the partners in Puig Bros. was discovered on board, as well as an escaped murderer. The Spanish consul once again complained of Butler's imperious manner, and Butler charged that Spain's vessels were unlawfully ferrying people out of New Orleans.[85] The *Blasco de Garay*, along with two other Spanish war steamers, eventually made it to Havana in early October. The Cuban press welcomed them. Many of the refugees on the *Blasco de Garay* were "of the best social position," observed the *Diario de la Marina*, a Havana newspaper; they came to Cuba to seek "the security they lack in their own land."[86] The arrival of the *Marigalanto* a few days later with another two hundred passengers from New Orleans prompted the *Diario* to gloat "that circumstances have made the Spanish flag the first to give aid and shelter to the citizens of Louisiana, while they have been suffering from the calamities which accompany civil war."[87] James De Hart could have been one of them.

It did not take long for De Hart to hang out his shingle in Havana. He announced his arrival by placing a notice in the *Diario* on November 4, 1862.[88] The ad informed readers that he had just arrived from New Orleans, where he had successfully practiced dentistry for many years. He was accepted into Havana's acclaimed Real Universidad, a center of science and medicine, and opened an office in his new dwelling at calle de Cuba 39, between Obispo and O'Reilly, just two blocks from the Palace of the Captain General and Plaza de Armas, the center of colonial authority in Cuba. (The site is now a parking lot.) Tapping into the progressive ideals of his prospective clients, De Hart informed readers that "by means of a process of his own invention he is able to fix most satisfactorily all artificial teeth that are not to the liking of their owners."[89] To be a dentist in a world made of sugar must have been a sweet line of work.

Mary De Hart was eager to follow her husband to Havana, and she did not want to leave her slaves behind. Rose Herera and her children made up the De Harts' most valuable assets. Herera's labor relieved Mary De Hart of the burdens of housework. Though very young, the children could soon be made to work. If the De Harts needed money, they could be hired out or sold. In the meantime, they could serve as playmates for their son. If Mary De Hart was anything like Ann Penrose and most other Southern slaveowners, she would have firmly believed that Herera and her children were better off as slaves in Havana than subject to the evil influences of Butlerism and the siren song of freedom in New Orleans. The challenge for De Hart was convincing Rose Herera to go. The children were too valuable to leave behind, but taking them without their mother would lead to inconvenience and expense in Havana. De Hart knew that it would be impossible to get permission from the Union authorities to take Herera to Cuba unless she agreed to the move, and it would be risky to smuggle Herera out of the country against her will. Before the Civil War, slaveowners often took trusted slaves with them to foreign destinations, but in Union-occupied New Orleans, practices that had been routine now became disputed.[90]

Rose Herera did not want to go to Havana. This claim is based on Herera's own testimony from three years later, when she petitioned the government for the arrest of Mary De Hart and the return of the children. After Mary De Hart's husband went to Cuba, Herera explained, "Mrs. A. V. De Hart spoke of following him to Havana, and frequently asked and urged your petitioner [Rose Herera] to go with her to that place, which petitioner constantly refused to do, not wishing to leave her husband, her mother, and her friends."[91] As slavery fell apart in New Orleans, Herera dared to assert her own identity as something other than her owner's property and servant. She was a wife, a daughter, a friend. These human ties of family and community endured within slavery and emerged as slavery receded, like sunken treasure revealed by a dried-up sea.

Mary De Hart had one more card to play. One or two weeks before Christmas, Rose Herera was thrown in jail after an altercation left De Hart's aunt Roland with a black eye. The older woman complained to the police that "her servant had beat her," so a policeman arrested Herera and put her in jail.[92] Herera told a different story. In the provost court in 1865, she testified that she did not hit the old woman. It was the other way around:

> Defendant [Mme. De Hart] had moved to Canal street with her aunt. She went out one evening and left me there. Mrs. Roland called to me to clean the house. I told her it was too late. She began to quarrel and says "Don't sauce me." I said I had been working all day and the little babies were crying. Defendant was not at home. She (Mrs. Roland) came and slapped me. She went out and came back with an officer, who said he had come to arrest me. She said. "Go! I want that man to take you." The policeman

Orleans Police Jail and Parish Prison during the Civil War.
From Marshall Dunham Photograph Album (Mss. 3241), Louisiana and Lower Mississippi Valley Collections, Louisiana State University Libraries, Baton Rouge, Louisiana.

told me to go with him. He took me to the parish jail, and I stayed there till the day they went away.⁹³

Upon cross-examination, Rose explained how Roland got her black eye. "I did not knock her in the face," she testified. "She came to me with the coffee pot, and it flew in her face." In other words, it was Roland's fault. Rose insisted that her real offense had been insolence: "I was put in jail because I was saucy."⁹⁴ No matter who attacked whom, Rose and Roland were combatants in the domestic war between slaves and masters that took place in kitchens across New Orleans as the old regime fell to ashes.

The New Orleans jail had always been fearsome to slaves. Owners sent unruly slaves there for bloodletting that they did not want to inflict with their own hands. After seeing the whipping of a slave woman at the New Orleans prison in 1842, the Northern reformer Samuel Gridley Howe wrote that what he witnessed at the prison "made me blush that I was a white man."[95] It was there that free woman of color Constance Perrine had been mistakenly and brutally whipped "as a slave." Captured runaways were lodged there until their masters claimed them, or else they were sold if they could not prove their freedom. Few could. It is likely, if not certain, that jailed free people of color who could not prove their freedom were sold into slavery. A group of inmates exposed the dreadful conditions that prevailed there upon the arrival of the Federals. Among other horrors, they informed Butler that a black woman had been tortured by the jailer, who tied her spread-eagled to the floor and deprived her of food and water for twenty-four hours. When that torture failed to produce the effect he desired, the jailor handcuffed her into a "crooked, painful" position and forced her to suffer in her own filth for another twenty-four hours.[96] The jail housed slaves throughout 1862 as municipal police functions remained in effect. In early November, Butler banned the arrest and confinement of slaves "unless the person arresting knows that such person is owned by a loyal citizen" and authorized the discharge of "all slaves not known to be the slaves of loyal owners," but the jail continued to house slaves taken there by the police.[97] Rose Herera and her two-month-old baby languished in this dungeon for a month while Mary De Hart pestered her to go to Havana with her children. She visited Herera several times in jail to try to convince her to go. De Hart even threatened to take the three oldest children without her, but their mother would not cave in. Rather, Herera "begged and demanded that her children should be left in New Orleans with her."[98]

Christmas passed and then a new year rolled in, bringing with it the Emancipation Proclamation and a new leader in New Orleans. Neither came to Rose's rescue. The Proclamation exempted New Orleans because it was no longer territory "in rebellion." Lincoln's "Preliminary Emancipation Proclamation" in September had threatened to free the slaves in any state or part of a state "in rebellion" as of January 1, 1863. On its surface, that threat (or promise) was intended to induce the people in rebellion to return to the Union, but nobody really believed it would accomplish that purpose. In fact, it had the opposite effect of fortifying Confederate resistance to the despotic power of an abolitionist president. The true purpose of the preliminary proclamation was to sharpen the axe of emancipation and get it ready to cut down the Confederacy. The preliminary proclamation did offer an escape hatch: any state represented in Congress by January 1 would, "in the absence of strong countervailing testimony," be deemed not in rebellion, and therefore exempt from emancipation. A skimpy electorate of confirmed loyal, white unionists in southern Louisiana satisfied that condition in December by electing two new congressmen, Benjamin Flanders and Michael Hahn. Their election began the political reconstruction of Louisiana, and it meant that the part of the state under Union occupation would not be included in the Emancipation Proclamation, despite some eleventh-hour debate on the matter. Rose Herera was still a slave and she remained in jail.[99]

New Orleans' exemption from the Emancipation Proclamation did not halt the unraveling of slavery there. The confiscation acts, the protection of runaways by Union authorities, and the recruitment of black soldiers continued to pull it apart, even as the Union government remained nominally committed to upholding loyal slaveowners' rights to their human property. Into this policy swamp waded a new Union commander for the Department of the Gulf, General Nathaniel Banks, who replaced Butler in mid-December 1862. Like Butler, Banks was a Massachusetts politico, but unlike Butler, he was a Republican with strong antislavery credentials. Despite his background, slaveowning New Orleanians saw Banks as a better alternative to their nemesis Butler. He came with a more conciliatory attitude toward them. "Kindness after the rod," one of his aides skeptically appraised it. This change did not bode well for Rose Herera. Quieting local citizens' fears of an impending slave revolt, Banks outlined his policy in a proclamation dated December 24. He declared that the Union did not wage war "for the overthrow of slavery" but to restore the Union. To that end he called upon slaves to "remain upon their plantations" and wait for the government to come to them. At the same time, he revealed that he was powerless to force the slaves to stay with their owners. "No encouragement will be given to laborers to desert their employers, but no authority exists to compel them to return." Soon, however, Banks would implement a set of labor policies that did compel (ex-)slaves to return to their plantations and work for food, clothing, and wages determined by yearly contracts.[100]

If Banks found himself in a "difficult position," as a Treasury agent noted in early January, Rose Herera's position was much worse.[101] Imprisoned in a New Orleans jail with her baby in the middle of winter, Rose fell sick while Mary De Hart packed to leave for Havana on the steamer *Bio Bio* in mid-January. Crucially, the local authorities granted a pass to "Mrs. E. Roland, son, servant, and four children" to go to Havana on the

Bio Bio.¹⁰² How Roland secured this permission from Union authorities remains a mystery. Did she have a friend in the provost marshal's office? Did she grease someone's palm? Perhaps there was some sleight-of-hand at work. It's worth noting that the pass did not identify the children as black or as slaves, nor did it indicate that the servant was the children's mother. This ambiguity may have been the secret to De Hart's success in getting them out of New Orleans. Roland also secured an order for Rose's release on January 7, but she was not actually let out until a week later.

De Hart stopped by the jail one last time on Thursday, January 15. She was on her way to the *Bio Bio* in a carriage with Roland, a "gentleman" named Fallon, and three of Herera's children. She sent Fallon into the jail with the order to release their mother. He gave it to a clerk who accompanied Fallon to Herera's cell. According to Fallon's testimony, the clerk told Herera she had been released, and Fallon told her that "the ladies were downstairs with the children" and that they were "going on the steamer Bio Bio to Havana." Herera replied that she was too sick to stand up. Fallon asked her whether she would go to Havana by the next steamer if she got better. She said yes and made "no objection to their going," so Fallon left her in jail. The party rode on to the levee where the steamer awaited. The children were boarded in full public view. Fallon and other witnesses claimed that they were not hidden. "There was no concealment of the children; they were playing about the boat; were apparently happy and contented," declared George Leveque.¹⁰³

With Rose Herera trapped in jail and weakened by illness, it fell to her mother Leocadie and husband George to try to stop the children from being taken away. Leocadie's owner had been dead for several years, and she had been free ever since. She lived in the city with her dead owner's sister and "had her own time." She saw Rose "rather often; sometimes two or three times a week, and every second Sunday," and admitted that the children "were pretty well treated." She had visited Rose in jail three times, including twice with De Hart, so she was privy to the discussions between them concerning the children. Leocadie was waiting on the *Bio Bio* when De Hart boarded with the children on the afternoon of January 15. Here is the scene as she described it in the provost court two years later:

> Witness [Leocadie] was on the ship when the children came. Defendant [Mrs. De Hart], Madam Fallon, and several other ladies, came with them. They were brought down to the ship in a carriage and taken on board by a little boy. Mrs. Roland asked for the mother of the child, and defendant stated that the mother was sick and could not come. Mrs. Roland said she would do better to turn the smallest child over to the grandmother (witness.) Defendant said no; if all the children were not brought to Havana Mr. De Hart would not be satisfied. Witness did not make any attempt to get the children, but as soon as the children saw witness defendant shoved the children away, and prevented them from getting near her.

Contrary to the assertion that the children appeared happy, Leocadie declared that the oldest was crying. Leocadie stayed on board the steamer as long as she could, but when Rose did not arrive, she left and took a cab to the jail. There she found Rose, too weak to stand, and escorted her home.[104]

George Herera also tried to intervene. Rose later testified that her husband "did everything he could" to rescue the children, but De Hart "acted mean to him." George Herera pleaded with the provost marshal to prevent the children from leaving but was informed that De Hart had received permission to take the children on the condition that she bring them back within three months.[105] On January 14, George Herera wrote a last-ditch letter to General Nathaniel Banks, the top Union brass in New Orleans, imploring him to stop the children from being spirited away to Cuba:

> Major General P. N. Banks
> Sir.
> My wife Rose belonging to Mrs Widow Rolland of this city, is now confined in prison by order of her mistress who is on the eve of her departure for Havana. As she intends to take with her, without their mother, my three children viz:
>> Ernest Seven years old
>> Mary four years"
>> & Josephine two years"
>
> I respectfully pray General, that according to the laws of God & man, my dear children shall not be separated from their mother.
>> I feel confident in your justice
>> I remain
>>> General
>>> Your devoted & grateful servant
>>> Georges Herera[106]

Herera's poignant letter affirmed the family ties that had been denied by slavery. *My wife Rose. My dear children. Their mother.* He tied his family's plight to transcendent principles of right and wrong. Rose and her children may have belonged to her owner as property, but they also belonged to him, and the mother and children belonged together. He invoked "the laws of God and man," and he appealed to the Union general's sense of "justice" to prevent the children from being taken to Cuba. Herera signed the letter in his own name, which suggests that he was literate, and the words were his own.[107]

Herera's letter adds a new dimension to the record of protest and activism among New Orleans' free people of color. Once the Federals regained control, the city's literate, propertied, and cosmopolitan free colored class became staunch unionists and pressed not only for abolition, but for racial equality, too. Many free men of color of fighting age joined the Union army and provided crucial leadership in Louisiana's Corps d'Afrique, though Herera was not one of them. In the fall of 1862, a cadre of activists founded a French-language newspaper called *L'Union*, which served as the mouthpiece of the free colored elite. Two years later it was replaced by the *Tribune*, the first daily newspaper published by African Americans in the United States. As Louisiana unionists rewrote the state constitution to abolish slavery, free people of color campaigned for civil and political equality. At times, their spokesmen complained that although the slaves were being freed, the already-free people of color were being denied their rights, including suffrage. George Herera's goal in writing this letter was more modest. He just wanted to keep his children from being separated from their mother. He failed.[108]

George Herera never saw Ernest, Mary, and Josephine again. Perhaps General Banks did not read the letter in time. Perhaps he never read it, or he read and ignored it. The wartime bureaucracy was, for many, a graveyard of hopes. Its archives are littered with unanswered pleas and dead letters like George Herera's.[109] The *Bio Bio* slipped its mooring on the afternoon of Friday, January 16, 1863, and headed down the winding Mississippi. Among its seventy-eight passengers were Mary De Hart, her son Edward, and Madam Roland. The three Herera children were also on board. The next morning, the *Bio Bio* would have crossed the bar at the mouth of the river and passed into the open sea, where the great river's brown, brackish water disappeared into the greens and blues of the Gulf. Four days later, the *Bio Bio* arrived in Havana's scenic harbor.[110]

The Herera children did not enter Havana unnoticed. The three black children ("negritos") on board the *Bio Bio* caught the attention of Havana's port authorities, who required De Hart to petition for permission to disembark them.[111] Cuba's laws prohibited the introduction of people of color into the island unless there were special circumstances that allowed for an exception. The laws were designed to staunch the smuggling of captive Africans into Cuba, as well as to prevent unwanted black people, whether free or slave, from coming in from Haiti, Jamaica, and other Caribbean islands and spreading notions of freedom to Cuban slaves.[112] The quarantine was not intended to prevent travelers and immigrants from bringing faithful domestic servants (often designated by the Spanish word *criado*) with them into Cuba. As refugees from New Orleans and other Southern ports thronged into Havana toward the end of 1862, Cuban authorities discussed what to do with the slaves they brought with them.¹¹³ They faced the same dilemma that officials in New Orleans had faced in 1809 when a convoy of French refugees, expelled from Cuba in the wake of Napoleon's invasion of Spain, showed up with black servants in tow. Back then the United States had carved a loophole in its new ban on slave importation to let them in, and now Cuba returned the favor.¹¹⁴ Two weeks after the *Bio Bio* arrived in Havana, De Hart was allowed to land the children, who were placed under the legal responsibility of a prominent Havanan named Juan Antonio Bances while they remained in the De Harts' (or perhaps Roland's) possession.¹¹⁵

The Herera children were just three among many thousands of slaves who were "refugeed" by their owners during the Civil War.¹¹⁶ Clara Walker was another. She was born into slavery in Arkansas and taken to California during the Civil War. Eighty years later, when an interviewer asked her "What is it to refugee?" she answered, "Well, you see, suppose you was afraid dat somebody goin' to take your property an' you run dem away off somewhere."¹¹⁷ Walker understood her master's motives. Fearful of losing their valuable property, owners forced, tricked, and talked their slaves into going where the Union army could not find them. Those who went along were lauded by their owners. A young Confederate woman escaping from Baton Rouge in late May 1862 met up with a band of hundreds of white and black people "all mixed together" walking in the road, fleeing from the Union troops. The slaves "deserve the greatest praise for their conduct," she thought, having saved their owners' belongings rather than their own.¹¹⁸ Shortly after the war, another displaced Louisianian recalled that many white women fleeing to Texas were "protected only by faithful negro servants."[119] Only a few of Frances Fearn's family's many slaves declined to accompany her father from Lafourche Parish to Texas. "They were often very short of food and had many hardships to endure," her mother marveled, "but not once did the slaves falter or cease in their vigilant care and consideration of him."[120] These stories complemented the dismal reports that circulated through the Confederacy of the doom that awaited slaves who stayed to greet the Union army, such as Confederate Governor Henry Watkins Allen's 1864 message to the Louisiana state legislature, which reported that slaves working on plantations seized by the Yankees had "died like sheep with the rot."[121]

Former slaves and their children interviewed in the 1930s remembered that their owners had tried to delay their freedom by hustling them out of the reach of Union power.[122] "Time dey ready for freedom in Louisiana," recalled Ella Washington, "dey refugees us to Texas, in de wagons. Us travel all day and half de night and sleep on de ground."[123] Fred Brown had been a boy in Baton Rouge during the war. "Jus' 'fore freedom come, de new overseer am 'structed to take us to Texas," he recalled. He and his comrades were taken to Kaufman County "and we is refugees dere."[124] Jake Walker was born in Mississippi after the war, so he never experienced slavery and emancipation, but his mother told him "she was refugeed to Texas and when they brung them back, Master Will Walker met them at the creek on his place and he said, 'You all are free now.'"[125] Andrew Smith's mother told him a similar story. She was "refugeed to Texas till the year of the surrender. They didn't know nothing 'bout freedom till a while after they got back from Texas."[126] These shared memories testified to the experience of wartime dislocation, the final chapter in the history of forced migration endured by enslaved African Americans. They articulated the knowledge that emancipation was an uneven process that took place sooner in some places than others, and that their former owners tried to keep them enslaved as long as possible by distance and isolation from the prospect of freedom. What makes Ernest, Mary, and Josephine Herera's story so extraordinary is that they were refugeed to Cuba, one of the last bastions of slavery in the Americas, and they continued to be held there as slaves even after slavery was abolished in the United States.

4

Justice

MARY DE HART returned from Havana by herself "to pay a visit to her friends" in New Orleans in January 1865.[1] The war was not over yet, but the Confederacy was reeling. Lincoln had been reelected in November, ending hopes for a negotiated peace. Sherman's army sliced through Georgia and took Savannah in time for Christmas. Grant laid siege to Petersburg, Virginia. So desperate was the Confederacy that its top officials made plans to arm slaves, but it was too late. Tens of thousands were already fighting for the other side, and the walls of slavery were tumbling down. Early in 1864, Union General Nathaniel Banks recognized that Louisiana's state constitutional provisions and laws concerning slavery were "inconsistent with the present condition of public affairs," and so he declared them "inoperable and void." Finally, after two years of Union rule in New Orleans, the ratification of Louisiana's new state constitution in September 1864 formally abolished slavery there. Rose Herera was no longer a slave. People of color clamored for civil and political rights, including the right to vote, but they faced powerful opposition to their dream of equal citizenship.² De Hart would not have been unaware of these sea changes. News from home arrived in Havana with every steamer from New Orleans. Yet she went back anyway. Two years is a long time to spend in exile, so it is understandable that she wanted to see her friends again. She could not have expected that she would be arrested, thrown in jail, and tried for kidnapping in a military court. However, these events did befall her and were a token of the upheaval that had taken place in New Orleans while she was gone. Nowhere was the change more on display than in the city's courts, where new concepts of justice arose from the wreckage of slavery.³

It had also been a long two years for Rose Herera to be apart from her stolen children. With emancipation came sorrow. George Herera died of disease in early May 1864.⁴ His was not a heroic death, like that of Captain André Cailloux of the Louisiana Native Guards, who fell at Port Hudson a year earlier. Cailloux's funeral drew thousands of Afro-New Orleanians into the streets to honor their "American Spartacus."⁵ Herera was one of countless black civilians who died during the war but do not count as casualties.⁶ Rose attested that he died on May 7. His burial on May 9—the same day that Louisiana's constitutional convention passed its emancipation ordinance—is noted in the death record book of the St. Louis Cemeteries, nos. 1 & 2.⁷ This grim source indicates that "George Herrera" had been born in New Orleans and was twenty-four years old when he died of "phthísié pulmonaire," or tuberculosis, a disease that many white doctors associated with black bodies. There was a "pretty general opinion," wrote one army doctor shortly after the war, "that tuberculosis is a scourge of the negro, especially the mulatto."

He hypothesized, fancifully, that the reason was that black people have a "tropical, or small lung."[8] Herera had been living at 241 Bourbon Street between St. Philip and Ursulines (the modern address of the same location is 1031 Bourbon; like De Hart's residence in Havana, it is now a parking lot.)[9] Rose may have lived there, too, after the De Harts left for Cuba. She carried on her husband's name after his death.

Four months after George died, Rose gave birth to a daughter named Louise Josephine, their fifth child. She was baptized at the St. Augustine Church in New Orleans' Tremé neighborhood in September 1864, just a few blocks away from where George Herera had lived.[10] Her baptismal record, which identifies her as "Louise Joséphine Elera," describes the girl as the "fille légitime de George Elera et de Marie Rose," or the legitimate daughter of George Elera (yet another spelling of that elusive name) and Marie Rose. Louise has a surname. This document is the first in which Rose does not appear as a slave. The record names both parents, not just the mother, and the reference to Louise as her parents' legitimate daughter indicates that the church recognized their marriage. For George this recognition was a posthumous honor. Louise's godparents are identified as Louis Forstall and Cecile Hypolite, but their race is not recorded. Compare this document to Rose's baptismal record from thirty years earlier: the watermarks of slavery have faded away.[11]

That Louise Josephine was baptized at St. Augustine Church is notable because that church had become a spiritual center for the city's "downtown" Catholic creoles of color. Rose Herera was part of a parish that promoted the religious instruction of women and children of color, and it would later harbor many of the city's

Tomb of the Unknown Slave, St. Augustine Church, New Orleans. Photograph by the author, 3 March 2012.

civil rights activists from Homer Plessy to A. P. Tureaud. One hundred and fifty years later, the church remained vital to New Orleans' enduring black Catholic community. In 2004, its congregation dedicated the *Tomb of the Unknown Slave*, a cross fashioned from a marine chain draped with shackles. It honors the memory of the "nameless, faceless, turfless Africans who met an untimely death" in a land without proper burials. A year later Hurricane Katrina swept away many hundreds more.[12] (See photograph.) The parishioners of St. Augustine have weathered many storms.

Rose Herera entered into freedom as a widow with two small children to take care of. Despite these unenviable circumstances, she wanted her other three children back and would take audacious steps to get them. Her refusal to abandon and forget them and her commitment to recovering them focus a spotlight on a crucial aspect of what freedom meant to newly emancipated people: the restoration of families shredded by kidnapping, sale, and forced migration. The quest to unite with long-lost loved ones was *central* to the meaning of freedom. Wives searched for their husbands, and husbands for their wives. Parents searched for their children, and children for their parents. They placed notices in newspapers, wrote letters to government officials and church leaders, and retraced their paths through the landscape of severance and sale. Some people found their kin, but more probably did not. "Dey was heaps of nigger families dat I know was sep'rated in de time of bondage dat tried to find dey folkses what was gone," recalled one hundred and four-year-old Tines Hendricks in the 1930s, "But de mostest of 'em never git togedder ag'in even after dey got free 'cause dey don't know where one or de other is."[13] Yet even when newly freed people could not find their kin, the act of searching for them offered testimony to slavery's devastating effect on their families.

Many newly freed people looked for their people in New Orleans, where so many slave families had been threshed apart. Thus did the archbishop of New Orleans receive a letter from Austin, Texas, in December 1866, asking him to look into the whereabouts of the children of an "old negro woman" whose children had been sold off before the war. "She only knows that the man who bought them was named Jones and that they went to New Orleans."[14] Some newly freed people in New Orleans did not have to look as far to find their kin. They knew exactly where they were—next door, down the street, or around the corner. As Ann Penrose Wilkinson discovered, black parents did not hesitate to claim their children from the children's owners, nor did they hesitate to appeal to the Union government for help in exercising their claims. "Applications to this Office by Parents for their Children are of daily occurrence," observed George Hanks, the city's Superintendent of Negro Labor, in April 1864. "Are not the Parents being free entitled to the Custody of their offspring. If not of what benefit is their freedom?"[15] Hanks grasped that for many newly freed people, getting their children out of slavery was the most urgent task at hand. It was a repudiation of one of American slavery's fundamental conceits. Proslavery dogmatists saw all slaves as figurative children and black people as a childish race, an indignity that justified the denial of parental rights to adult slaves. Incapable of taking care of themselves, slaves could not be expected to take care of their own children without white supervision. One prominent proslavery spokesman went so far as to argue that slavery actually protected slave children from being abused by their parents. White Southern slaveowners numbed themselves to the harm they inflicted upon slave families. They convinced themselves that the affective bonds of family—love, pride, dignity, pain, and sorrow among others—did not matter very much to slaves. ("Their griefs are transient," Thomas Jefferson once wrote.) It was all a massive, self-serving lie erected as truth on the scaffolding of social power.[16]

So many enslaved parents clung to their children as tightly as they could despite constant reminders that those children did not "belong" to them as a matter of law and could be taken away

JUSTICE

from them with impunity. At those life-changing moments when an owner's estate was divided among his heirs; or slaves were sold to satisfy creditors, or moved to a new labor camp on the southwestern frontier, or rented out for another year's work; or when a master called a boy into the "big house" to be raised as a valet, or whipped a girl in front of her parents—the point was driven home. Your children are not your children. They belong to someone else, who can do whatever he wants with them. As ex-slave Caroline Hunter put it in 1937, "During slavery it seemed lak yo' chillun b'long to ev'ybody but you."[17] It can be hard to fathom how enslaved mothers and fathers coped with this trauma. It is easy to suspect that a cold fatalism crept into their hearts as insulation against inevitable heartbreak, but there is scant evidence of this attitude taking hold. One cannot read the many narratives of former slaves, or the twentieth-century interviews with those who had been slaves as children, without being moved by the depth of feeling between parents and children. The enduring love that enslaved parents had for their children impelled them to recover their children from owners who would not let them go.[18]

Children are seldom heard or seen in history. The exceptions are times when parental authority breaks down, and children perturb the social order. Disasters like war, which manufacture and displace large numbers of orphans, are such times. There are also eras when parental authority is fractured not by an immediate shock such as war, but by more fundamental shifts in the structure of authority that leave children exposed to new forms of power, as when Christian missionaries established schools for Indian children for the purpose of "civilizing" them and saving their souls.[19] Wartime emancipation combined the shock of war with an overturning of slaveowners' paternalism. This one-two punch knocked slave children loose from their masters' households. The intimate disputes that then broke out between freed parents and former owners over the fate of children became intensely public, both in the sense that they were widely publicized in local and northern newspapers and periodicals, and that they drew the government into the novel task of deciding the children's fate. As the historian Mary Mitchell has shown, abolitionists toured the North with freed children in tow. They circulated postcards featuring images of slave children who were so light-skinned they looked white. Do-gooders established orphanages and schools that drew newly freed children into a new vision of black childhood after slavery that floated dueling hopes of uplift and control. America's racial future, embodied by children, was up for grabs.[20]

The case that prompted Hanks's attention involved one Madame Cougot, who had been granted possession of a little girl by the Union authorities. Cougot complained that the girl's mother was hanging around and using "threatening language." She wanted the mother removed "so that she could not come and trouble her." Upon investigating the case, Thomas Conway, a Union official with the formidable title of Inspector of Vagrants, discovered that although the girl said she wanted to stay with Madame Cougot, she had been influenced by "strong pressure and the exercise of considerable cunning." He found that Cougot was "not in any sort of sympathy with our Government," whereas the girl's father had been a Union soldier and her mother was an "industrious person" who had taken good care of her daughter.

JUSTICE

"The return of the child to slavery is an outrage," protested Conway. "I found the girl on her knees washing a brick side walk at 11 o'clock in the morning. Whereas, if she were left with her mother, she would have been at school reaping the sweetest fruits of liberty."[21] Variations on this scene played out thousands of times across the South in the aftermath of slavery. Herera's case was special only because her children had been taken to Cuba. This international dimension placed extra legal and logistical obstacles on her road to reunion.

News traveled fast along the banquette descending from the levee to the back o' town. Hearing that Madame De Hart had returned from Cuba, Rose Herera sought her out on January 2 and "begged the restoration of her children, which Mrs. De Hart refused."[22] One can only imagine that tense meeting. After De Hart refused to promise to return the children, Herera found a lawyer to press a case against her. He had De Hart arrested on January 6 and hauled into a civilian court on charges of kidnapping.[23] The reversal of fortune was stark. Just two years earlier, Herera had languished in jail. Now it was De Hart's turn. That De Hart was thrown in jail on charges levied by her former slave reveals the new politics of justice after slavery.

The politics of justice was complicated by tension between civilian and military authority and the many dilemmas involved in righting the wrongs of slavery. In Lincoln's words, Louisiana's judiciary had been "swept away" by the war, and its reconstruction was still under way as De Hart's case proceeded through the courts.[24] After Union troops took New Orleans in May 1862, the city's six "recorder's courts," which had handled criminal cases, were replaced by a provost court, a military court that handled virtually all criminal cases under martial law. A civilian judiciary slowly returned. Two recorder's courts reopened in 1863 with new judges who had sworn an oath of allegiance to the Union. Criminal cases involving civilians shifted back to the recorder's courts, whereas criminal cases involving military personnel (including black soldiers), and many cases involving slaves and freedpeople who were not soldiers, remained under the jurisdiction of the provost court. A Union official reported that early in 1864, the civilian courts were in a state of "shocking confusion" when it came to the rights of freedpeople, who had "no other recourse than that furnished by the military authorities." Fraught with jurisdictional and political tension, a two-headed system of civilian and military criminal justice remained in place until federal troops were removed from New Orleans at the end of Reconstruction.[25]

De Hart's case started out in a civilian court and ended up in a military one. After five days in jail, De Hart was released on a $1,000 bond—the same sum that James De Hart had paid for Rose Herera and her children. Because it involved civilians only, the case was heard in the Second District Recorder's Court in February. The judge, F. A. Woolfley, quickly dismissed the case on the grounds that "there was no statute applicable in such a criminal prosecution, and that no statute had been violated." No law ever prohibited an owner from taking her slave out of the country, so there was nothing to charge her with. De Hart could not be tried for doing something that was not a crime. In normal circumstances, that ruling would have closed the matter, but with the provost court still in operation to enforce an alternative sense of justice, Herera had not exhausted her legal remedies.[26]

JUSTICE

It helped a great deal that Herera had prominent lawyers on her side. She could not have taken her case to court without lawyers versed in the arcane technicalities of law who were willing to represent her. Their job was to translate her sense of justice into the language of the law and guide her through the law's gauntlet. Although it was De Hart who was on trial (and she had lawyers, too), navigating the city's inchoate judicial system would have been no less of an ordeal for the illiterate, newly freed Herera. First she went to Henry Train, whose office was centrally located at 13 St. Peter Street on Jackson Square. She might have known him from his political activities in support of freedpeople. He was a director of the biracial Freedmen's Aid Association and a member of the Central Executive Committee of the Friends of Universal Suffrage, a major radical organization.[27] It was Train who advised Herera to have De Hart arrested in early January and charged with kidnapping, and it was Train who unsuccessfully represented her in the recorder's court. But after Judge Woolfley dismissed the case, Herera and Train enlisted the aid of Thomas Jefferson Durant, of Durant and Hornor, to champion her cause. This was a crucial move, because Durant happened to be the leading white egalitarian in Louisiana. He would take her case to the next level and beyond.[28]

Thomas Jefferson Durant was a formidable ally. Born in Pennsylvania, Durant moved to New Orleans as a teenager in the early 1830s and gained a name for himself as a newspaper editor, workingmen's advocate, Democratic politician, and lawyer. At thirty he won a coveted appointment as U.S. district attorney for the eastern district of Louisiana. One admirer called him "the architect of his own fortunes," which was another way of saying that he was the classic Jacksonian type, a self-made man. It should not be surprising, then, to learn that Durant purchased a slave woman and her three children in 1845. Nevertheless, Durant had some unorthodox views on slavery. He took an interest in the ideas of Charles Fourier, an influential French socialist, whose elaborate theories of "association" led to the founding of utopian communities in Europe and America. Durant himself was no utopian; he preferred "thorough and practical reform." Like his namesake, Thomas Jefferson Durant thought slavery was "an evil affecting the white race even more than it does the black," but he abhorred abolitionism. "This slavery question seems to make rabid all who touch it," he warned the leader of the American Fourierists in 1847.[29]

The slaveholders' rebellion altered Durant. He metamorphosed from a respected, if eccentric, member of the Louisiana bar into one of the leaders of Louisiana's wartime movement for black equality. During the secession crisis, Durant opposed the fire-eaters. "I fear the future will be full of horrors," he wrote in private correspondence. When the war came, he served in the Louisiana militia, but did not stray very far from his home at the corner of Canal and Dryades streets in New Orleans, just a block away from where the De Harts lived.[30] The arrival of federal troops allowed Durant to express his true political allegiance to the Union, but he earned Lincoln's ire by defending New Orleans' loyal slaveowners in the summer of 1862. Durant soon turned against slavery. He legally manumitted his own slaves Roseanna, her daughters Elizabeth and Sally, and Elizabeth's sixteen-month-old baby Henrietta in March 1863.[31] A rival unionist, the dentist A. P. Dostie, criticized Durant for having owned slaves and then "ostentatiously" emancipating them once slavery was already practically dead.[32] In October 1863 Durant wrote to Lincoln that "we, in Louisiana, are now so situated that we must choose between the systems of Slavery and freedom: I do not hesitate to choose the latter, for, after the Proclamation it would be a great crime and a great error to establish slavery again."[33] He warned Lincoln that many slaveowners thought otherwise and would return newly freed people to slavery if they could. This point is important because the wartime movement from slavery to freedom seems in hindsight to have been so inexorable that the real fear of reversal has been forgotten. The reason that Durant formally manumitted his slaves was to ensure that they could not be reenslaved if New Orleans fell back into Confederate hands. By the end of 1863, Durant was publicly proclaiming himself to be a firm unionist and a "radical abolitionist."[34]

Durant played a big, controversial part in the political drama of Louisiana's wartime reconstruction. He was appointed as the state's attorney general in 1863 and had the task of registering loyal voters for an election to select delegates to a convention that would write a new "free-state" constitution that abolished slavery. The task was slow and difficult because most of the state remained in Confederate hands, and Durant complained that the Union army refused to aid him in registering loyal voters in the places it did possess. But Lincoln did not want excuses; he wanted a new state built upon a "tangible nucleus" of the electorate as fast as possible. With that goal in mind, Lincoln transferred power to organize a new state government into General

Nathaniel Banks's hands at the end of 1863, and Banks swiftly seized the reins. Banks cut out Durant and engineered the election of Michael Hahn, a German-American unionist, as Louisiana's governor in February 1864. When Durant and his allies turned against the Banks-Hahn regime, free-state unionism in Louisiana cracked apart. Whether it was the question of suffrage for free men of color (Durant supported it; Banks was more hesitant) or merely a scramble for power that pushed Banks and Durant apart, the schism damaged unionism in the state, and helped pave the way for ex-Confederates to return to power at the end of the war.[35]

Durant is best known as a radical for advocating voting rights for free men of color, but his radicalism had important other dimensions that have not attracted as much attention from historians. Durant joined the free colored activists and editors of the *Tribune* who criticized Banks's 1864 labor policy as a return to slavery. He helped to organize the Freedmen's Aid Association early in 1865 to loan money, rent land, and provide other support to freedpeople who were trying to work for themselves.[36] Visiting New Orleans in the spring of 1865, New York journalist Whitelaw Reid met Durant at a dinner with Chief Justice Salmon Chase. "Tall, thin, sallow, cadaverous," the New Orleans lawyer was an "intense Radical," Reid told his readers. "He speaks at negro meetings, demands negro suffrage, unites with negroes in educational movements, champions negroes in the courts."[37] Late in 1865, at one of those meetings, Durant gave a speech to the Freedmen's Aid Association that pronounced a capacious view of black liberty. Liberty meant more than the right to work, he claimed. It meant "the right to enjoy the fruits of one's labor . . . the right to own the soil that he tills and the marriage right, the right to have your children around you, and above all to have one's rights respected by his neighbor."[38]

Among those Durant championed in the courts were freedwomen seeking to recover their children. Rose Herera's case was not the first he had argued. In October 1863, Durant (with Henry Train) represented a newly freed woman named Virinda who was trying to recover two of her children from her former owner, ex-Recorder Joseph Soloman. Virinda had gained her freedom as a reward for revealing "concealed weapons" to the Union authorities, and now that she was free, she thought she was entitled to her children. The case was heard in Judge Atocha's provost court, where Virinda herself seemed to be on trial. Witnesses for Soloman maligned her as a bad character. They testified that she kept company with "colored women of bad repute," was a "lewd and abandoned woman," and a thief. One of the children took the stand and indicated that she preferred to stay with Soloman because "I did not have enough to eat when I was with my mother." Other witnesses defended Virinda's character as a steady worker. "Her conduct is good," testified Colonel Hanks.[39] The arguments on both sides of Virinda's case epitomized the rival claims of parents and owners. "A mother's claim to her child is the highest known to the laws," Durant asserted, "no stranger has a right to keep a child from the mother merely because he could furnish it with better food, clothing, and shelter." Soloman retorted that he was no stranger to the children. Rather, he had been a surrogate father: "They were born under his roof; he had raised them, paid their doctor's bills for them, treated them as kindly as he did his own children, and claimed them by virtue of laws which had never been repealed."⁴⁰

Judge Atocha's decision was, well, Solomanic. He dismissed the mother's right to her children and opted to "consider the future welfare of the children." This principle allowed for broad judicial discretion in custody cases. Finding that the respectable white man could care for the children better than their working mother, the judge awarded custody to Soloman but granted Virinda visiting rights for two hours on Tuesdays and Fridays. Soon even that was taken away. In an episode reminiscent of the Cougot case, Soloman kept Virinda from seeing the children and then had her arrested for using "violent language" against him. She had to give up her visitation rights to get out of jail. Virinda's case demonstrates that newly freed people faced an uphill climb to recover their children through the courts. Rose Herera would learn the same lesson.⁴¹

After striking out at the recorder's court, Herera took her case to the Union military authorities, whom she hoped would be more sympathetic to her plight than Judge Woolfley. Banks had moved on, so she had to appeal to the new Union military commander of the Department of the Gulf, Major General Stephen A. Hurlbut, to take up the case.⁴² Henry Train prepared a petition on her behalf, which she signed with an *X*. In the petition, and in all other government documents relating to the case, her last name is spelled "Elyra," an Anglicized version of the Spanish "Herera." The petition adds that she was *"sometimes called Mrs. George Elyra,"* emphasizing her status as a wife.⁴³ The petition explained who she was, laid out the basic story of the taking of the children against her will, and drew a sharp contrast between the De Harts' treason and her own loyalty. It alleged that the De Harts were "enemies to the United States and rebels to the government," whereas it insisted that Herera and her children "are free and entitled to the rights of American citizens, and to the protection of the government of the United States."[44] The petition filtered Rose Herera's voice through Henry Train's pen, so we cannot be sure the words were her own. Still, it is remarkable to find counsel for a recently freed woman in the South insisting on her rights of citizenship and demanding the protection of the U.S. government.[45]

At that moment, the citizenship rights of recently freed men and women were far from settled. The Supreme Court's controversial *Dred Scott* decision of 1857 had denied citizenship to black people, but in November 1862, Lincoln's attorney general Edward Bates publicly opined that free men of color, if born in the United States, were citizens. Despite his authority, Bates's opinion did not quell debate over black citizenship. African Americans and their allies had to fight for it during the war and long afterwards. It took the Civil Rights Act of 1866 and ratification of the Fourteenth Amendment two years after that to confirm—on paper at least—that "all persons born or naturalized in the United States, and subject to the jurisdiction thereof, are citizens of the United States." Yet the contours of national citizenship were poorly defined. Bates admitted that "eighty years of practical enjoyment of citizenship, under the Constitution, have not sufficed to teach us either the exact meaning of the word, or the constituent elements of the thing we prize so highly." For black people in New Orleans, citizenship meant many things, from the right to hop onto any streetcar to the right to vote. Rose Herera's petition insisted that being a citizen meant getting her children back.[46]

Two days after receiving the petition, Hurlbut ordered De Hart arrested again. She was locked up in the Julia Street women's prison, a private house that had been confiscated by Union authorities and (in the recollection of one of its inmates) "converted into a prison for the ladies of the city who should offend those mighty potentates, Butler and Banks, and the rest."[47] Hurlbut ordered that the case be tried under military jurisdiction in the provost court, which was administered at that time by Major G. Norman Lieber, son of the famous author of the country's first comprehensive laws of war, Francis Lieber.[48] Provost courts were military tribunals established by the Union army as part of its police powers. Many of the cases involved infractions by soldiers, and black soldiers not infrequently found themselves on trial for offenses such as drunkenness and assault. The provost courts also heard cases involving white Southerners who attacked Union soldiers and agents or used seditious language in public, such as drunkenly damning old Abe Lincoln to hell or insulting Union soldiers as sons of bitches. Wherever Union authorities held sway, newly freed people brought their grievances to the provost courts because they had no hope of justice in civilian courts dominated by white Southerners. A half century after the war ended, General Oliver Otis Howard, the head of the Freedmen's Bureau, recalled in his autobiography that although the provost courts were usually fair to freedpeople, they were not immune to "infectious prejudice against the negro."[49]

JUSTICE

Like all courts, the provost court was more than a legal venue. It was also a political and social theater where ideas of justice were staged and enacted by judges, lawyers, witnesses, plaintiffs, and defendants.[50] Perhaps the most important new idea of justice to be introduced into the South via the provost court was the idea that people of color should be able to testify against white people in a court. The old laws died hard. "Many Judges of Courts have been known to say openly that 'they did not want to hear d—d nigger testimony,'" complained Thomas Conway (now elevated to the title of General Superintendent of Freedmen) in an 1865 report on the condition of freedpeople in Louisiana.[51]

The first provost court judge in New Orleans, Major Joseph Bell, allowed a black witness in one of the earliest cases to come before the court. The defendant's lawyer objected to this violation of Louisiana law. "Has Louisiana gone out of the Union?" asked Bell. "Yes," replied the lawyer. "Well, then, she took her laws with her," observed the judge, "Let the man be sworn!"[52] This anecdote comes from a partisan source—James Parton's admiring account of Butler's reign in New Orleans in 1862—yet Parton relied on eyewitnesses with fresh memories of recent events, and his description of the business of New Orleans' provost courts is unrivalled.

The provost judges heard a full spectrum of cases, from "a street broil to questions of constitutional law, from petty larceny to high treason, from matrimonial squabbles to suits for divorce."[53] Justice moved swiftly. Some cases would only take one or two minutes to process; a few would last as long as an hour.

The De Hart case took longer than most. When it came to deciding cases in New Orleans, the judges drew on an eclectic array of legal sources and authorities. Bell "had to ransack all books and all the by-ways of his memory for law and precedent to guide him in his novel situation. French law, Spanish law, admiralty law, the slave code, state law, municipal law, common law, were all laid under contribution," explained Parton, "and when these failed to meet the case, he drew upon the ample resources of his own common sense."[54]

Nowhere did "common sense" matter more than in cases involving slaves and freedpeople. The provost judges jettisoned the state's black code (although it was hauled back in for the De Hart case), which had fixed the subordinate legal status of slaves and free people of color before the arrival of the Union army. This left a hole in the law, which was filled partway by the judges' own "common sense" of justice. Yet what was common sense to the Union officers who presided over the provost court was lawless despotism to the slaveowners in New Orleans. Just as Tom Paine's *Common Sense* had marked a revolutionary challenge to colonial power in 1776, the provost court judges' commonsense understandings of justice for people of African descent also posed, at times, a revolutionary challenge to the local slave power.[55]

The case Parton chose as a "specimen of the provost court slave cases" resembled Rose Herera's in several respects. It was a child custody case featuring a poisonous compound of family and property. The case involved a free man of color named John Montamal who married a slave woman and then purchased her for six hundred dollars. "Both were light mulattoes," wrote Parton, possibly to hint at the whiteness of their daughter, "an intelligent girl eleven years old, who had been sent to school and had been received into the Catholic church." Having fallen into debt, the husband-father-owner had to mortgage his daughter to creditors. When his finances worsened, the mortgage was foreclosed and his daughter auctioned off at a sheriff's sale. The arrival of the Union army brought hope. Montamal went to the provost court to plead for her return. The judge presiding over the case, Colonel J. B. Kinsman, "decided the girl was free and gave her back to her parents." Parton observed that the decision "was manifestly contrary to the laws of Louisiana, which would have doomed the girl to slavery," but Kinsman agreed with Bell that "when Louisiana went out of the Union she took her black laws with her." Parton hinted that his account of the case just scratched the surface of Montamal's story, "which, fully related, would furnish the material for an Uncle Tom novel." He urged his white readers to cross the mental boundary of race by imagining "a favorite child, sister, niece, or ward of their own" in the position of Montamal's daughter.[56]

Like Montamal and Virinda, Rose Herera asked the Union government to rescue her children from slavery. This step took courage because it invited retaliation. As night fell on March 6, two strangers visited Herera's house on the corner of Burgundy and Barrack and "tried to induce her, by expostulation and by threats of injury to her children in Havana, to abandon the effort to procure their restoration."[57] The men warned her that her lawyers were out to rob her. They offered to guarantee that the children would be returned after the war, but they also said "she would be made to suffer for it when the war was over."[58] She did not bow to the threat.

Judge Advocate Fenton Rockwell informed Durant that the case was scheduled for Friday, March 10, at 10 a.m. "Will you have the kindness to be ready at that time with witnesses," he directed, adding, "The case is too important to admit of any delay."[59] Durant needed more time to gather evidence to support Herera's claim that the children were taken without her consent, so he asked for a postponement. Then he requested from the police jail the orders for Rose's arrest and discharge and the name of the officer who had arrested her. He also requested from the provost marshal general copies of De Hart's passports permitting her to go to Havana with the children "and a statement of the means, if known, by which Mrs. De Hart could get a pass for three colored children of such tender years." From Warneken and Co., the shipping agents for the steamship *Bio Bio* that carried De Hart and the children to Havana, Durant requested "what their books show about the three children."[60] Durant seems to have taken Herera's case seriously and represented her diligently. At the same time, the longer he took to amass evidence, the longer De Hart sat in jail.

United States v. Mrs. De Hart opened in the provost court on Saturday, April 8, 1865, and concluded on Thursday, April 13, 1865, four days after Lee surrendered at Appomattox.[61] No less than Lee and Grant, the two women who confronted each other in Lieber's courtroom were enemies. They looked at the world from profoundly different angles. From Mary De Hart's perspective, the proceedings in the provost court must have seemed deeply unjust. Here was an unfaithful, insolent domestic challenging her former mistress for the possession of her lawful property. Added to this indignity was her shoddy treatment by the Union military authorities. New Orleans' ex-Confederate community would have regarded her incarceration as yet another insult to Southern ladyhood by the Union authorities. From Rose Herera's perspective, on the other hand, the injustice was that anyone would deprive a mother of her children by kidnapping them and holding them as slaves in a foreign country, and then have the audacity to proclaim innocence in open court. As a moral drama, nothing less than slavery itself was on trial. From a legal standpoint, however, the case revolved around more specific questions concerning the facts, the law, and the authority of the court to decide these matters.

First of all, did the children leave with their mother's consent and the government's permission? The prosecution depended on two witnesses of color who would not have been allowed to testify before the arrival of Union troops. One was Rose Herera, and the other was her mother, Leocadie. Herera testified that she never agreed to the children's departure. She told the story of her quarrel with Madame Roland; her arrest and incarceration; her negotiations with De Hart in the parish jail; her mother's and husband's unsuccessful attempts to keep De Hart from sailing with the children; and her release from jail a little too late to stop them. Leocadie then corroborated her daughter's story and clarified her own role in the affair. She had visited the *Bio Bio* on the afternoon that it sailed. She "did not make any attempt to get the children," she testified, "but as soon as the children saw witness defendant [De Hart] shoved the children away and prevented them from getting near her." She added that De Hart had asked her to go to Havana, too, and even promised to pay her way, but Leocadie had her own charges to attend to. Leocadie's testimony exhibited an air of defiance. "Witness cannot read or write," runs the transcript, "but is sufficiently instructed to defend herself when attacked."[62]

To dispute the government's case that the children were taken without permission, the defense witnesses testified to three main points: (1) nobody objected to De Hart taking the children; (2) the children had not been concealed on board the *Bio Bio;* and (3) the provost marshal had issued passports for De Hart to sail to Havana with the children. J. A. Letton, who had been the clerk of the police jail in the winter of 1862–63, remembered Rose from the jail. He recounted the conversation between J. G. Fallon and Rose Herera about her going to Havana with De Hart and the children. "I heard her make no objection to the children going to Havana, nor any remonstrance," he asserted.[63] Fallon's wife testified that George Herera, whom she saw at the *Bio Bio*'s mooring on the day before it left, "made no complaint or objection to the children going." She also testified to seeing Leocadie bid farewell to her grandchildren on board the vessel. "I did not see the children cry when she left," she recalled. Leocadie "kissed them when she left and bid them good-bye."[64] Fallon, the shipping agent for Warneken and Co., concurred with his wife. He had seen Leocadie on the *Bio Bio,* and "she did not make any objection to the children going." Similarly, George Leveque "did not hear the grandmother say or do anything to protest against the children going off, or show any dissatisfaction."[65] Missing from the trial record was the one irrefutable piece of tangible evidence that George Herera objected to the children's departure—his January 14 letter to General Nathaniel Banks urging him to prevent Mrs. De Hart from taking the children to Havana. He did complain. He was not satisfied.

Witnesses for the defense testified that De Hart and Roland had not hidden the children away on the *Bio Bio*. If the children were playing out in the open on board the vessel, who could suspect De Hart of kidnapping or any other malice? "There was no concealment of the children; they were playing about the boat; were apparently happy and contented," recalled George Leveque. Mrs. Hickman agreed, "Everyone coming aboard could see them." Hickman testified that she did not know whether the children were "satisfied," but she observed that they were "playing, and not crying." Fallon said that he found the children in De Hart's "state-room" on the *Bio Bio*, but insisted "they were not hid away." One of the children was sitting on Mrs. Roland's knee eating a cracker.[66] According to defense witnesses, the scene on board the *Bio Bio* reflected the affectionate relationship between the De Harts and the slave children.

Friends and neighbors testified that the De Harts doted on the slave children. A Mrs. Blossman averred that the slaves "were treated like white children." Roland told her "they were never to be sold; they were to be free." One Mrs. Stockton confessed that they "were treated so well in the family that I was jealous." She too heard Roland say that the children "were to be free." Moreover, it was common knowledge "that the children were spoiled. I have seen her [Roland] hold the children in her lap and kiss them." Mrs. Fallon testified that "the children were treated very well by Madam Roland," and their parents never complained. George Leveque, "an intimate friend of De Hart," similarly declared that "the children were treated very well." A.

F. Hickman, a wholesale grocer who lived on Julia Street, testified that he often saw that children at Roland's, where they "were treated as well as [her] own children; not treated as slaves are generally treated; were petted and treated kindly." On cross-examination, Hickman realized that he had said too much. The children "were kindly treated, as all slaves are," he corrected himself. "I did not intend to say they were treated differently from other slaves."[67] All these protestations were essential to the benevolent image prescribed by proslavery dogma, but whether the De Harts treated the children well or cruelly was beside the point of whether they unlawfully took the children to Cuba without their mother's consent.

The lawyers clashed over the evidence of consent and the credibility of the witnesses. Durant insisted that the testimony of Rose Herera and her mother proved that she had not consented to the children's departure "but protested with the vehemence of a mother against the outrage." He impeached "the female witnesses on the other side, who, trained in the fashionable female accomplishments of treason, see but dimly the cause of justice when presented under a dark skin." They were blinded by their racism. Even if Herera had appeared to consent, Durant argued, such consent would have been a "mere delusion" created by the dire circumstances in which she found herself: "Rose was treated as a slave, was sick and in prison. She was in no condition, mental or physical, to give a valid consent."[68] De Hart's lawyers Holland and Baer retorted that their witnesses "are all well-known and respected citizens of this city, of unimpeachable character . . . true and loyal, though unfortunately differing with the counsel in his exalted ideas and eutopian theories relative to the race to which his client belongs."[69] Trying to clinch the case for their client, De Hart's lawyers concluded that "Rose consented positively to the children's going, and agreed to join them as soon as she got well."[70]

To show that De Hart did not act unlawfully, the defense offered further testimony and written proof that Roland got permission from Union authorities to transport the children to Cuba and had paid for the passage. Defense introduced into evidence a pass issued to Roland by the provost marshal general's office on January 12, 1863, which granted "Mrs. E. Roland, son, servant, and four children" permission to travel from New Orleans to Havana on the *Bio Bio*. The pass contained a crucial ambiguity. It did not specify that the four children were not Roland's own, nor did it indicate that they were children of color. The children were sufficiently dark-skinned to be recognized as "negritos" by port officials in Havana, so it is unlikely that anybody would have mistaken them for white children. Conveniently, the shipping agent Fallon could not remember who signed the pass, but he remembered giving it to the Captain Nichols of the *Bio Bio*, who said it was "all correct."[71] Adding to the confusion, E. F. Stockmeyer, an agent of Warneken and Co., testified that the firm's books showed no passengers "described as colored, or of African descent" for that particular voyage, but he also testified that the company did not usually record its passengers' servants' race in its books. "We took colored servants to Havana," he admitted, and as long as they were paid for, the company didn't ask questions.[72]

Even if the children had been taken against their mother's wishes, could De Hart be held responsible? The defense argued that because Madam Roland owned Rose and her children, Mary De Hart was not responsible for them and should not be punished for Roland's taking them to Cuba. It was Roland who "appeared to have control" of the children on the *Bio Bio*, testified J. G. Fallon.[73] In contrast, Durant argued that the transfer was a sham designed to elude the De Harts' creditors and the authorities. Aiding the prosecution was P. A. Snaer, a New Orleans dentist who had served in James De Hart's militia company, and, like Captain De Hart, went to Havana in the fall of 1862, where the two men saw each other again. He testified that a few days before he left New Orleans, Mrs. De Hart "proposed to me to take one of the children to Havana," but he had rejected the proposal. Snaer's testimony implied that after her husband left, Mrs. De Hart rather than Roland had been in control of the children.[74]

Another prosecution witness, Dr. J. L. Riddell, strengthened the case that the sale to Roland was a sham. Riddell was a renowned if controversial professor of chemistry at the Louisiana Medical College (now Tulane.) He also happened to be a close neighbor of Durant, as well as the De Harts' landlord at 17 Baronne Street. The De Harts had fallen behind on rent in 1862, and whenever Riddell visited them to ask for payment, he took notice of the valuable Rose. "I had my eye upon her," he testified. After James De Hart fled to Havana, and Mrs. De Hart moved to another house along with Roland, Herera, and the children, Riddell filed suit for the year's rent he was owed. It was only then that he learned to his surprise that De Hart had sold her to Roland. "I had seen nothing to show that De Hart had ceased to become her owner, or that she belonged to Mrs. Roland," he testified. "Circumstances in the house remained the same as to apparent control of the girl by the defendant." Riddell felt cheated; he got his revenge by testifying against De Hart.[75]

Supposing that the children were taken by De Hart without their mother's consent, the question remained: Was the act a crime? Yes, argued Durant, as he dusted off the slave code for a novel purpose. Article 43 of French Louisiana's original 1724 Code Noir prohibited the separation of children under the age of fourteen from their parents. This was one of many paper protections for slaves written into the code. After the Louisiana Purchase, that colonial provision was modified and integrated into the 1806 Black Code, which prohibited slave children under the age of ten from being sold apart from their mothers. The change favored buyers and sellers over parents and children. The revised law lowered the age of nonseparation from fourteen to ten, and changed the language from "parents" to "mothers," thereby denying fathers parental rights to their young children.[76]

A subsequent law enacted in 1829 prohibited any slave child under the age of ten from being brought into Louisiana for sale without its mother, unless the seller provided affadavits that the child's mother was dead. The law was supposed to protect slave families—defined as mothers and children—from being torn apart by the interstate slave trade. Louisiana was nearly alone among the Southern states in prohibiting the sale of children away from their mothers (Alabama enacted a similar law in 1852), and it may have deterred separations, but the law was only invoked in a handful of cases, and nobody was ever punished for violating it. How could they be, when black people were not allowed to testify against whites? Historian Walter Johnson suggests that slave dealers simply marketed slave children as orphans in order to sell them legally, whether the children's parents were dead or not.[77]

Pointing to these provisions in the law, Durant contended that De Hart had violated "the spirit" of Louisiana's slave code by separating the Herera children from their mother.[78] It was an ingenious, if dubious, effort to avoid inflicting an ex post facto punishment on De Hart—that is, punishing her for doing something that was not a crime when she did it. The taboo against ex post facto punishments is a basic legal principle rooted in fairness. People should be able to know if what they are doing is legal, and if it is legal at the time they do it, they should not be punished for it if it later becomes illegal.[79] How did this principle apply to slavery and emancipation? As far back as 1787, slavery's defenders in the Ohio valley had criticized the Northwest Ordinance's prohibition on slavery as an ex post facto law. The same argument cropped up from time to time in debates over abolition and emancipation and reappeared during the Civil War as the Union adopted its policies of confiscation. The taboo on ex post facto laws did not bar emancipation, but it did prevent former slaveowners from being punished for having done things that were cruel yet legal. By alleging that De Hart had violated the "spirit" of the slave code's protective clauses, Durant was acknowledging that she had not violated the letter of the law.[80]

De Hart's lawyers, Buchanan and Gilman, pounced on Durant's shaky argument. They argued, futilely, that the provost court was not a "competent tribunal" for the prosecution of an offense against the criminal laws. More persuasively, they argued that the provisions of the slave code simply did not apply to the facts of the case. The Herera children had been born in

Louisiana, not brought from somewhere else, and they had not been sold apart from their mother. By law and custom, slaveowners could separate mothers from children as long as they didn't sell them apart. That had never been a crime, despite Durant's creative interpretation of the law's spirit. How slaveowners managed their slave property was their own business. It was only when that property changed hands that the law could step in and regulate the transaction, and even then the law had to step carefully.[81]

The argument over whether De Hart had broken the slave code was irrelevant, however, if Durant could prove that Herera and her children were free in January 1863. If they were free, then the crime of kidnapping clearly applied, and all the prosecution had to do was demonstrate that the children's parents had not consented to their departure. But the status of Rose and her children turned out to be a thorny question, and its thorniness reveals the ambiguities of the piecemeal policy of emancipation in New Orleans during the war. Durant's case for their freedom relied on the Second Confiscation Act of July 17, 1862, which obliged the government to seize the property of "any person hereafter acting as an officer of the army or navy of the rebels in arms against the United States." James De Hart fit that description, argued Durant, because he had served as an officer in the Confederate forces before the capture of New Orleans, and there was no proof that he had ever resigned. The act also prohibited any sale of property eligible for confiscation after sixty days from the passage of the act. That provision, argued Durant, meant that De Hart's sale of the slaves to Madam Roland had been "null and void." Moreover, the act barred military authorities from deciding on "the validity of the claim of any person to the service of labor or another person." This meant that the De Harts' defense could not base their case on Herera and the children having been slaves.[82]

Naturally, De Hart's lawyers disputed these allegations. Turning around Durant's argument about the inability of military tribunals to decide on the validity of claims to slaves, Buchanan and Gilman argued that this constraint meant the provost court had no authority to decide the case at all. If the court could not find that Herera and her children were slaves, neither could it find that they were free. This was a clever argument, but it ignored the intent of the law, which was to prevent military authorities from returning fugitive slaves to their owners. De Hart's lawyers followed up by contending that her husband had ceased to be a rebel before passage of the Second Confiscation Act by returning to civilian life when the Union took over New Orleans. His sale of the slaves to Roland, they pointed out, took place less than sixty days after the passage of the act, which made it legal. And finally, Herera and her children had never been "seized" by the government and so had not been made free under the terms of the act.[83] By the time these arguments were aired in April 1865, the passage of Louisiana's new state constitution abolishing slavery had superseded the Second Confiscation Act, so there was no question that Rose Herera and her two children in Louisiana were now free, but just how and when they got that way was murky. For Rose Herera and her children, and many others, wartime emancipation did not follow a straight line from slavery to freedom. The experience was more like wandering in a maze.[84]

Although she had entered from the opposite side, De Hart also found herself trapped in a maze of federal power. De Hart's lawyers used the case to criticize the system of federal military rule that continued to trespass on local civilian government in Louisiana. Any person charged with violating the criminal laws of the state of Louisiana, they insisted, should be tried "in the first district court of New Orleans, before a jury of the vicinage, upon an indictment found by a grand jury, according to the course of proceeding in criminal cases at common law." It was not merely Louisiana's new state constitution that required the regular forms of law. They argued that she had been deprived of the right of due process and trial by jury guaranteed by the federal Constitution. Noting that the kidnapping charge against De Hart had already been dismissed in the recorder's court, Buchanan and Gilman argued that although Herera could have appealed to the district attorney or state attorney general to try the case in the district court, the provost court had no business taking it up. "We formally deny that any military commander or military tribunal is competent to try offenses against the State laws by a citizen when there is a regularly organized and constitutional tribunal in session for the trial of such offenses."[85] But what De Hart's lawyers did not say—what everyone would soon grasp—is that Louisiana's new governor, James Madison Wells, who replaced now-Senator Michael Hahn in March, had begun to put Confederate sympathizers in positions of power. For starters he had appointed Edmund Abell as judge of the First District Court. Defending slavery at the state's 1864 constitutional convention, the racist Abell had asked his fellow delegates to "look at the free negro in his native jungles, sir, what do you find? A mere bug-eater; a fruit-eater." One informant reported to Banks that Wells had filled the courts with "the rankest kind of Copperheads" (Confederate sympathizers). Black people could hardly expect justice from that quarter.[86]

Ten days before he was assassinated, President Lincoln sent General Nathaniel Banks back to Louisiana to replace Stephen Hurlbut, who had resigned as commander of the Department of the Gulf. Banks arrived in New Orleans on April 20.[87] Deciding on the De Hart case was not his highest priority. More urgent was the task of keeping Governor Wells from handing Louisiana back to the rebels, while at the same time remaining in the good graces of the new president, Andrew Johnson. The threat of Confederate resurgence brought Banks closer to radicals like Durant and could have made him more amenable to Durant's persuasion in the De Hart case. Rose Herera worried that he was being pulled the other way. In late April, she stopped by Durant's office to let him know that "one of Mrs. De Harts friends told her that they was trying to fix it with Gen Banks & the mayor for their side."[88] While Mary De Hart sat in the female prison on Julia Street awaiting a verdict, twenty-two of her friends, "ladies and gentlemen, citizens of the United States," submitted a petition to Banks on May 9 asking him to grant De Hart an interview and calling for her "immediate pardon." The petitioners worried that "there has been an effort to prejudice the minds of those in authority against Mrs. De Hart" by impugning her husband as an officer of the rebel army and the sale of his slaves to Roland as a "sham . . . for the purpose of defrauding his creditors." The petition insisted the charges were false, but even if they were true, "certainly, general, you will not hold his wife responsible for his actions."[89] The petition may have prodded Banks to action, but not with the result the petitioners hoped for.

On May 13, Banks issued his ruling. He found that Rose Herera and her children had been slaves owned by James De Hart. The sale to Roland was probably fraudulent, but it didn't matter, because Mrs. De Hart had been an "active party" in the taking of the children. Banks believed that the children were taken against their mother's will, and he agreed with Durant that even if she had consented, her consent would have been invalid because she was "in duress, and in such condition that her hopes and fears would naturally influence her answers and actions." Banks accepted certain minor aspects of the defense argument. De Hart had not violated General Orders Nos. 44 and 88. Herera and her children had never been seized and freed by the government. And the children had not been secretly whisked away. But these, too, were irrelevant. Swallowing Durant's line on the slave code, Banks found that the act constituted a "forcible taking, thereby separating the mother from children of less than ten years of age, contrary to the spirit if not to the letter of the statute of the State, and in furtherance of a practice too unnatural and cruel for toleration." He scoffed at De Hart's lawyers' arguments on the jurisdiction of the provost court, insisting that the proceeding "is entirely the action of the commanding general, who in time of war is the highest local executive power existing." Banks ruled that Mrs. De Hart was "not guilty of kidnapping, within the meaning of the statute, but is guilty of improperly and unlawfully separating the children of less than ten years of age from the mother."[90] It is scarcely necessary to point out the deep and obvious irony of a Union general enforcing Louisiana's slave code after slavery had been abolished. The protective aspects of the slave code had never been taken seriously as long as slaveowners were in the saddle. The codes were violated with impunity and rarely enforced. For Banks now to enforce the slave code and evoke its benevolent "spirit" revealed not the continuity from slavery to emancipation, but a fundamental rupture of law and power masked as continuity.

Still the case was not done. General Banks ordered De Hart's release from jail once the children were returned to their mother, but the children did not arrive, and so De Hart remained in jail for almost two more months. Then politics intervened in De Hart's favor. Moving rightward, President Johnson backed Governor Wells and dismissed Banks from his post, leaving Major General Edward R. S. Canby in charge of the Department of the Gulf. De Hart then appealed to Canby to reconsider her case. In early June, her new lawyer (formerly a Union officer) sharply criticized Banks's action as "a gross assumption of power." Neither military law nor Louisiana law justified his conduct toward De Hart. The general "had no right to imprison and arrest the accused; his court had no right to try her, and he had no right to condemn her to be a hostage for the return of property, which she never owned or had in her possession." She was the innocent victim of double jeopardy.[91] Later in June, De Hart reiterated her innocence. She swore before a notary public and justice of the peace that the children had been taken to Cuba "with the consent of both father and mother, and with the promise on the part of the mother to go with them." She insisted that the children did not belong to her, she was not in control of them,

JUSTICE

and she could not get them back from Cuba. Her friends attested that she was "truthful and reliable."[92] Soon after, Canby released De Hart from jail and placed her under the supervision of the provost marshal general.[93]

Desperate, Rose Herera sped to Durant when she heard that De Hart was free. A note in Durant's files dated June 30 indicates that she told the lawyer that De Hart "is expecting to go up the coast today and preparing to slip away to Havana. She says she is going to Havana & that Rose will never see her, nor her children any more." She implored Durant to "keep his eye" on her.[94] Durant must have sent an inquiry to Canby, because the general wrote to Durant the same day explaining his course of action. Canby expressed "no doubt as to the enormity of the crime that was committed in separating these children from the care and guardianship of the mother, and none whatever as to the duty of the Government to restore them . . . by whatever legal and proper means can be used for that purpose." But he questioned the "legality and expediency" of the judicial proceedings against De Hart. The Provost Court was "without jurisdiction" and the charge against her was "not proven." He thought that the proper and more effective course of action would have been to apply to the Cuban government "for the restoration of the children now held in that Island in violation of the laws of Spain."[95] Then, on July 1, Canby formally revoked Banks's order against De Hart on the grounds that the provost court lacked jurisdiction in the case. He freed her on bond, and she rejoined her husband in Cuba later in July with instructions to have the children sent back to their mother. Now Rose Herera could only wait for their return.[96]

United States v. Mrs. De Hart was not the trial of the century. It was an obscure child custody case that barely made the local papers, eclipsed by the news of Lee's surrender at Appomattox and Lincoln's assassination. Yet the confrontation between De Hart and Herera in New Orleans over the three slave children in Cuba is significant because it illuminates the ad hoc structure of local justice in the twilight of slavery. The revived civilian court dismissed the charges against Mary De Hart because what she had done in taking the children to Cuba was not a crime in January 1863. But the Union army still governed New Orleans, so the case did not go away. With the help of her radical white lawyers, Henry Train and Thomas Jefferson Durant, the children's mother appealed to the military authorities, who were more receptive to her plea. Mary De Hart was tried in a provost court, a military tribunal where Herera was allowed to tell her side of the story. The Union commander, General Nathaniel Banks, concluded from the evidence that De Hart was indeed guilty of forcibly taking the children to Cuba, but he needed some legal rationale to pin her with a crime. Durant's creative reading of Louisiana's antebellum slave code gave Banks the veneer of legal justification that he needed to punish De Hart for kidnapping the children. Soon after, a new Union commander overturned Banks's ruling and set De Hart free. The shifting sands of military rule provided an unstable foundation for justice. As a result, Mary De Hart wasted more than three months in jail. Rose Herera got her day in court, but she did not get her children back. Justice was not done—not yet.

5

Reunion

WITH PEACE CAME a flurry of reunions. The United States reunited with the defeated Confederacy. Soldiers reunited with their families. Freedpeople, too, grasped at the chance to reunite with lost kin. They placed ads in newspapers. They sent letters to the Freedmen's Bureau. They went to court. They took to the road. As if time, distance, and poverty were not big enough obstacles to the restoration of their families, many freedpeople endured harassment and hostility in their quest. A committee of black leaders in Richmond, Virginia, protested to President Andrew Johnson in June 1865 that men and women visiting the city "in search of long lost wives or children, who had been separated by the cruel usages of slavery," had been arrested as vagrants, thrown in prison, and forced into labor, "thus preventing the reunion of long-estranged and affectionate families." Such scenes were repeated across the South.[1] The virtual reenslavement of black people in Richmond who were searching for their families and their appeal to the president for help underscore the link between the political struggle for national reunion and black people's struggle for reunions of their own.[2]

Rose Herera sought to recover her children from slavery in Cuba at the same time that emancipation took root in the United States. The military conquest of the Confederacy, new state constitutions that abolished slavery, and the passage and ratification of the Thirteenth Amendment ended the legal existence of chattel slavery throughout the country by the end of 1865. Meanwhile, countless struggles waged by newly freed people against their former masters across the slave states accelerated the overthrow of slavery and transformed the legal victory of abolition into the "social revolution" of emancipation. The revolutionary achievement of those whom the historian Ira Berlin called the "freedom generation" seems even more impressive when one recognizes that emancipation could have been stalled or even reversed if the terms of national reunion had tilted in a more reactionary direction.[3] Throughout the slave states, newly freed people stared down the prospect of renewed enslavement as white Southerners tried to resuscitate their power. The fear of a return to slavery found expression, above all, in stories and rumors of kidnapping that circulated across the South in the early days of Reconstruction. It was in this cauldron that the plight of Rose Herera's children entered the realm of national politics and international diplomacy.

After releasing Mary De Hart from jail in mid-July, Major General Edward Canby advised Secretary of War Edwin Stanton of the "abduction of three colored children" from New Orleans. He relayed the circumstances of the case of the Herera children to Stanton and requested that he pass the information along to Secretary of State William Seward for transmission to the Cuban authorities. Canby hoped that the Cubans would send the children back to their mother in New Orleans. "I do not see any other way in which this result can be obtained," he explained.[4] Stanton relayed Canby's information to Seward on August 10, and nineteen days later, Seward dryly instructed Thomas Savage, the U.S. vice-consul general in Havana, to "make such inquiries in regard to the matter as may be in your power, and report the result to this department, in order that, if the children can be identified, proper measures may be adopted with a view to their return to New Orleans." As it turned out, Savage already knew all about them.[5]

Thomas Savage, along with the U.S. consul general in Cuba, William T. Minor, kept close tabs on the Confederate blockade runners, spies, diplomats, and expatriates who passed through Havana. For example, in July 1864 Savage reported to Seward that "certain notorious rebels" had slipped out of New Orleans on an English schooner and were now in Havana "trying to get upon our Steamers bound North."[6] Later that summer, Savage reported that Pierre Soulé had arrived in Havana from Charleston, looking very "dejected." Savage surmised that Soulé intended to join his family on St. Thomas.[7] The Polish Confederate Valery Sulakowski applied to the U.S. consulate in Havana in February 1865 for permission to travel to New Orleans to collect his sick wife and move to Mexico, but the State Department rejected his request.[8] Even after the war ended, the consuls continued to track ex-Confederate movements in and through Havana as the losers fled into exile. "John C Breckenridge, Col Wood Taylor, Captain Wilson, Wood the commander of the pirate Tallahassee one other white person and a negro servant of Breckenridge landed at Cardenas on this Island on the morning of the 11th Instant, in an open boat after a passage of eight days from the coast of Florida. They are now in Havana," reported William T. Minor in early June 1865. Later that month Minor reported that Breckinridge, the Confederacy's last secretary of war, was still lurking in Havana among "persons who, during the war, have been, and continue to be very bitter in their hostility to the Government." Breckinridge's postwar flight to Cuba and subsequent three-year exile are familiar to scholars of the Civil War, while in contrast, nothing is known of the fate of his "negro servant."[9]

Other people of color came to the consuls' attention. One was a man named William Perry, who had been brought to Havana from Mobile by a Captain Godfrey and was "held in slavery here which of course was unlawful," wrote Savage. Perry found the consulate and claimed his freedom; Savage sent him to Key West so that he could return home. Similarly, a man named Alexander Poke had been brought from New Orleans three years earlier by a Captain Bunkin. The captain soon departed, leaving Poke "in bondage, in charge of Mrs Brewer, a person notoriously hostile to the United States." (This person was probably Sarah Brewer, proprietor of the Hotel Cubano, which one traveler called the "head-quarters of the Secessionists" in Havana.) Expecting more cases to come to light, Savage suggested that the State Department raise the matter with the Spanish legation in Washington.[10]

More cases did come to light, including the Herera children. After Mary De Hart's lawyer sent word of the decision in her case to her husband, her aunt Mme. Roland offered to send the children back to New Orleans so that her niece could return to

Havana.[11] Taking responsibility for the "three little negroes, named Ernest, Maria, and Josephine, who were brought by me into this city in the month of January 1863," Roland informed Thomas Savage that she was willing to deliver the children to him or anyone else he designated as an agent. The vice-consul sent Roland's message to the authorities in New Orleans, along with a letter of his own indicating that the children were now "virtually under my control" and that he would send them to New Orleans "when a proper conveyance shall offer." He added that the children had been treated "with all the kindness and affection that their mother could desire"—indeed, Roland appeared to treat them "as if they were her own children." Of course, that was precisely the problem. From Rose Herera's perspective, they were not her children, but she had been acting as if they were. If it ever reached Canby, Savage's communication may have convinced him to allow De Hart to leave New Orleans later that month under the expectation that the children's return was imminent.[12] Their return did seem imminent. John Holland, De Hart's lawyer, wrote to Durant on July 22 reporting that the children were now in the consul's possession "to be returned to this city by the first opportunity." He asked Durant to relay the news to Herera "so that she can be on the lookout for them."[13]

That was where matters stood when Savage received Seward's inquiry in early September. On September 15th, Savage replied with copies of the documents he had conveyed to New Orleans a month earlier. The vice-consul again reassured his boss that the children were "very kindly treated" by Roland, "in fact, the same as if they were her children." Pressing the point too far,

Savage noted that Roland "is very fond of them, and seems to feel keenly the threatened separation." It is not impossible, of course, that Roland actually was fond of the children and did not want to part with them, but for Savage to say so suggests that he had fallen for the proslavery fiction of family feeling between masters and slaves. In the same report, Savage also called attention to the case of a girl named Delia, who had been brought to Havana from New Orleans a year earlier by a "Mrs. Whittimore . . . who sold her at Matanzas," a town east of Havana. (Savage reported that Whittimore died somewhere in the United States shortly after selling Delia, but he may have been misinformed, because a Mrs. C. J. Whittemore—evidently the same person—signed the petition to General Banks calling for De Hart's release in early May.) The American consul in Matanzas investigated Delia's case and referred it to Cuba's Captain General, who freed her and ordered her to be placed in the consul's custody. "In justice to the man who purchased the girl," wrote Savage, "it is proper to state that she has been looked upon and in every respect treated as one of his family. She has been quite happy, but she must be sent to the United States, the law of this country so requiring it."[14]

But it was not Savage's sympathy for Roland that prevented him from sending back the children. He was looking out for them, or so he said. The logistics of travel between Havana and New Orleans in mid-September demanded patience: "At this season of the year, with no proper conveyances running between this port and New Orleans, and a very severe quarantine at the latter named place, it would have been cruel in me to embark them." He preferred to wait until the quarantine had been lifted and steamships ("the most proper conveyance for children of a tender age") were again ferrying between Havana and New Orleans. Thus he would not send the children home for a few more months, and in the meantime, their mother had to wait.[15] Savage elaborated in a letter to Durant dated October 28, which reported that the quarantine at New Orleans had blocked vessels from Havana throughout the summer, and nothing but small schooners "entirely unfit to send small children by" were running between the two ports. Savage decided to wait until the Star Line steamers began to run again between New York and New Orleans.[16]

The year ended without any sign of the children's arrival in New Orleans. Thomas Durant wrote to General Canby in New Orleans and Consul Minor in Havana demanding answers. He claimed to have heard nothing from the government since Secretary of War Edwin Stanton informed him in mid-October that the case had been placed in the hands of the State Department. But in late December, a man "lately arrived from Havana" who had just stayed with James De Hart there told Durant that he had seen Herera's son and youngest girl in De Hart's house, while the older girl (who was only seven) had been "hired out." He also told Durant that the consul in Havana had declared that he would not send the children to New Orleans unless the $115 for their passage was paid. Adding to Rose Herera's frustration was the fact that she had gone to see General Canby twice about her children but was not let in to see him.[17]

The intelligence that one of the girls had been hired out in Havana hints at a more complex story of the children's experience in Cuba than the one told by Thomas Savage and friends of the De Harts. No matter how well they appeared to be treated, the children were still kept as slaves in a city with a thriving market for their labor. Children under the age of fifteen made up about 30 percent of Havana's slave population, and about a quarter of all slave sales there in the 1850s and 1860s involved children. As in New Orleans, a high proportion of Havana's slaves worked in domestic service, and most domestic servants were women and girls. Moreover, the average price paid for slave children in Havana increased sharply in the 1850s, reflecting buyers' fears of the end of importation. The upward trend made the Herera children, and especially the two girls, all the more valuable. Despite the consul's assertions that the children were treated well by Roland, the hiring out of the seven-year-old Mary Herera suggests that she was isolated from her siblings and her labor turned into a commodity at a tender age.[18]

When Durant pressed Canby for the children's return, the general assured him that the consul would send the children "by the first proper opportunity," and he promised to make arrangements with the Star steamship line to pay for their passage.[19] Later that month, Canby passed along the worrisome news that the consul in Havana had decided to send the children home with Mrs. De Hart, who expected to return to New Orleans "in a few days." Canby confessed that he would not have chosen her as the children's escort, "but I presume that no trouble will result from the selection."[20] William Minor corroborated Canby's message in a letter sent from Havana in January, which revealed that "Mrs De Hart intends to go to New Orleans by the first steamer of February and I will send them with her."[21]

REUNION

On New Year's Day 1866, an exasperated Durant also wrote to Secretary of State William Seward to ask what was going on, or as he put it, to "beg to be informed what steps have been taken to redress so enormous a wrong, committed on a poor mother, in violation of every written and unwritten rule." Speaking for Rose, Durant implored Seward "to redress one of the most grievous injuries that the crimes of a departed system have left evidence of."[22] An enormous wrong, a grievous injury, a crime—Durant's indignant language contrasted sharply with Savage's complacency. Coincidentally, though, as Durant posted his letter to Washington, William Seward embarked on a Navy steamship for a recuperative tour of the Caribbean that included three festive days in Cuba. He could have strolled by the Herera children in one of old Havana's narrow streets, or glimpsed them through a parlor window thrown open to celebrate a "charming tropical evening," but there is no evidence that they crossed his path or his mind.[23]

As Seward's steamer anchored in Havana on January 20, 1866, William Minor came on board to deliver mail and last week's newspapers from New York.[24] The New York–Havana connection remained tight, and people, goods, and information chugged back and forth between the two ports. That same day, having read the same newspapers from New York, Cuba's Captain General Domingo Dulce fired off an angry letter to Spain's ambassador in Washington, Gabriel Tessara. The papers were reporting that Charles Sumner, the radical Republican senator from Massachusetts, had charged that "freed negroes from the southern states are now kidnapped and taken off to this island

[Cuba] and to Brazil, to be held in slavery, and that in this manner, a new traffic had been inaugurated on the shores of the south." Expressing surprise and dismay at Sumner's allegation of human trafficking from the United States to Cuba, Dulce fumed that "a case cannot be made out, even of a solitary individual." It does not appear that Dulce raised the issue with Seward in person, but soon after the secretary returned to Washington, Tessara sent him a copy of Dulce's letter along with a copy of Cuba's regulations for the "safe-keeping" of people of color who arrived from foreign countries. Its provisions "have always been faithfully complied with," he insisted.[25]

Sumner's allegation about the kidnapping of freedpeople for sale in Cuba and Brazil reflected a widespread fear of kidnapping and enslavement among Southern black people and, moreover, an awareness that their freedom was not fully secure as long as slavery endured in other places in the Americas.[26] Collective memories of kidnapping haunted the age of emancipation. Newly freed people did not forget that Africans had been snatched and traded to Atlantic slavers, free people of color waylaid and sold in the slave states with no questions asked, enslaved people plucked from their cabins and "sold down the river" never to see their families again. Now the war etched fresh memories of the kidnapping of black people. Confederate raiders committed egregious cases of mass kidnapping. The most infamous occurred during Lee's assault on Pennsylvania in 1863, when Confederate soldiers seized dozens, and possibly hundreds, of African Americans and shipped them south into slavery.[27] At the very same time as Lee marched toward Gettysburg, a naval officer reported from the opposite end of the war that Confederate raiders at the

Battle of Goodrich's Landing had "carried off about 1,200 negroes who were employed working on the so-called Government plantations" along the Mississippi River in northeast Louisiana. Although we tend to have an image of wartime emancipation as an unstoppable forward march, many black people did not experience it like that at the time. They learned that the forward march of freedom was erratic and could be reversed.[28]

Kidnappers kept busy in New Orleans. The antislavery soldier Rufus Kinsley of the Eighth Vermont proudly recorded that he "rescued a slave from the hands of a kidnapper, at the French Market" on May 26, 1862. Later that year, he did it again: "Rescued, with the help of my trusty pistol, a slave woman from the hands of a kidnapper."[29] James Parton, the first chronicler of Benjamin Butler's reign over New Orleans, recounted the kidnapping of Jeff, a barber who was awarded free papers for working at an army hospital. Jeff was nabbed in the street, "overpowered after a desperate fight, thrust into a carriage, and driven off to Foster's slave pen." From there he was conveyed to a plantation below the city and put in irons. He managed to escape and the next morning, though still shackled, he swam to the safety of a Union gunboat. His former owner was convicted of kidnapping and sentenced to two years in the parish prison, but Jeff was later thrown in the same prison for stealing liquor from the hospital, and there his former owner connived to sell him. Butler put the man on bread and water until he revealed Jeff's whereabouts, and when the barber was finally rescued a second time, Butler "took him into his own service" and escorted him to Massachusetts, far from his nemesis.[30] Colonel George Hanks, the Superintendent of Negro Labor in the Department of the Gulf, testified to the American Freedmen's Inquiry Commission (AFIC) early in 1864 that planters "make great efforts to recover their own negroes; they even hired men to steal them from my camp." One planter, he said, offered him $5,000 to return his slaves. Hanks claimed that he ordered his men to "shoot anyone caught in this business," but other Union officials may not have been so pure of heart.[31]

As the Herera case indicates, women and children were especially vulnerable to wartime kidnapping.[32] Early in 1863, the quartermaster of the New-Orleans, Opelousas, and Great Western Railroad complained to Banks that the wife and daughter of one of his employees had been seized by policemen in Gretna "and forcibly carried to their mistress in New Orleans." A provost guard recovered them, but the mayor demanded their release and return to their putative owner.[33] Later that year, Banks received an anonymous tip from "Justice" that four white men "kidnapped" Arana Johnson, the wife of a soldier in the Second Native Guards. The men took her to a plantation where they "beat her unmercifully with a Stick," then pulled her clothes over her head and whipped her naked body more than fifty times. When the plantation's driver protested, one of the men pulled out a gun and threatened to kill him and keep on killing. "God damn you, if you say another word. I'll blow your brains out. the Yankee's have turned all you Niggers fools. and I intend to Kill all the niggers I can, and it will not be long. before all the Yankee's in Louisiana were killed off. and those who were not Killed. would have to run off."[34] Officers suspected a conspiracy to ensnare the wives of colored soldiers. A few days later a colonel in the Fourth Native Guard reported that "Nearly every day the wife of some Soldier is spirited away" to St. Bernard Parish.[35] A year later, the *New York Times* reported that the kidnapping of colored children was a "frequent occurrence" in New Orleans. The *Times*' correspondent cited the story of a mother who complained to the Union authorities that a French woman had stolen her little girl. An investigation revealed that the girl had been kidnapped by her old owner, and the child was handed back to the mother.[36]

Slaveowners were not the only culprits. Not only did civil authorities conspire to kidnap black people, but critics protested that Union soldiers and officers did so too. Some of the allegations arose from the contradictory efforts of the Union authorities to respect loyal slaveowners' rights to their human property, and at the same time rake people of color into military service and public works. Other allegations involved sheer venality. Criticizing Banks's rule in June 1863, one "gentleman" in New Orleans protested that Northern soldiers "are everywhere standing guard over kidnapped negroes, or aiding to kidnap them."[37] A detective who investigated conditions in St. Bernard Parish discovered several men who claimed to have been arrested and sent to the provost marshal of the parish, Captain Sawyer, who had treated them brutally and hired them out to local planters.[38] Late in 1864, more than fifty "free colored citizens of Baton Rouge" protested that they had been "forcibly dragged from home & business" and impressed into labor on the levee at Morganza. Already free before the war, they objected not only to their seizure by government agents but also to the insult of being lumped together with "the lowest and most degraded class" of "contrabands, or those who have heretofore been slaves."[39] Black

Southerners had ample reason to mistrust Union agents, who were often hostile and even vicious toward them. Wartime emancipation cannot be sugar-coated. It was mayhem.

Widespread kidnapping pointed toward the ultimate prospect of the restoration of slavery. It signaled slaveowners' reluctance to accept emancipation, their relentless pursuit of lost human property, their capacity for savage violence. Tracking her family's former slaves in New Orleans in April 1863, Ann Penrose confided to her journal that "we keep them in view, when we know where they work, until, as we hope, better times will come when we can enforce our authority."[40] Union officials testified to the stubbornness of this mood among white planters in the Deep South early in 1864. "I talked to a pro-slavery and secession planter, who lives in the La Fourche district," General James S. Wadsworth told the AFIC. "He avowed his hope and expectation that slavery would be restored there in some form." The planter scoffed at the suggestion that slavery could not be revived: "It would take a great while to restore the excellent discipline that existed before the war; but still, they could be returned to slavery." Wadsworth agreed.

> I know that any energetic man could go on to a plantation, crack his whip, tell these people that all this talk about freedom was bosh and they must go to work, and make them obey him. Some of those who have been in the army would go North, others would go to the swamps, and the whites would have a great deal of trouble; but they would hunt the fugitives up, and capture or kill them, and in ten years they would have a system of slavery even more

severe than before, because they would have to exercise greater severity in order to maintain their authority.[41]

Hanks told the AFIC much the same thing: "The planters see that Slavery is dead but the spirit yet lives; they are even more rampant to enslave the negroes than ever before."[42] Heeding these eyewitnesses, AFIC Commissioner James McKaye urged the national government to guarantee the freedmen's civil and political rights. Nothing less would allow them to defeat "the machinations and schemes of any class or power to subject them again to any form of slavery or serfdom."[43]

Black Southerners were adamant that they would not be pushed back into slavery. On New Years' Day 1863, the day of the Emancipation Proclamation, Union soldier John Burrud observed that the "contrabands" at a Union army camp outside New Orleans "say heare that they will ly down and have there heads cut off before they will go into slavery."[44] Two months later, he had proof. "The poor cretures are willing to do anything rather than to go back to servitude," he wrote to his wife. "I saw a slave at Tibadeaux jump into the Bayou and drowned himself to get away from his Hellish Master who was trying to take him back to slavery."[45] Few black people actually went to the extreme of suicide to avoid enslavement, but they did risk death to escape slavery, help the Union, and fight for their freedom. They protested and resisted the many tactics that white Southerners used to revive slavery in fact if not in name, including the enactment of new "black codes" in 1865, which threatened to reenslave black Southerners through vagrancy, apprenticeship laws, and oppressive contracts. As a Freedmen's Bureau agent in Shreveport noted, the freedmen "were willing to enter into written agreements, provided they could be assured that there was no trap laid to ensnare them and force them back to slavery."[46]

As the black labor market shifted from slavery to contract and wage labor, newly freed people watched out for kidnappers and enslavers disguised as labor agents and recruiters.[47] Employers scoured the South for workers after the war, mobilizing recruiters and agents to attract freedpeople with offers of work under good conditions at decent wages in distant places. They often met with suspicion. Most freedpeople did not exactly jump at the chance to travel a long way with someone they didn't know for an uncertain reward. A wary Freedmen's Bureau agent in Virginia in 1867 thought the "Negro-Labor-factors" combing through his area for workers bore the "cloven foot of the 'nigger trader.'"[48] Yet other officials colluded with recruiters because they were eager to put freedpeople to work or to get rid of them altogether. Many freedpeople signed up in the hope of higher wages and land or to escape dire circumstances of violence and poverty. When the gears of the new Southern labor market meshed with the old cogs of Atlantic slavery, rumors of the kidnapping of freedpeople for sale to Cuba and Brazil spun across the South.

Rumors often illuminate shadowy aspects of reality and popular consciousness. They reveal a horizon of plausibility—what some people think actually happened, is happening, or could happen. Admittedly, this claim presumes that people circulate rumors because they think they might be true, and not because they think they are funny or outrageous, which is often the case with "urban legends." Whether the thing being rumored about is actually true is not an unimportant question, but it is not the only question to ask. One must also ask: Why is the rumor plausible? How does it get around? What is its impact? Rumors flourish amid uncertainty and the absence or mistrust of authoritative sources of information. They can and do function as one of oppressed people's "arts of resistance," to use the political scientist James Scott's well-known phrase, but elites may also propagate rumors that serve their own interests (to manipulate financial markets, for instance). Rumors may express the hopes of oppressed people, but then again, they may also express their fears, and rumors may themselves be tools of oppression.[49]

A short note in Durant's papers provides a glimpse into the circuit of rumor within Rose Herera's network of acquaintances in New Orleans. As we saw in Chapter 4, a note dated June 30, 1865, and possibly written by Durant or one of his associates revealed that Herera had come to warn Durant that Mary De Hart had been released from jail and was planning to steal away to Havana. How did she know? The note explained that Aimée, a midwife and the mother of Dr. Louis Charles Roudanez, told Herera "that Mrs. Riddell told her it was Dr. R. who got Mrs. De Hart out of jail, and that he would get her off to Havana, and that he was a great friend of General Canby."[50] This convoluted snippet discloses three intriguing facts. One is that Herera's informant was the mother of an influential and outspoken free man of color, Dr. Louis Charles Roudanez, who was one of the founders of New Orleans' radical newspaper the *Tribune* and a political associate of Durant.[51] Another is that Herera's grapevine telegraph was composed of women: Dr. Riddell's wife told Dr. Roudanez's mother, who told Rose Herera the story of

Riddell securing De Hart's release. Through this relay, Herera learned that the chemistry professor Riddell, who served as a witness at De Hart's trial, had Canby's ear and was now using his influence to help Mary De Hart escape from justice.

In the immediate post–Civil War context, historian Steven Hahn argues, rumor "may be imagined as a field and form of political struggle." Hahn examines the widespread hope among freedpeople across the South late in 1865 that the government was going to give them land and the corresponding fear among Southern whites that freedpeople were going to rise up and seize the lands by force when the government did not fulfill its promise. He explains that the insurrection scare "dramatized the political sensibilities and resources that ex-slaves possessed and built upon in the aftermath of emancipation."[52] The kidnapping rumors were nowhere near as broad and deep as the rumors of land distribution and black insurrection; nevertheless, they imply an anxious mood and defensive posture among freedpeople.

The kidnapping rumor tapped into freedpeople's fear of reenslavement, their knowledge of the persistence of slavery and the slave trade outside the United States, and the ties of trade and travel that linked Southern ports to the Atlantic's last remaining slave societies, Cuba and Brazil.[53] It seems to have originated early in the war as a scare tactic used by slaveowners to keep their human property from running off. In the fall of 1861, *Harper's Weekly* ran a cartoon mocking Confederates for warning their slaves that the Yankees would sell them in Cuba.

Reports from the South showed there was some validity to the scene *Harper's Weekly* depicted. In December 1861, a man named Abram in Hilton Head, South Carolina, told a *New York*

REUNION

SOUTHERN PLANTER. "Pomp, you Rascal! do you see any of those Cussed Yankee Ships coming this way?"

POMP (*suddenly becoming Serious*). "Lor' bress you, Massa, I'se so awful scared since you was a-tellin me de Yankees would sell me into Cuba, dat I can't see nuffin' at all."

CÆSAR (*behind the door*). "That's so. Yah! yah!"

"Pomp, you Rascal!"
From Harper's Weekly, *November 9, 1861. LC-USZ62-138109. Prints and Photographs Division, Library of Congress, Washington, D.C.*

Times correspondent that his master had warned that "de Yankees would take de niggers and sell us in Cuba, and want us to fight, but we talk it over, and agreed to come to de Yankees."⁵⁴ A correspondent for the abolitionist *Liberator* reported that the slaves were not gulled by their owners' threats. "Few negroes are so dull as to be imposed upon by the fictions of their masters that they are to be sold to Cuba, or would be worked day and night harder than ever, or other such inventions."[55] Later in the war, the heroic Robert Smalls testified to the AFIC that slaveowners in coastal South Carolina "told us that we must fight the Yankees who intended to catch us and sell us to Cuba to pay the expenses of the war." Smalls refused to believe it, but he said that "a great many" of his fellow slaves did.[56] Long afterward, schoolteacher Elizabeth Botume recalled the story told of an overseer on a Combahee River plantation in South Carolina who warned his charges to run and hide from the Union gunboats steaming toward them. "I tell you them Yanks are the very devil! If they catch you they will sell you to New Orleans or Cuba!" But it was the overseer who ran, while the slaves welcomed the Yankees.[57] The rumor cropped up again in May 1863 in Virginia, when the superintendent of contrabands at Fortress Monroe met with a delegation of people of color who asked if the Union army "put black men in irons and sent them off to Cuba to be sold or set them to work and put balls on their legs and whipped them, just as in slavery; because that was the story up there, and they were frightened and didn't know what to do." He corrected the misconception.[58]

The rumor of African Americans sold in Cuba took on a new life after the war in the context of what Northern newspaper editor Whitelaw Reid called "labor experiments." Touring the postwar South, Reid came across a Missourian prospecting for workers in Georgia. The man boasted that "he had no trouble in getting as many as he wanted, except from the apprehension of the negroes throughout all that region, that any one who proposed to take them away anywhere to labor, really mean to run them over to Cuba and sell them." Other white men "entertained no doubt of his being a negro smuggler" and envied his chance of success.[59] With their ears to the ground, government agents in the military and Freedmen's Bureau (created in March 1865) began to report similar rumors of kidnapping and investigated suspicious movements of shady characters and vessels in Gulf ports. The agents took the rumors seriously and investigated them diligently but turned up no hard proof of widespread slaving.

In mid-September 1865, Alabama's governor Lewis Parsons received a letter from a correspondent in Clarke County, north of Mobile, alleging that "persons in that vicinity and some of them in our uniform, and perhaps elsewhere, were collecting parties of freedmen under alleged contracts to work for them near the coast, but that when there they were shipped off to Cuba and to Brazil, and sold as slaves." Parsons read the letter to Freedmen's Bureau assistant commissioner Wager Swayne, who reported its content to General O. O. Howard, the head of the Bureau. Parsons did not believe the allegation at first because it had come from an "irresponsible source," but he took it more seriously after a trustworthy delegate to Alabama's constitutional convention assured him that "it was in all probability true." The delegate said that he had been "approached on the subject, and that from $50 to $100 was paid to former owners of able bodied men for each person secured by their cooperation." To thwart the slavers, Parsons and Swayne requested that an officer from Mobile visit Clarke County with "some mounted men and a force of colored troops, which will enable him to get to the bottom of the matter." The allegation was so serious that Swayne and Parsons had considered sending a telegraph message directly to President Johnson, but they decided to avoid the inevitable publicity and wait until they had gathered more evidence of the affair. In the meantime, they called on Howard to advise the president to deploy the Navy to patrol the coast for traffickers. Swayne seemed to think that a plot to ensnare and enslave the freedmen was entirely plausible, as he explained to Howard: "You will readily see how a bad man in any part of the South, used all his life to buying and selling slaves, might seek in this way redress for what he considers a wrongful taking away what once belonged to him."[60]

William Kobbe, a captain in the 178th New York stationed in Greenville, Alabama, heard the same rumor and passed it to the Freedmen's Bureau. "I have been informed in confidence that on the coast of Alabama & Florida, parties having contracts for lumber, employ freedmen in large numbers, ship them as hands offering large wages ($3. per day), take them to the West Indies & there sell them into slavery," he reported. He insisted that his information comprised "more than vague rumours, & a successful trip, by which 700 negroes were carried off, is spoken of." And although he admitted that "the accounts may have been changed & exaggerated before they reached me," he thought they were "reliable enough to justify me in reporting such atrocities." As with Swayne, Kobbe's report rested on hearsay, but he thought it was sufficiently noteworthy to pursue. Parsons and Swayne got corroboration from a more reliable source than the original letter, whereas Kobbe seems to have been impressed enough with the specific details of the story he heard and the severity of its allegation to advance it.[61]

The government agents who passed around the kidnapping rumor preferred to keep it quiet so they could catch the culprits. Heeding the appeal from Swayne and Parsons, Major General Charles Woods sent a Freedmen's Bureau agent with an "ample force" from Mobile to Clarke County to break up the plot and arrest anyone connected to it. He also warned General Philip Sheridan, who was then commander of the Division of the Gulf, of the affair.[62] Writing to President Johnson from Natchez in late September, Carl Schurz reported that Woods also sent a telegram to General Canby in New Orleans. He assured Johnson that Swayne and Woods believed the reports of kidnapping were "well founded" and that "measures were at once taken by the military authorities to prevent the execution of such nefarious designs. Strict secrecy was to be observed with regard to this business in order to insure the arrest of the guilty parties."[63] In early October, the secretary of war received a letter informing him of a plot "to convey from our southern Coast five or six hundred Freedmen to Cuba." The freedmen had been hired to chop wood, and their employers intended to "run them into Cuba" in vessels manned by "late Junior officers in the rebel navy." All they needed was a hefty $5,000 advance. The letter was forwarded to the Freedmen's Bureau and then transmitted to Swayne in Alabama "for thorough investigation" with instructions to be careful "not to scare off the originators and movers in this scheme."[64] A month later, General Howard received word from the head of the Freedmen's Bureau in Tallahassee, that the kidnapping rumor "which was for a time prevalent in some circles" had been put to rest. It was either "without foundation," or else the scheme had been "abandoned as impractible or for fear of discovery."⁶⁵ But the fear of kidnapping lingered. A Northern teacher appointed to report on conditions in Florida in October 1866 worried that some freedmen "are decoyed away under various pretenses for the real purpose of sending them to a market—perhaps to Cuba."⁶⁶

Kidnapping rumors also surfaced in Rose Herera's New Orleans. One swirled around an ex-Confederate cavalry officer named Archibald Dobbins, who was lurking in the city. In a letter to his wife in June 1865, Dobbins asserted that he was on his way to Texas, "where my negros are. I expect to send them to Cuba if possible and go to Mexico with my brigade." What became of this scheme is not known.⁶⁷ But six months later, a Union general in Mobile heard that Dobbins was "at the head of the plan to run off several hundred Freedmen to Cuba and sell them as slaves."⁶⁸ This intelligence was passed on to the provost marshal in New Orleans, who put a detective on Dobbins's trail. Disguising himself as a Cuban planter, the detective snooped for Dobbins's tracks around New Orleans. He learned from "parties at the St. James Hotel" that Dobbins had gone to Clarke County, Alabama, the locale of the earlier rumor, and that Dobbins was "into a speculation that he will either make all the money he wants or go higher than a kite," meaning perhaps he would hang for it. While in New Orleans, Dobbins frequented Jennie King's brothel "where he was often engaged with the proprietress & wanted her to invest some money in what he called an Outside Speculation." King, who had been the source of the information about Dobbins that reached Woods in Mobile, told the detective that she knew "two or three persons who were engaged in getting Labourers to work plantations in Cuba."

He eavesdropped on malevolent conversations. At the St. James Hotel, he overheard a friend of Dobbins say "he would bet that in six months from now that there would not be as many niggers in the South as there is now & a man who I did not know replied with a laugh = no not by a damn sight." But the detective could not find hard proof of trafficking: "I have made a thorough investigation in regard to report of a schooner leaving the New Basin with (60) Sixty negroes on board &c. I cannot trace it to any reliable source. If any such party left the City it was by some other route than the Basin." Nevertheless, by late December he was convinced that something major was afoot, and that it was linked to Confederate emigration to Brazil.

> I am <u>well satisfied</u> and do firmly believe that there is an Extensive Organization extending throughout the States of Mississippi Georgia Alabama Florida Louisiana & Texas composed of men who never was worth any property & those who lost every thing by the war that are engaged in running negroes to Brazil in connexion with the <u>Brazil Colonization Society</u> or <u>Company</u> I base my convictions on what I know & learned in the Rebel lines during the last week in investigating the subject of this report.

He asked for more time and manpower. Investigators needed to be sent to Texas, Alabama, and Florida, he thought, and they needed to go to the plantations where the recruitment was actually taking place.[69]

The detective pursued the case into 1866. In early January, one of Dobbins' associates told him "there was <u>more money to be made by running niggers to Cuba than at anything else</u>." Two freedmen complained that a man named Hodges "has hired a great many Colored Persons within the last six months (from 75 to 100) and that they sudenly disappear and except some old woman & young children they have never seen any of the Hands employed by the said Hodges." The detective suspected collusion between the traffickers and the governor of Louisiana, who had been "mentioned" as providing passports "for the purpose of takeing negroes out of the United States."[70] He overheard a man at the St. Charles Hotel tell another that "it was the easiest thing in the world to get them over to some of those turpentine orchards on the coast and decoy them on board of a small vessel." He caught wind of "parties who go by the steamers that run from here to Havana and take one or two body servants and return without them," which is precisely what De Hart and Roland had done with the Herera children. His reports never mentioned the Herera children, though. The detective never caught any kidnappers in the act, yet he remained sure that "this nefarious business is going on."[71] One thing is certain: Dobbins did eventually migrate to Brazil. A scientist with a Smithsonian-sponsored expedition found him "prospecting on the Tapajos river" in Santarem in 1867.[72]

The rumors of kidnapping finally escaped from this grapevine and became public knowledge when Charles Sumner took to the floor of the Senate on January 9, 1866. The Massachusetts radical was Congress's foremost champion of equal rights, so it is not surprising that he would be the one to publicize the allegations. Sumner read excerpts from two letters decrying kidnapping. One, from a correspondent in Alabama whom Sumner would not name but said was well known to members of the

House, referred to a "big trade" in "running negroes to Cuba and Brazil." The letter alleged that men in Yankee clothing, including men reputed to be Federal officers, were hiring workers at exorbitant wages to make turpentine or sugar, sending them to the coast, and embarking them on steamers that ferried them back to slavery. "They are just cleaning out this section of the country of the likeliest men and women in it," protested Sumner's informant. The second letter, from a judge in Florida, passed along reports that "certain parties here intend to make a business of importing negroes into Cuba." These letters were not Sumner's only sources of information. He claimed to have received "verbal communications" from across Texas, Louisiana, and Mississippi "that in each of those States a system of kidnapping has already been commenced, and a new slave-trade started on that coast." He introduced a resolution directing the Judiciary Committee to look into the necessity of passing new laws to prevent the kidnapping of freedmen, and he called upon the entire national government, including the president and the State, Navy, and War departments, to stop "this unexpected enormity of outrage."[73] Sumner's speech upset Captain General Domingo Dulce when the New York papers arrived on his desk in Havana.

Paradoxically, Dulce's objection stemmed from his own efforts to stop the slave trade to Cuba. He was part of a new breed of Spanish and Cuban reformers who believed that ending the slave trade and encouraging European immigration would civilize and whiten Cuba and allow Spain to keep its grip on the colony. The Civil War helped the reformers in one important way. With eleven slave states out of the Union, the Lincoln administration negotiated a new antislave trade treaty with Great Britain in 1862 that allowed the British navy to search vessels flying the American flag. The new treaty was a heavy blow to the Cuban slave trade, but did not immediately end it. Demonstrating that the Cuban authorities could effectively police slave smuggling into the island remained crucial to breaking the power of Cuba's slave traders and fending off British intervention. Yet Dulce had to tread carefully and not overstep his authority or embolden the slaves. The Spanish government's paramount interest in Cuba was preserving its colonial order. This imperative required that Cuba be isolated as much as possible from the emancipation in North America. The Spanish minister to the United States made this policy abundantly clear in a letter to Dulce in late December 1865 warning him about the rumored Christmas insurrection: "Serious are the risks that arise from this state of things, not only for the southern states of this country, but what is even worse, for the Antilles."[74] Just like their North American counterparts, Cuban planters and policy makers tried to keep their slaves from getting wind of the slave revolt in St. Domingue in the 1790s and abolition in the British West Indies in the 1830s. Now war and emancipation in the United States, along with British pressure against the Atlantic slave trade, sparked renewed vigilance in Cuba in the 1860s.[75]

Dulce cracked down on slave smuggling into Cuba when he became Captain General in 1862, but slavers still managed to land Africans on the island. In one highly publicized case in 1863, a Cuban official named José Augustín Argüelles received a handsome bounty for capturing a slaver, but was later discovered to have sold the Africans into slavery for his own profit. Argüelles's crime was discovered while he was in New York on business. The U.S. government shipped him back to Cuba, where he was convicted of "stealing negroes."[76] Dulce's testy response to Sumner reflected more than just his interest in defending his administration's probity and competence. He may also have been reassuring Cuban planters and the Spanish government that the island was not being infiltrated by freedmen from the United States. Unable to substantiate the rumors of kidnapping, U.S. consul William Minor explained to Seward in mid-February that Cuban planters were not eager to buy black Americans. "The impression is quite general here that, by recent events in the United States, even the most ignorant slave has been educated into some idea of personal liberty," he wrote, "and that, consequently, even if again reduced to a state of slavery, his examples and teachings would be dangerous on the plantations." Minor did admit, however, that some refugees from New Orleans had brought slaves to Cuba during the war. He reported that seven had been reclaimed through the consulate. Four had already been sent home, "and three children are now here, at the control of the consulate, awaiting a proper opportunity to go to New Orleans, which will be about the 1st of March."[77] Those three children were Rose Herera's.

As the Herera children waited for a steamer to take them home, the record of their ordeal became embedded in the legislative history of Sumner's effort to prevent the kidnapping of freedmen. On February 9, the Senate's Judiciary Committee reported a bill (S. No. 132) "to prevent and punish kidnapping," and the following week, Sumner presented new testimonials of an ongoing traffic in freedmen from Florida, Texas, and Louisiana. "In this way the proclamation of emancipation is set at defiance, and a new slave trade is opened," he lamented. Calling the bill a "necessity," Senator Daniel Clark of New Hampshire added that "reports in the newspapers and other quarters" indicated that kidnappings were taking place, and the Judiciary Committee had found "no sufficient protection in the statutes of the United States against it." The law governing the coastal slave trade had offered "slight protection" against the practice, but had been repealed, leaving "no provision at all" to guard against it. It would have been bitterly ironic if the abolition of slavery spurred a revival of the slave trade. The bill was intended to defuse an impending scandal.[78]

On March 5, Edwin Morgan, a Republican from New York, introduced a resolution to the Senate requesting the president to communicate "if not incompatible with the public interest, any information which may be in possession of the Executive in regard to the alleged kidnapping of colored person in the southern States for the purpose of selling them as slaves in Cuba or elsewhere." It passed with no objection.[79] Ten days later, in response to the resolution, President Johnson submitted a report from the secretary of state "upon the subject of the supposed kidnapping of colored persons in the southern States for the purpose of selling them as slaves in Cuba." Most of the State Department's report was devoted to documents, probably supplied by Durant, pertaining to the case of Rose Herera and her children.[80] This publication is the source that has provided much of the evidence at the heart of this book. The press barely noticed the report, and it seems to have made no impact on the great debates over Reconstruction that raged in the nation's capital.[81] Considered as a piece of propaganda, the State Department's report minimized the extent of kidnapping and reassured the public that the government was doing everything it could to locate and recover people victimized by kidnappers. Nevertheless it inserted the story of Rose "Elyra"—her name was spelled like that throughout the report—into the public record at the highest level, and thus elevated one freedwoman's lowly struggle to recover her children into a matter of national significance.

Spurred by Sumner, Congress quietly moved on the antikidnapping bill. Unlike other aspects of Reconstruction policy, it sparked little debate and progressed easily. All Republicans could agree that freedpeople should not be sold into slavery in Cuba and Brazil. A few dissident voices sniped that the danger was blown out of proportion or, as Kentucky's Senator Garrett Davis insinuated, perpetrated by the "Yankees" themselves. The House passed the Senate's antikidnapping bill two months later, and despite his widening rift with congressional Republicans in the months following his provocative veto of the Civil Rights and Freedmen's Bureau bills, President Andrew Johnson signed "an act to prevent and punish kidnapping" in May 1866. The law promised to protect the nation's newly freed people from the vortex of Atlantic slavery. It had no practical effect and was largely a symbolic antislavery gesture.[82]

The wheels of the government turned too slowly for Rose Herera. The children did not arrive in January or February. On March 1, Durant appears to have written to Seward one more time in the hope of recovering the children. Frederick Seward replied on his father's behalf three weeks later, and by then it was all over.[83] In mid-March, the steamship *Evening Star* chugged out of Havana with Ernest, Mary, and Josephine Herera on board. In a final irony, the U.S. Consul William Minor sent them home in the care of Mrs. De Hart, who was moving back to New Orleans. He put the very person who had kidnapped the children from their mother in charge of returning them to her. They arrived in New Orleans on March 17, 1866.[84] The children had not seen their mother in over three years. Their father was dead. Ernest would have been nine years old, Mary seven, and Josephine five. The returning children would have barely remembered their brother George, who was just an infant when they were stolen away. They would have met their little sister Louise for the first time. Without any sources to document the occasion, we can only imagine their reunion.

Rose Herera disappears from view until 1880, when a census taker named her as the head of a household at 32 St. Anthony Street in New Orleans' Seventh Ward, just a few blocks from where her husband George had lived during the war. According to the census, she was forty-two years old, a washwoman, and a mother. Four of her five children lived with her: Mary (22), Joseph (19), George (17), and Louise (15). Mary's occupation was listed as "Home," Joseph and George as "laborers," and Louise as "attending school." Also living with them was their grandmother, Leocadie, now identified as Mary Cadet (77). Only the eldest son Ernest, who would have been twenty-four, was missing from his mother's household. One oddity is that the census lists Rose's second daughter Josephine as a son named Joseph. The census taker probably made a simple mistake; such errors often crept into the census. Three generations living together under their own roof is a small testament to the profound difference between slavery and freedom, as well as to the resilience of Rose Herera's family.[85]

The reunion of Rose Herera and her children contrasts with two disasters that befell New Orleans later in 1866. On July 30,—"bloody Monday" in the annals of New Orleans—police stormed the Mechanics' Institute on Dryades Street, between Canal and Common (just a block from where the De Harts had lived), where twenty-five delegates to an interracial state constitutional convention were preparing to enfranchise black men and strip ex-Confederates of the right to vote. In one of the worst episodes of violence during Reconstruction, the police massacred many of the delegates and their supporters in the hall and mopped up the rest in the streets. Nearly forty people were murdered that day. One witness would later condemn it as "wholesale slaughter." The event helped Republicans in Congress to wrest control of Reconstruction from President Johnson. From his office window facing Carondelet Street, two blocks from the Mechanics' Institute, Thomas Jefferson Durant heard the rising murmur of a mob. Then he saw the police marching down the street "two-by-two" with revolvers in hand, shooting "indiscriminately" and beating up black people. He watched blood run in the street. Although he had opposed the convention as "injudicious and dangerous," he knew the blood could just as well be his. Durant slipped out of his office and fled to a friend's plantation in nearby Carrolton, where he jumped on board a steamboat heading upriver and left New Orleans behind, never to return.[86]

For sheer loss of life, the fate of the *Evening Star*, the vessel that carried the Herera children from Havana to New Orleans, was a greater catastrophe. En route from New York to New Orleans in early October 1866, the *Evening Star* sank in a hurricane off the coast of Georgia with almost three hundred passengers on board. All but thirty perished, including most of the singers of a Parisian opera company on its way to New Orleans to revive the new French Opera House. Among the other notable casualties were James Gallier Jr., the architect of the Mechanics' Institute, and Louisiana planter Henry Palfrey, along with his "lady, child, and servant," returning from a brief exile in Canada. Also on board, reported the always reliable *New York Times*, were "from seventy-five to a hundred prostitutes" heading south for the winter.[87] A poet mourned for the *Evening Star*'s dead:

> Oh wave of the sea that came rolling this way,
> Looking so grand at the close of day,
> What tidings of wrecks are these you have brought?[88]

The Herera children were lucky to make it home.

Epilogue

THE RUMOR THAT African Americans were being kidnapped and trafficked to Cuba was what sociologists call a "diving rumor"—one that surfaces at intervals like a whale. It bobbed up again in 1878, when a government agent who was investigating reports of trespassing on timber lands in Florida sent word to President Rutherford Hayes that black people were being kidnapped and sold in Cuba. The agent's information was supported by an affidavit from a Cuban engineer, Fernando Lopez de Queralta, who had served in the U.S. army and then went on to become a general with the insurgents in the civil war that broke out in Cuba in 1868. Queralta testified that he had met a man in Santiago de Cuba who claimed that he had been taken from Louisiana with four other people in 1866 and worked as a slave on a sugar plantation ever since. President Hayes sent Congressman John Leonard, a Republican from Louisiana, to Cuba to investigate the allegation. Leonard died of yellow fever in Havana before he could report his findings. When Cuban authorities conducted their own inquiry, they did not find Queralta's man, but they made another startling discovery. On a plantation in Güines, about thirty miles southeast of Havana, lived a slave woman known as Juana la Americana, who claimed to have come from the United States during the Civil War. Her fellow slaves corroborated her story.[1]

Like the Herera children, Juana la Americana was from New Orleans. She told investigators that she had been the property of a Mr. Smith, who also owned her mother, Margarita. Smith sold five-year-old Juana and her mother to William Bisby in 1859 in New Orleans. Bisby took them to Havana in a steamboat sometime around 1864. Juana would have been ten at the time. The authorities substantiated Juana's story by locating a notarized bill of sale in New Orleans for Margarita and Juana from James Simkins to William Henry Smith for $650 in 1859, as well as a bill of sale from Smith to William Bisby in Havana for 350 pesos in 1865. Bisby, it appears, then sold Juana to Leon de Martiarter, the owner of the Dolores sugar plantation in Güines. She languished there for more than a decade. She gave birth to three children, but all died, and she had no other family around her. The U.S. consuls overlooked her. Emancipation eluded her. It took the Ten Years' War in Cuba—another war with corrosive effects on slavery—to bring her story to light. One wonders how many other Juanas were never discovered.[2]

Even if few African Americans were taken to Cuba by their owners during the U.S. Civil War, the significance of the stories of Juana and the Herera children exceeds their numbers. Their experiences demonstrate slaveowners' dogged efforts to hang onto their human property as long as possible. They exemplify the disruptive impact of the Civil War on enslaved people who were uprooted from their homes and severed from their families. They draw attention to the plight of slaves who worked as domestic servants, and the dire vulnerability of enslaved children. They dredge up an unknown connection, like an abandoned undersea cable, between Southern slavery and its Cuban counterpart. Although the overthrow of slavery in the United States fed abolitionist hopes in Cuba, the persistence of slavery in Cuba after the Civil War posed a threat to newly freed people in the United States, as the diving rumor of kidnapping signified. The kidnapping rumors reflected more than the immediate fear of being sold into slavery in Cuba. The rumors drew upon black people's collective memory of the Atlantic slave trade and forced migration in North America, thus calling attention to the shock and violence of enslavement, and they registered the precariousness of the quasi-freedom achieved by emancipation.

Yet the contrast between the Herera children, who made it home safely in 1866, and Juana la Americana, who remained stranded in Cuba, highlights the extraordinary political process that led to the Herera children's return. Confronting her former owner, their widowed mother took a bold stand to get them back. She found allies among the cadre of activists fighting for African Americans' civil and political rights in New Orleans, who helped to guide her case through the ad hoc system of military justice managed by the Union authorities in the city. When local institutions failed to provide satisfaction, her advocate, Thomas Jefferson Durant, used his influence to bring her case to the attention of leading politicians in Washington, D.C. That the State Department managed to recover the children early in 1866 is a testament to the new recognition by the United States government of the rights and needs of African American families as Reconstruction lurched forward.

Rose Herera's legacy is a spark of hope in dark times. She was born into slavery and lived through war. She was bought and sold and thrown in jail. Three of her children were taken from her and spirited away to a foreign land. Her husband died just as she was about to become free. Despite the hardships of her life, she did not concede her right to her children or give up the hope that she would get them back. She set events in motion that would lead to their return, and thus she made history. After a long ordeal, her three kidnapped children came home to their bereaved mother in New Orleans. Now that they were free, Rose Herera's children finally belonged to her.

Appendix

Abbreviations

Notes

Acknowledgments

Index

APPENDIX

Rose Herera's Petition

*F*ROM U.S. CONGRESS, SENATE, *Message of the President of the United States, Communicating, in Compliance with a Resolution of the Senate of the 5th Instant; A Report from the Secretary of State, upon the Subject of the Supposed Kidnapping of Colored Persons in the Southern States for the Purpose of Selling Them as Slaves in Cuba,* 39th Cong., 1st Sess. (1866), S. Ex. Doc. 30, ser. 1238, pp. 18–19.

To Major General S. A. Hurlbut, commanding department of the Gulf:

The petition of Rose Elyra, who resides in New Orleans, respectfully represents: That she is of African descent, and was born a slave in the family of Octave Leblanc, in the parish of Pointe Coupee, in Louisiana, being now about twenty-five years of age, as she believes, and was brought to New Orleans some twelve years ago. That since she arrived in New Orleans she has become the mother of four children, viz: Joseph Ernest, born on the 14th day of January, 1857; Marie Georgiana, born the 27th of December, 1858; Marie Josephine, born the 7th of December, 1860; and Joseph George, born the 2d of September, 1862; that the father of all these children was George Elyra, a free man of color, born in this city, to whom she was married by Mr. Costi, a Catholic priest, at the Cathedral in this city, between the dates of the births of her second and third child, as above set forth, and the said husband died in this city on the 7th day of May last, 1864.

Now your petitioner further shows that about the time of her said marriage her former owner, Octave Leblanc, was compelled, by his being in debt, to part with her, and did sell her and two children to J. A. De Hart, a dentist, residing then at No. 17 Baronne street, in this city, where she continued to reside in said De Hart's family as a domestic servant until the latter part of December, 1862, and during her residence there her third and fourth children were born.

Your petitioner further shows that the said De Hart and his wife, Amelie Valcour De Hart, were enemies of the United States and rebels to the government; that the said De Hart was captain of a rebel military company, and a few months after the occupation of the city of New Orleans by the national forces, viz: in the month of October, 1862, he left this city for Havana, Cuba, where he has ever since remained; that after the departure of De Hart Mrs A. V. De Hart spoke of following him to Havana, and frequently asked and urged your petitioner to go with her to that place, which petitioner constantly refused to do, not wishing to leave her husband, her mother, and her friends; that on one evening after dark about the 18th of December, 1862, Mrs. De Hart caused a police officer to enter the house, who took off your petitioner, with her baby three or four months old, and lodged them in the parish prison of New Orleans, where they were kept in confinement about a month, or until the middle of January, 1863; that during this time, the said Mrs. De Hart frequently visited her in the prison, bringing petitioner's three other children with her, urging her to go with her to Havana, and threatening to take off with her to Havana petitioner's three eldest children if petitioner refused to go; but your petitioner always did so refuse, and begged and demanded that her children should be left in New Orleans with her; and finally, the said Mrs. De Hart did go off to Havana, taking with her petitioner's three eldest children, whom petitioner has never seen since, and who are now held unlawfully by the said De Hart and his wife as slaves in Havana.

Petitioner further shows that when the said children were thus illegally taken off from New Orleans the eldest, Joseph Ernest, was six years old, the second, Marie Georgiana, four years old, and the third, Mary Josephine, two years old; that your petitioner was utterly helpless and powerless to prevent this gross outrage and violation of her natural and civil rights by reason of her condition and her imprisonment, from which she was only released by an order left behind by the said Mrs. De Hart on her departure aforesaid.

APPENDIX

Petitioner further shows that on the 2d of January of this year the said Mrs. De Hart returned to New Orleans, when petitioner immediately called upon and begged the restoration of her children, which Mrs. De Hart refused; and thereupon, acting under the advice of counsel, petitioner caused the said Mrs. De Hart to be arrested and brought before Recorder F. A. Wolfley, of this city, on a charge of having kidnapped the said children, but on the 28th of February the said recorder dismissed the case, deciding there was no law of Louisiana applicable to it.

Petitioner further shows that her arrest and imprisonment, above stated, was in violation of General Orders No. 88 from headquarters of the department of the Gulf, dated the 1st of November, 1862, to which your petitioner now appeals.

Petitioner avers that by the fifteenth and sixteenth sections of the act of 31st January, 1829, of the State of Louisiana, (see acts, p. 48,) it is not only forbidden to bring into Louisiana, without the mother, any slave child under ten years of age, but it was also forbidden to any owner of slaves in Louisiana to sell any slave children under ten years of age, without the mother; the humane idea of the legislator having been to prevent the separation of children of tender years from their mother, and the spirit of the law discountenancing such separation by whatever means brought about.

Petitioner further shows that herself and her aforesaid three children are free and entitled to the rights of American citizens, and to the protection of the government of the United States, to which she now appeals, and avers that the said Mrs. A. V. De Hart is bound in law and equity and good morals to restore to her her three children whom she wrongfully took away.

Wherefore your petitioner prays, the premises considered, that you will be pleased to cause the said Mrs. Amelie De Hart to appear before you, and that she may be prevented from leaving this city, as she is soon about to do, and that she may be ordered to cause to be brought back from Havana your petitioner's three children, viz: Joseph Ernest, Mary Georgiana, and Mary Josephine, and that the said Mrs. A. V. De Hart be held in confinement until she shall have complied with this order; and your petitioner will ever pray, &c.

her

ROSE x ELYRA,

mark

Sometimes called Mrs. George Elyra

H. Train, Durant & Horner,

Of counsel for Petitioner.

New Orleans, *March* 4, 1865.

Abbreviations

ANHC — Archivo Nacional, Havana, Cuba

BC — *Private and Official Correspondence of Gen. Benjamin F. Butler, during the Period of the Civil War*, 5 vols. (Norwood, Mass.: Plimpton Press, 1917)

FSSP — Freedmen and Southern Society Project, University of Maryland, College Park

Limongi Papers — Felix Limongi Papers, Library of Congress, Washington, D.C.

NARA — National Archives and Records Administration, Washington, D.C.

OR — *War of the Rebellion: A Compilation of the Official Records of the Union and Confederate Armies* (Washington, D.C.: U.S. Government Printing Office, 1886)

PD — Ann Wilkinson Penrose Diary and Family Letters, 1861–1865, Louisiana and Lower Mississippi Valley Collections, Louisiana State University Libraries, Baton Rouge

Report — U.S. Congress, Senate, *Message of the President of the United States, Communicating, in Compliance with a Resolution of the Senate of the 5th Instant; A Report from the Secretary of State, upon the Subject of the Supposed Kidnapping of Colored Persons in the Southern States for the Purpose of Selling Them as Slaves in Cuba*, 39th Cong., 1st Sess. (1866), S. Ex. Doc. 30, ser. 1238

Notes

PROLOGUE

1. Eric Foner, *The Fiery Trial: Abraham Lincoln and American Slavery* (New York: W.W. Norton, 2010), 240–242.
2. The main source for my narrative of the events of Rose Herera's life and the kidnapping of her three children is U.S. Congress, Senate, *Message of the President of the United States, Communicating, in Compliance with a Resolution of the Senate of the 5th Instant; A Report from the Secretary of State, upon the Subject of the Supposed Kidnapping of Colored Persons in the Southern States for the Purpose of Selling Them as Slaves in Cuba*, 39th Cong., 1st Sess. (1866), S. Ex. Doc. 30, ser. 1238 (hereafter cited as *Report*).
3. Stephanie McCurry, *Confederate Reckoning: Power and Politics in the Civil War South* (Cambridge, Mass.: Harvard University Press, 2010), ch. 6.
4. Quintin Hoare and Geoffrey Nowell Smith, eds., *Selections from the Prison Notebooks of Antonio Gramsci* (London: Lawrence and Wishart, 1971), 276.
5. See especially Thavolia Glymph, *Out of the House of Bondage: The Transformation of the Plantation Household* (New York: Cambridge University Press, 2008), chs. 3–4; Leslie A. Schwalm, "Between Slavery and Freedom: African American Women and Occupation in the Slave South," in *Occupied Women: Gender, Military Occupation, and the American Civil War*, ed. LeeAnn Whites and Alecia P. Long (Baton Rouge: Louisiana State University Press, 2009), 137–154.

6. George Washington Cable, *Dr. Sevier* (Boston: James R. Osgood, 1885), 175–176; Roulhac Toledano and Mary Louise Christovich, *New Orleans Architecture: Faubourg Tremé and the Bayou Road* (Gretna, La.: Pelican, 1980), 63.

7. *Report*, 23.

8. Randy J. Sparks, *The Two Princes of Calabar: An Eighteenth-Century Atlantic Odyssey* (Cambridge, Mass.: Harvard University Press, 2004); Rebecca Scott and Jean M. Hébrard, *Freedom Papers: An Atlantic Odyssey in the Age of Emancipation* (Cambridge, Mass.: Harvard University Press, 2012); Jon F. Sensbach, *Rebecca's Revival: Creating Black Christianity in the Atlantic World* (Cambridge, Mass.: Harvard University Press, 2005); Annette Gordon-Reed, *The Hemingses of Monticello: An American Family* (New York: W. W. Norton, 2009); David S. Cecelski, *The Fire of Freedom: Abraham Galloway and the Slaves' Civil War* (Chapel Hill: University of North Carolina Press, 2012). Microhistory was pioneered by social historians of early modern Europe. The touchstones are Carlo Ginzburg, *The Cheese and the Worms: The Cosmos of a Sixteenth-Century Miller* (Baltimore: Johns Hopkins University Press, 1980), and Natalie Zemon Davis, *The Return of Martin Guerre* (Cambridge, Mass.: Harvard University Press, 1983). On the value of biography (and microhistory) for historicizing Atlantic slavery, see Joseph C. Miller, "A Historical Appreciation of the Biographical Turn," in *Biography and the Black Atlantic*, ed. Lisa A. Lindsay and John Wood Sweet (Philadelphia: University of Pennsylvania Press, 2014), 19–48.

9. Peter Bardaglio, "The Children of Jubilee: African American Childhood in Wartime," in *Divided Houses: Gender and the Civil War*, ed. Catherine Clinton and Nina Silber (New York: Oxford University Press, 1992), 213–229. On the importance of children in the history of American slavery, see Wilma King, *Stolen Childhood: Slave Youth in Nineteenth-Century America*, 2nd ed. (Bloomington: Indiana University Press, 2001); Jennifer L. Morgan, *Laboring Women: Reproduction and Gender in New World Slavery* (Philadelphia: University of Pennsylvania Press, 2004); Marie Jenkins Schwartz, *Born in Bondage: Growing Up Enslaved in the Antebellum South* (Cambridge, Mass.: Harvard University Press, 2000).

10. The essential starting point for such an analysis is Ira Berlin, Barbara J. Fields, Steven F. Miller, Joseph P. Reidy, and Leslie S. Rowland, *Slaves No More: Three Essays on Emancipation and the Civil War* (New York:

Cambridge University Press, 1992), and the ongoing documentary series published by the Freedmen and Southern Society Project as *Freedom, A Documentary History of Emancipation, 1861–1867* (New York: Cambridge University Press, 1982–2013).

11. On kidnapping as a method of enslavement, see Orlando Patterson, *Slavery and Social Death: A Comparative Study* (Cambridge, Mass.: Harvard University Press, 1982), 115–122. For recent assessments of the significance and complexity of kidnapping as a feature of the Atlantic slave trade, see G. Ugo Nwokeji, *The Slave Trade and Culture in the Bight of Biafra: An African Society in the Atlantic World* (New York: Cambridge University Press, 2010), 126–132; Rebecca Shumway, *The Fante and the Transatlantic Slave Trade* (Rochester, N.Y.: University of Rochester Press, 2011), 59–61; Randy J. Sparks, "Gold Coast Merchant Families, Pawning, and the Eighteenth-Century British Slave Trade," *The William and Mary Quarterly*, 70 (April 2013): 317–340. On stories of kidnapping in the oral history of enslavement, see Anne C. Bailey, *African Voices of the Atlantic Slave Trade: Beyond the Silence and the Shame* (Boston: Beacon Press, 2005), 79–82, 108–112.

12. Ottobah Cugoano, *Thoughts and Sentiments on the Evils of Slavery* (London, 1787), 93.

13. Frederick Douglass, *My Bondage and My Freedom* (New York: Miller, Orton, and Mulligan, 1855), 91.

14. Edward E. Baptist, "'Stol' and Fetched Here': Enslaved Migration, Ex-slave Narratives, and Vernacular History," in *New Studies in the History of American Slavery*, ed. Edward E. Baptist and Stephanie M. H. Camp (Athens: University of Georgia Press, 2006), 243–274 ("We are stolen" 261). For the full context of the song, see William Wells Brown, *Narrative of William W. Brown, an American slave* (London: Charles Gilpin, 1849), 50–51; *Documenting the American South*, http://docsouth.unc.edu/fpn/brownw/brown.html. On the kidnapping of free people of color in the United States, see Carol Wilson, *Freedom at Risk: The Kidnapping of Free Blacks in America, 1780–1865* (Lexington, Ky.: University Press of Kentucky, 1994).

15. The only sustained examination of the post–Civil War kidnapping rumors is José B. Fernandez and Jerrell H. Shofner, "Kidnapping of Freedmen from the United States for the Cuban Slave Trade," in *Homenaje a Lydia Cabrera*, ed. Reinaldo Sanchez, Jose Antonio Madrigal, Richardo Viera, and Jose Sanchez-Boudy (Miami: Ediciones Universal, 1978),

295–302. On kidnapping and reenslavement in the Atlantic world, see among others Scott and Hébrard, *Freedom Papers;* Sidney Chalhoub, "Illegal Enslavement and the Precariousness of Freedom in Nineteenth-Century Brazil," in *Assumed Identities: The Meanings of Race in the Atlantic World,* ed. John D. Garrigus and Christopher Morris (College Station: Texas A & M University Press, 2010), 88–115.

16. Karl Marx to Lion Phillips, 29 November 1864, in Karl Marx and Friedrich Engels, *Collected Works,* vol. 42 (Moscow: Progress Publishers, 1987), 48.

17. W. E. B. Du Bois, *Black Reconstruction: An Essay Toward a History of the Part Which Black Folk Played in the Attempt to Reconstruct Democracy in America, 1860–1880* (New York: Harcourt, Brace, 1935), 121. The revolution of emancipation is at the core of more recent interpretations of the era. See Eric Foner, *Reconstruction: America's Unfinished Revolution, 1863–1877* (New York: Harper and Row, 1988); Bruce Levine, *The Fall of the House of Dixie: The Civil War and the Social Revolution that Transformed the South* (New York: Random House, 2013). For comparative perspectives, see Steven Hahn, "Class and State in Postemancipation Societies: Southern Planters in Comparative Perspective," *American Historical Review,* 95 (February 1990): 75–98; Barrington Moore, *Social Origins of Dictatorship and Democracy: Lord and Peasant in the Making of the Modern World* (Boston: Beacon Press, 1993).

18. *Report,* 48.

1 POINTE COUPÉE

1. *Report,* 18.

2. Frederick Douglass, *Narrative of the Life of Frederick Douglass, an American Slave* (Boston: Anti-Slavery Office, 1845), 1, http://docsouth.unc.edu/neh/douglass/douglass.html. For masters' control over slaves' biographies, see Walter Johnson, "Possible Pasts: Some Speculations on Time, Temporality, and the History of Atlantic Slavery," *Amerikastudien/American Studies,* 45, no. 4 (2000): 491–492.

3. Orlando Patterson, *Slavery and Social Death: A Comparative Study* (Cambridge, Mass.: Harvard University Press, 1982), 5–8 (quotation on 7). For a critique of the concept of social death, see Vincent Brown, "Social

Death and Political Life in the Study of Slavery," *American Historical Review*, 114 (December 2009): 1231–1249.

4. Sacramental records, St. Francis Church, Pointe Coupée, Louisiana, vol. 6, p. 350, entry 123, Diocese of Baton Rouge Archive. An invaluable resource for genealogical research into people of African descent in Pointe Coupée is *Diocese of Baton Rouge Catholic Church Records: Pointe Coupée Records, 1770–1900; Individuals without Surnames* (Baton Rouge: Catholic Diocese of Baton Rouge, 2007). Rose is listed on p. 260.

5. L. Virginia Gould, "Urban Slavery—Urban Freedom: The Manumission of Jacqueline Lemelle," in *More Than Chattel: Black Women and Slavery in the Americas*, ed. David Barry Gaspar and Darlene Clark Hine (Bloomington: Indiana University Press, 1996), 301. Johanna Lee Davis Smith, "Mulatto Bend: Free People of Color in Rural Louisiana, 1763–1865" (PhD diss., Tulane University, 2012), 112. On the paternalist denial of slave fatherhood, see Walter Johnson, *River of Dark Dreams: Slavery and Empire in the Cotton Kingdom* (Cambridge, Mass.: Harvard University Press, 2013), 194.

6. On godparenthood among people of African descent in Louisiana, see Kevin Roberts, "Slaves and Slavery in Louisiana: The Evolution of Atlantic World Identities, 1791–1831" (PhD diss., University of Texas at Austin, 2003), 122–129; Emily Clark and Virginia Meacham Gould, "The Feminine Face of Afro-Catholicism in New Orleans, 1727–1852," *William and Mary Quarterly*, 3rd ser., 59 (April 2002): 424–438. For comparative perspective, see Stuart B. Schwartz, *Slaves, Peasants, and Rebels: Reconsidering Brazilian Slavery* (Urbana: University of Illinois Press, 1992), ch. 5.

7. Anthony E. Kaye, *Joining Places: Slave Neighborhoods in the Old South* (Chapel Hill: University of North Carolina Press, 2007).

8. This number is derived from *Pointe Coupée Records, 1770–1900: Individuals without Surnames*. Out of the twenty-one baptisms, only Rose had a godparent who was a free person of color.

9. Quoted in Michael Pasquier, *Fathers on the Frontier: French Missionaries and the Roman Catholic Priesthood in the United States, 1789–1870* (New York: Oxford University Press, 2010), 178. See also Joe Gray Taylor, *Negro Slavery in Louisiana* (Baton Rouge: Louisiana Historical Association, 1963), 134–136.

10. Mary Frances Seibert, *Zulma: A Story of the Old South* (Natchez: Natchez Printing and Stationery, 1897), 19.

11. For a useful overview of the history of Pointe Coupée, see Brian J. Costello, *A History of Pointe Coupée Parish Louisiana* (New Roads, La.: New Roads Printing, 1999). For Pointe Coupée's emergent slave society, see Gwendolyn Midlo Hall, *Africans in Colonial Louisiana: The Development of Afro-Creole Culture in Louisiana in the Eighteenth century* (Baton Rouge: Louisiana State University Press, 1992), ch. 8.

12. On the conspiracies of the 1790s, see Hall, *Africans in Colonial Louisiana*, chs. 10–11; Ulysses S. Richard Jr., "The Pointe Coupée Slave Conspiracy of 1791," *Proceedings of the Meeting of the French Colonial Historical Society*, 15 (1992): 116–139; Jack D. L. Holmes, "The Abortive Slave Revolt at Pointe Coupée, Louisiana, 1795," *Louisiana History*, 11 (Autumn 1970): 341–362.

13. The rate of growth of the slave population in Point Coupée for each decade was as follows: 16 percent in the 1820s, 29 percent in the 1830s, 44 percent in the 1840s, and 65 percent in the 1850s. Statistics derived from the University of Virginia's Historical Census Data Browser, http://mapserver.lib.virginia.edu/index.html. The rate of growth of the white population exceeded the slave population until the 1850s.

14. In a rigorous analysis, Michael Tadman estimates a 13 percent rate of natural decrease (deaths over births) per decade in the thirteen leading sugar parishes in Louisiana in the 1840s and 1850s. See Michael Tadman, "The Demographic Cost of Sugar: Debates on Slave Societies and Natural Increase in the Americas," *American Historical Review*, 105 (December 2000): 1553–1554. Pointe Coupée, being split between sugar and cotton, may not have such a dismal record as this. But even if Pointe Coupée had a typical rate of increase for the United States (about 25 percent per decade), importation would have accounted for more than half of the increase in the 1850s. For the typical rate, see Tadman, "Demographic cost," 1549 (table 1).

15. Tadman, "Demographic cost."

16. On "increase" in the slave labor force, see Jennifer L. Morgan, *Laboring Women: Reproduction and Gender in New World Slavery* (Philadelphia: University of Pennsylvania Press, 2004), ch. 3.

17. Lunsford v. Coquillon, 2 Mart. (n.s.) 401 (La. 1824). For more on the Lunsford case, see James D. Hardy Jr. and Robert B. Robinson, "Freedom and Domicile Jurisprudence in Louisiana: Lunsford v. Coquillon," *Louisiana History*, 39 (Summer 1998): 293–317. For the importance of law in fixing the status of the offspring of slaves, see Kathleen Brown, *Good Wives, Nasty Wenches, and Anxious Patriarchs: Gender, Race, and Power in Colonial Virginia* (Chapel Hill: Institute of Early American History and Culture / University of North Carolina Press, 1996); Thomas D. Morris, "'Villeinage . . . as It Existed in England, Reflects but Little Light on Our Subject': The Problem of the 'Sources' of Southern Slave Law," *American Journal of Legal History*, 32 (April 1988): 95–137.

18. Camillia Cowling, *Conceiving Freedom: Women of Color, Gender, and the Abolition of Slavery in Havana and Rio de Janeiro* (Chapel Hill: University of North Carolina Press, 2013), 55–59.

19. For variations on this story, see Ronnie W. Clayton, *Mother Wit: The Ex-Slave Narratives of the Louisiana Writers' Project* (New York: Peter Lang, 1990), 61 (Francis Doby), 72 (Octavia Fontenette), 137–138 (St. Ann Johnson), 190 (quotation from Robert St. Ann). See also Richard Follett, *The Sugar Masters: Planters and Slaves in Louisiana's Cane World, 1820–1860* (Baton Rouge: Louisiana State University Press, 2005), 75.

20. Records of burials compiled from *Pointe Coupée Records, 1770–1900: Individuals without Surnames*, 258–260. On the severe challenges of reproduction among slaves in Louisiana's sugar parishes, see Richard Follett, "Gloomy Melancholy: Sexual Reproduction among Louisiana Slave Women, 1840–1860," in *Women and Slavery*, ed. Gwyn Campbell, Suzanne Miers, and Joseph C. Miller, vol. 2, *The Modern Atlantic* (Athens: Ohio University Press, 2008), 54–78. On the rearing of slave children, see Marie Jenkins Schwartz, *Born in Bondage: Growing Up Enslaved in the Antebellum South* (Cambridge, Mass.: Harvard University Press, 2000); Wilma King, *Stolen Childhood: Slave Youth in Nineteenth-Century America*, 2nd ed. (Bloomington: Indiana University Press, 2001).

21. In contrast, more than half of the free people of color were female. Census data drawn from the University of Virginia's Historical Census Browser, http://mapserver.lib.virginia.edu/collections/stats/histcensus/index.html (accessed July 17, 2013).

22. Slave schedule, Pointe Coupée, Louisiana, Seventh Census of the United States, reel 245, M432, National Archives and Records Administration, Washington, D.C. (hereafter cited as NARA). Rose is also described as "mulatto" in several of the notarial records included in *Report*, 7, 13, 17. Only four of the forty-two slaves enumerated on the Leblanc slave schedule are marked as mulatto, and the sixteen-year-old is the one closest to Rose's age.

23. Jennifer L. Hochschild and Brenna Marea Powell, "Racial Reorganization and the United States Census, 1850–1930: Mulattoes, Half-Breeds, Mixed Parentage, Hindoos, and the Mexican Race," *Studies in American Political Development*, 22 (March 2008): 66–68.

24. An exception were the Pueblo Indians in Taos, who were listed in the 1850 census as "copper" in color. James P. Collins, "Native Americans in the Census, 1860–1890," *Prologue*, 38 (Summer 2006): n1, www.archives.gov/publications/prologue/2006/summer/indian-census.html (accessed June 11, 2014).

25. Jennifer M. Spear, *Race, Sex, and Social Order in Early New Orleans* (Baltimore: Johns Hopkins University Press, 2009), esp. 180–182.

26. Adéle v. Beauregard, 1 Mart. (o.s.) 183 (La. 1810), quoted in Judith Kelleher Schafer, *Slavery, the Civil Law, and the Supreme Court of Louisiana* (Baton Rouge: Louisiana State University Press, 1994), 20.

27. J. D. B. DeBow, *Statistical View of the United States* (Washington: A. O. P. Nicholson, 1854), 83. On free people of color in rural Louisiana, see Carl A. Brasseau, Keith P. Fontenot, and Claude F. Oubre, *Creoles of Color in the Bayou Country* (Jackson: University Press of Mississippi, 1994); Gary B. Mills, *The Forgotten People: Cane River's Creoles of Color* (Baton Rouge: Louisiana State University Press, 1977). For the history of Mulatto Bend, see Smith, "Mulatto Bend," and for free people of color in Pointe Coupée, see Costello, *A History of Pointe Coupée Parish*, ch. 7.

28. "Sale of Plantation and Slaves," February 24, 1853, in Joseph Stinson v. Julius V. Winter, filed January 15, 1859, 9th District Court, No. 2232, Pointe Coupée Parish Courthouse. By "unnamed," I mean only that these children were not identified by name in the bill of sale. On slave families in Louisiana, see the seminal Herbert G. Gutman, *The Black Family in Slavery and Freedom, 1750–1925* (New York: Vintage Books, 1976); Ann Patton Malone, *Sweet Chariot: Slave Family and Household Structure in*

Nineteenth-Century Louisiana (Chapel Hill: University of North Carolina Press, 1992). On husbands and wives in the slave market, see Walter Johnson, *Soul by Soul: Life in the Antebellum Slave Market* (Cambridge, Mass.: Harvard University Press, 1999), 34–35, 181.

29. Data on slaveholding compiled from Slave schedule, Pointe Coupée, Louisiana, Seventh Census of the United States, reel 245, M432, NARA. Octave Leblanc was born in Pointe Coupée in 1803 to Alexandre Leblanc and Charlotte Allain; see *Diocese of Baton Rouge Catholic Church Records*, vol. 2, *1770–1803* (Baton Rouge: Catholic Diocese of Baton Rouge, 1980), 480. He married Julie Bouis in 1830. Their daughter Ann, who is listed on the 1850s census, was born in 1832. Julie died sometime before 1850. *Diocese of Baton Rouge Catholic Church Records*, vol. 5, *1830–1839* (Baton Rouge: Catholic Diocese of Baton Rouge, 1984), 90.

30. Frederick Gerstäcker, *Wild Sports in the Far West* (Boston: Crosby, Nichols, 1859), 377. For background, see Irene S. Di Maio, trans. and ed., *Gerstäcker's Louisiana: Fiction and Travel Sketches from Antebellum Times through Reconstruction* (Baton Rouge: Louisiana State University Press, 2006), 1–16.

31. Gerstäcker, *Wild Sports*, 378. For a good description of the damage done by a major break in the levee in Pointe Coupeé in 1850 and the use of slave labor to repair the levee, see the "Letter from the Interior," *New Orleans Daily Picayune*, 22 June 1850. On flooding in Pointe Coupée, see Brian J. Costello, *Desolation Unmeasured: The Tragic History of Floods in Pointe Coupee Parish* (New Roads, La.: New Roads Printing, 2007).

32. Gerstäcker, *Wild Sports*, 379. On travelers' sympathies with the proslavery argument, see Elizabeth Fox-Genovese and Eugene Genovese, *Slavery in White and Black: Class and Race in the Southern Slaveholders' New World Order* (New York: Cambridge University Press, 2008), 106–121.

33. William Still, *Still's Underground Rail Road Records* (Philadelphia: William Still, 1886), 403–406. A newspaper account of the event, which Still includes in his memoir, also appeared in the *New York Daily Times*, 29 July 1857. Parlange appears in the 1850 census as the owner of 171 slaves, third most in the parish. "Vincent Turner" must be the Vincent Ternant Jr., whose widow married Parlange. The Parlange plantation still exists.

34. Still, *Still's Underground Rail Road Records*. On the activities of William Still and Philadelphia's Vigilance Committee, see Elizabeth

Varon, "'Beautiful Providences': William Still, the Vigilance Committee, and Abolitionists in the Age of Sectionalism," in *Antislavery and Abolition in Philadelphia: Emancipation and the Long Struggle for Racial Justice in the City of Brotherly Love*, ed. Richard Newman and James Mueller (Baton Rouge: Louisiana State University Press, 2011), 229–245.

35. "Les enfans d'Eulalie . . . etaint tres polis vers les blans," Deposition of Louis Hubert, Eulalie, f.w.c., et al. v. Long et al., p. 66, Docket 3979, New Orleans, June 1856, 11 La. Ann. 463, Supreme Court of Louisiana Historical Archives, Earl K. Long Library, University of New Orleans, http://libweb.uno.edu/jspui/handle/123456789/5285. News of proceedings against Long and Mabry appeared in the New Orleans *Daily Picayune*, 3 March 1853 and 13 March 1853. The French material in these records was translated for me by Professor Paul Young of Georgetown University.

36. Deposition of E. E. Short, pp. 38–39, Eulalie, f.w.c., et al. v. Long et al.

37. Deposition of E. W. Robertson, pp. 40–42, Eulalie, f.w.c., et al. v. Long et al.

38. On the "Anglo" influx, see Costello, *History of Pointe Coupee Parish*, 70–71.

39. Judith Kelleher Schafer, *Becoming Free, Remaining Free: Manumission and Enslavement in New Orleans, 1846–1862* (Baton Rouge: Louisiana State University Press, 2003), esp. ch. 7 on freedom suits by those who claimed to have been kidnapped. See pp. 123–124 for Eulalie v. Long and Mabry.

40. Prescription did not apply to slaves who ran away from their owners.

41. Solomon Northup, *Twelve Years a Slave* (Auburn, N.Y.: Derby and Miller, 1853), 321, http://docsouth.unc.edu/fpn/northup/northup.html.

42. On communication among slaves via the "grapevine," see Phillip Troutman, "Grapevine in the Slave Market: African American Geopolitical Literacy and the 1841 *Creole* Revolt," in *The Chattel Principle: Internal Slave Trades in the Americas*, ed. Walter Johnson (New Haven, Conn.: Yale University Press, 2004), 206.

2 NEW ORLEANS

1. *Report*, 18 ("brought to New Orleans"); [William Robinson], *Diary of a Samaritan* (New York: Harper and Bros., 1859), 150 ("hospital"). On the 1853 yellow fever epidemic in New Orleans, see John Duffy, *Sword of Pestilence: The New Orleans Yellow Fever Epidemic of 1853* (Baton Rouge: Louisiana State University Press, 1966); Jo Ann Carrigan, *The Saffron Scourge: A History of Yellow Fever in Louisiana, 1796–1905* (Lafayette: Center for Louisiana Studies, University of Southwestern Louisiana, 1994); Ari Kelman, *A River and Its City: The Nature of Landscape in New Orleans* (Berkeley: University of California Press, 2003), ch. 3.

2. On Louisiana's classifying slaves as real estate, see Thomas D. Morris, *Southern Slavery and the Law, 1619–1860* (Chapel Hill: University of North Carolina Press, 1996), 74–77; Judith Kelleher Schafer, *Slavery, the Civil Law, and the Supreme Court of Louisiana* (Baton Rouge: Louisiana State University Press, 1994), 8, 21–26 (quotation from *State v. Seaborne, alias Moore* [1843] on 21). For determinants of slave prices, see Lawrence Kotlikoff, "The Structure of Slave Prices in New Orleans, 1804–1862," *Economic Inquiry*, 17 (October 1979): 496–518. On how slaves lived with a price on their heads, see Walter Johnson, *Soul by Soul: Life inside the Antebellum Slave Market* (Cambridge, Mass.: Harvard University Press, 1999).

3. The classic historiography of the American slave community begins with John Blassingame, *The Slave Community: Plantation Life in the Antebellum South* (New York: Oxford University Press, 1979); Eugene Genovese, *Roll, Jordan, Roll: The World the Slaves Made* (New York: Vintage Books, 1972). More recently, see Anthony E. Kaye, *Joining Places: Slave Neighborhoods in the Old South* (Chapel Hill: University of North Carolina Press, 2007); Dylan C. Penningroth, *The Claims of Kinfolk: African American Property and Community in the Nineteenth-Century South* (Chapel Hill: University of North Carolina Press, 2003). Localized histories of particular slaves and their communities include Annette Gordon-Reed, *The Hemingses of Monticello: An American Family* (New York: W.W. Norton, 2008); Lorena Seebach Walsh, *From Calabar to Carter's Grove: The History of a Virginia Slave Community* (Charlottesville: University Press of Virginia, 1997); David E. Paterson, "Slavery, Slaves, and Cash in a Georgia

village, 1825–1865," *Journal of Southern History*, 75 (November 2009): 879–930.

4. *Report*, 18. For Octave and Martin O. Leblanc's sale to Joseph Stinson in 1853, see the copy of the bill of sale filed with Joseph Stinson v. Julius V. Winter, filed January 15, 1859, 9th Dist. Ct., no. 2232, Point Coupée Parish Courthouse. On slave mortgages in Louisiana, see Richard Kilbourne Jr., *Debt, Investment, Slaves: Credit Relations in East Feliciana Parish, Louisiana, 1825–1885* (Tuscaloosa: University of Alabama Press, 1985), ch. 3; Bonnie Martin, "Slavery's Invisible Engine: Mortgaging Human Property," *Journal of Southern History*, 76 (November 2010): 817–866.

5. Louisiana, vol. 11, p. 188, R. G. Dun & Co. Credit Report Volumes, Baker Library, Harvard Business School. Street numbers are indicated in Robinson's Atlas (1883), available online through the New Orleans Notarial Archives, www.notarialarchives.org/robinson/index.htm. A guide to New Orleans street numbers before 1890 is available online through the City Archives of New Orleans Public Library, http://neworleanspublicli-brary.org/~nopl/info/louinfo/numberchanges/numberchanges.htm.

6. *New Orleans Daily Picayune*, 7 November 1858. For the historical geography of New Orleans, see Richard Campanella, *Geographies of New Orleans: Urban Fabrics before the Storm* (Lafayette, La.: Center for Louisiana Studies, 2006); Peirce F. Lewis, *New Orleans: The Making of an Urban Landscape* (Charlottesville: University of Virginia Press, 2003).

7. *Gardner's New Orleans Directory for 1861* (New Orleans: Charles Gardner, 1861), 8, 10. For a comprehensive statistical overview of the commerce of New Orleans from 1820–1860, see Thomas E. Redard, "The Port of New Orleans: An Economic History, 1821–1861" (PhD diss., Louisiana State University, 1985). On the aspirations and frustrations of New Orleans merchants, see Scott Marler, *The Merchants' Capital: New Orleans and the Political Economy of the Nineteenth-Century South* (New York: Cambridge University Press, 2013); Walter Johnson, *River of Dark Dreams: Slavery and Empire in the Cotton Kingdom* (Cambridge: Harvard University Press, 2013).

8. Data compiled from Historical Census Browser, http://mapserver.lib.virginia.edu/index.html. For comparative statistics, see Richard C. Wade, *Slavery in the Cities: The South, 1820–1860* (New York: Oxford University Press, 1964), app. Salvador exemplifies the trend in Brazil. See Mieko

Nishida, "Manumission and Ethnicity in Urban Slavery: Salvador, Brazil, 1808–1888," *Hispanic American Historical Review*, 73 (August 1993): 366.

9. For the debate over the decline of urban slavery in the United States, see Wade, *Slavery in the Cities*, esp. ch. 9; Claudia Dale Goldin, *Urban Slavery in the American South 1820–1860: A Quantitative History* (Chicago: University of Chicago Press, 1976), esp. ch. 5; Barbara Jeanne Fields, *Slavery and Freedom on the Middle Ground: Maryland during the Nineteenth Century* (New Haven, Conn.: Yale University Press, 1985), ch. 3; Midori Takagi, *Rearing Wolves to Our Own Destruction: Slavery in Richmond, Virginia, 1782–1865* (Charlottesville: University Press of Virginia, 1999); Frank Towers, "The Southern Path to Modern Cities: Urbanization in the Slave States," in *Old South's Modern Worlds: Slavery, Region, and Nation in the Age of Progress*, ed. L. Diane Barnes, Brian Schoen, and Frank Towers (New York: Oxford University Press, 2011), 145–165. The debate would benefit from a wider lens that examines slave cities elsewhere in the Atlantic world, such as Havana, Rio, and Lagos.

10. Frederick Law Olmsted, *The Cotton Kingdom: A Traveller's Observations on Cotton and Slavery in the American Slave States, 1853–1861*, ed. Arthur M. Schlesinger (New York: Da Capo Press, 1996), 233.

11. *Report*, 18. On the social structure of slavery in pre–Civil War New Orleans, see Virginia Meacham Gould, "'The House That Was Never a Home': Slave Family and Household Structure in New Orleans, 1820–1850," *Slavery & Abolition*, 18, no. 2 (1997): 90–103 (data from estate inventories, 91). On immigrants in the formation of the urban working class in Southern cities before the Civil War, see Ira Berlin and Herbert G. Gutman, "Natives and Immigrants, Free Men and Slaves: Urban Workingmen in the Antebellum American South," *American Historical Review*, 88 (December 1983): 1175–1200.

12. *New Orleans Daily Picayune*, 7 October 1856.

13. *New Orleans Daily Picayune*, 15 January 1857.

14. *New Orleans Daily Picayune*, 3 March 1857.

15. On the vocabulary of the slave market, see Johnson, *Soul by Soul*, esp. ch. 4. Johnson does not put much credence in slave traders' descriptions of the skills attributed to slaves in their advertisements; he represents them largely as an index of the fantasies of paternalism that the traders peddled to buyers (pp. 124–126). However sophisticated this analysis, it passes too

quickly over the quotidian reality that buyers were purchasing people to work for them.

16. *New Orleans Daily Picayune,* 4 March, 1856. Judith Kelleher Schafer, "New Orleans Slavery in 1850 as Seen in Advertisements," *Journal of Southern History,* 47 (February 1981): 33–56. I have supplemented Schafer's findings with my own analysis of more than a hundred sale and wanted ads from the *Daily Picayune* from 1851 to 1860. For an elegant analysis of domestic service in a slave city with parallels to New Orleans, see Sandra Lauderdale Graham, *House and Street: The Domestic World of Servants and Masters in Nineteenth-Century Rio de Janeiro* (New York: Cambridge University Press, 1988). On the rape of domestic servants, see Wilma King, "Within the Professional Household: Slave Children in the Antebellum South," *Historian,* 59 (Spring 1997): 530–531. On the rape of light-skinned slave women by slave traders, see Edward E. Baptist, "'Cuffy,' 'Fancy Maids,' and 'One-Eyed Men': Rape, Commodification, and the Domestic Slave Trade in the United States," *American Historical Review,* 106 (December 2001): 1619–1650.

17. On conflict within the plantation household, see Thavolia Glymph, *Out of the House of Bondage: The Transformation of the Plantation Household* (New York: Cambridge University Press, 2008).

18. George Washington Cable, "The 'Haunted House' on Royal Street," in *Strange True Stories of Louisiana* (New York: Charles Scribner's Sons, 1889), 192–232; Harriet Martineau, *Retrospect of Western Travel* (London: Saunders and Otley, 1838), 2:136–143. The most thorough analysis of the Lalaurie case is Carolyn Morrow Long, *Madame Lalaurie, Mistress of the Haunted House* (Gainesville: University Press of Florida, 2012).

19. Martineau, *Retrospect of Western Travel,* 2:136 (revelation), 144–145 (so white). Other cases of the torture of slave children in New Orleans can be found in the *National Era,* 16 November 1854; *New Orleans Daily Picayune,* 1 June 1856.

20. *New Orleans Daily Picayune,* 6 March 1856. Lawrence E. Kotlikoff found only forty examples of husbands and wives being sold together out of a sample of 5,785 slaves sold in New Orleans in the nineteenth century. Kotlikoff, "The Structure of Slave Prices in New Orleans, 1804–1862," 512.

21. Schafer, "New Orleans Slavery in 1850," 35–42; Johnson, *Soul by Soul,* 91–93, 122–123, 151–154.

22. Fredrika Bremer, *Homes of the New World; Impressions of America* (New York: Harper and Brothers, 1853), 2:206–209.

23. *New Orleans Daily Picayune*, 20 August 1853.

24. Ads from *New Orleans Daily Picayune*, 15 October 1856. Kotlikoff, "Structure of Slave Prices in New Orleans, 1804–1862," 515–17, finds a "light colored female premium." See also Johnson, *Soul by Soul*, 113–115; Baptist, "Cuffy." For slave hiring, see Jonathan Martin, *Divided Mastery: Slave Hiring in the American South* (Cambridge, Mass.: Harvard University Press, 2004). On the hiring of slaves for household labor, see Keith C. Barton, "'Good Cooks and Washers': Slave Hiring, Domestic Labor, and the Market in Bourbon County, Kentucky," *Journal of American History*, 84 (September 1997): 436–460.

25. C. S. Knapp to Joseph Copes, 2 December 1854 (valuable mulatto man); Mrs. Harris to Joseph Copes, April 1853 (Chloe); George Beard to Joseph Copes, 9 October 1854 (Mary); Emma L. C. Beard to Joseph Copes, 23 June 1855 (Hester), all in Joseph S. Copes Papers, Manuscripts Collection 733, Tulane University Libraries, New Orleans, Louisiana.

26. *New Orleans Daily Picayune*, 26 February 1852 (Susan); 28 June 1854 (Mildred Ann Jackson); 6 December 1854 (Elizabeth); 15 January 1857 (Sarah). See also the analysis of runaway ads in Schafer, "Slavery in New Orleans Slavery in 1850," 42–55.

27. Theodore Guyol, Acts, vol. 39, July–December 1857, no. 547, O. Le Blanc & Son to Valerien Allain, September 2, 1857, New Orleans Notarial Archives. The sum is the equivalent of roughly $150,000 in today's dollars.

28. On local sales, see Steven Deyle, *Carry Me Back: The Domestic Slave Trade in American Life* (New York: Oxford University Press, 2005), ch. 5; Thomas Russell, "Sale Day in Antebellum South Carolina" (PhD diss., Stanford University, 1993). For the life histories of commodities, see Igor Kopytoff, "The Cultural Biography of Things: Commoditization as Process," in *The Social Life of Things: Commodities in Cultural Perspective*, ed. Arjun Appadurai (New York: Cambridge University Press, 1986), 64–94.

29. *Report*, 18. Perhaps to recoup some of their losses, in 1857 the Leblancs sued a free man of color from Pointe Coupée, Laurent Julien, who had failed to pay off a $150 debt to them for "articles of merchandize furnished and monies advanced." See PAR20885722 (microform), in *Race, Slavery,*

and Free Blacks, ser. 2, *Petitions to Southern County Courts, 1775–1867*, ed. Loren Schweninger (Bethesda, Md.: LexisNexis, 2002–2005), reel 17.

30. Louisiana, vol. 11, p. 188, R. G. Dun & Co. Credit Report Volumes.

31. Edward E. Baptist, "Toxic Debt, Liar Loans, Collateralized and Securitized Human Beings, and the Panic of 1837," in *Capitalism Takes Command: The Social Transformation of Nineteenth-Century America*, ed. Michael Zakim and Gary J. Kornblith (Chicago: University of Chicago Press, 2012), 79; Johnson, *Soul by Soul*, 38. On the "smooth and profitable functioning of the southern economy" in the wake of the Panic of 1857, see James L. Huston, *The Panic of 1857 and the Coming of the Civil War* (Baton Rouge: Louisiana State University Press, 1987), 33–34, 60–65, 79–97.

32. *New Orleans Daily Picayune*, 13 March 1858. V. Allain & Co. is listed in *Gardner's Directory for 1861*, 32.

33. *Gardner's Directory for 1861*, 71 (Bouligny); A. Oakey Hall, *The Manhattaner in New Orleans* (New York: J. S. Redfield, 1851), 17 (St. Louis Exchange, gloominess); Mrs. Houstoun, *Hesperos: or, Travels in the West* (London: John Parker, 1850), 2:56 (good fortune).

34. *Report*, 18; Felix Grima, Acts, vol. 43, June 5, 1857–December 29, 1858, nos. 36, 37, 38, 40, 61, 139, New Orleans Notarial Archives. Sosthene Allain is listed at 11 St. Peter St. in *Gardner's Directory for 1861*, ii.

35. Felix Grima, Acts, vol. 45, January 4–April 30, 1860, no. 100, New Orleans Notarial Archives. Praise for Mercer from a biographical sketch in Edwin L Jewell, *Jewell's Crescent City Illustrated* (New Orleans, 1873), n.p.

36. William Newton Mercer Diary, April 5 and 17, 1860, May 7, 1860, William N. Mercer Papers, Louisiana State University, in Records of Ante-Bellum Southern Plantations from the Revolution through the Civil War (microform), ed. Kenneth Stampp, ser. 1, pt. 3, reel 3, University Publications of America, Frederick, Md.

37. Felix Grima, Acts, vol. 49, January 16, 1861–June 14, 1862, no. 4, New Orleans Notarial Archives.

38. Grace Elizabeth King, *Creole Families of New Orleans* (New York: Macmillan, 1921), 446–449. On the interlaced genealogy of the Leblancs and Allains, see Stanley Clisby Arthur, *Old Families of Louisiana* (New Orleans: Harmanson, 1931), 35–40. Sosthene Allain had a son, Theophile, with one of his slave women in West Baton Rouge. Allain took an interest

in his son's upbringing, and Theophile Allain went on to become a successful businessmen and politician after the Civil War. William J. Simmons, *Men of Mark, Eminent, Progressive and Rising* (Cleveland: Geo. M. Rewell, 1887), ch. 19; Documenting the American South, http://docsouth.unc.edu/neh/simmons/simmons.html.

39. Robert H. Gudmestad, *A Troublesome Commerce: The Transformation of the Interstate Slave Trade* (Baton Rouge: Louisiana State University Press, 2003).

40. *Report*, 24.

41. Leocadie became free after the death of her new owner in 1860 or 1861. She continued to live with her owner's sister, took care of her children, and "had her own time." *Report*, 25.

42. De Hart Passport, July 11, 1876, Passport no. 50396, Passport Applications, 1795–1905, reel 214, M1372, General Records of the Department of State, Record Group 59, NARA; for confirmation of the date of De Hart's naturalization, see Card Index to Naturalizations in Louisiana, reel 4, P2087, Records of the District Courts of the United States, Record Group 21, NARA. James De Hart's obituary appears in the *New Orleans Daily Picayune*, 22 May 1890.

43. A. Oakey Hall, *The Manhattaner in New Orleans; or, Phases of "Crescent City" Life* (New York: J. Redfield, Clinton Hall, 1851), 32.

44. Fredrick Marcel Spletstoser, "Back Door to the Land of Plenty: New Orleans as an Immigrant Port, 1820–1860" (PhD diss., Louisiana State University, 1978), 299.

45. Richard Campanella, *Geographies of New Orleans: Urban Fabrics before the Storm* (Lafayette: Center for Louisiana Studies, 2006), esp. 205–262; Joseph Tregle, "Creoles and Americans," in *Creole New Orleans: Race and Americanization*, ed. Arnold R. Hirsch and Joseph Logsdon (Baton Rouge: Louisiana State University Press, 1992), 164–165. See also Paul Lachance, "The Foreign French," in Hirsch and Logsdon, *Creole New Orleans*, 101–130.

46. *New Orleans Daily Picayune*, 23 September 1843.

47. Robert P. Swierenga, *Faith and Family: Dutch Immigration and Settlement in the United States, 1820–1920* (New York: Holmes and Meier, 2000), 133 (table 4.4). The 1860 U.S. census counted 262 Dutch inhabitants of Louisiana, out of 28,261 in the United States. Robert P. Swierenga and

Harry S. Stout, "Dutch Immigration in the Nineteenth Century, 1820–1877: A Quantitative Overview," *Indiana Social Studies Quarterly* 28, no. 2 (1975): 27–28.

48. H. Berendregt, "Letter from St. Louis, Missouri, December 14, 1846," quoted in Henry S. Lucas, *Dutch Immigrant Memoirs and Related Writings* (Grand Rapids, Mich.: William B. Eerdmans, 1997), 2:515.

49. *New Orleans Daily Picayune*, 23 September 1843. For the record of the De Hart's marriage on 25 October 1854, see Orleans Parish (La.) Third Justice of the Peace, Marriage Licenses, 1848–1880, vol. 2, p. 708, City Archives, New Orleans Public Library.

50. *New Orleans Daily Picayune*, 23 November 1852. The *Daily Picayune* noted De Hart as having arrived at the St. Louis Hotel.

51. Within a few months, Davidson had disappeared from De Hart's ads. See, for instance, *New Orleans Daily Picayune*, 29 April 1852.

52. *New Orleans Daily Picayune*, 20 December 1859; *Gardner's Directory for 1861*, 129.

53. *Jackson Mississippian*, 15 November 1859, quoted in *New Orleans Daily Picayune*, 24 November 1859.

54. Louisiana, vol. 11, p. 207, R. G. Dun & Co. Credit Report Volumes.

55. David A. Chernin, "The Beginnings of Professional Dental Institutions in 19th century America," *Journal of the History of Dentistry*, 57 (Spring 2009): 3–14; J. E. Dexter, ed., *History of Dental and Oral Science in America* (Philadelphia: Samuel S. White, 1876), 190–191. On the professionalization of medicine in the nineteenth-century South, see Jonathan Daniel Wells, "Professionalization of the Southern Middle Class," in *Southern Society and its Transformations*, ed. Susanna Delfino, Michelle Gillespie, and Louis M. Kyriakoudes (Columbia: University of Missouri Press, 2011), 157–175.

56. *Gardner's Directory for 1861*, 477. On the same page as De Hart in the 1860 federal census are four other dentists: Theophilus Anfoux, A. White, F. H. Knapp, and Ferdinand McLain. Two doors down from De Hart was Anfoux & Robinson's New Orleans and Southern Dental Depot, "dealers in all kinds of dental materials, dental furniture, etc." (*Gardner's*, 23).

57. Emily Hazen Reed, *Life of A. P. Dostie; or, The Conflict in New Orleans* (New York: Wm. P. Tomlinson, 1868), 17.

58. Elliot Ashkenazi, ed., *The Civil War Diary of Clara Solomon: Growing Up in New Orleans, 1861–1862* (Baton Rouge: Louisiana State University Press, 1995), 88. On proslavery suspicions of "outsiders," see Dennis C. Rousey, "Friends and Foes of Slavery: Foreigners and Northerners in the Old South," *Journal of Social History*, 35 (Winter 2001): 373–396. On slavery and the Southern middle class, see Jonathan Daniel Wells, *The Origins of the Southern Middle Class, 1800–1861* (Chapel Hill: University of North Carolina Press, 2004), ch. 9.

59. Eugene Genovese and Elizabeth Fox-Genovese, *Fatal Self-Deception: Slaveholding Paternalism in the Old South* (New York: Cambridge University Press, 2011), 126–127; Allison Dorsey, *To Build Our Lives Together: Community Formation in Black Atlanta, 1875–1906* (Athens: University of Georgia Press, 2004); Franklin M. Garrett, *Atlanta and Environs: A Chronicle of Its People and Events, 1820s–1870s* (Athens: University of Georgia Press, 1969), 1:453 ("aggrieved").

60. William Still, *Still's Underground Rail Road Records* (Philadelphia: William Still, 1886), 254–295. For Bayne's political career, see the entry in John T. Kneebone, ed., *Dictionary of Virginia Biography* (Richmond: Library of Virginia, 1998), 1:409–411.

61. *Gardner's Directory for 1861*, 240; Eighth Census of the United States, 1860, reel 417, p. 198, M653, Records of the Bureau of the Census, Record Group 29, NARA; Rachel Kranz, ed., *African-American Business Leaders and Entrepreneurs* (New York: Facts on File, 2004), 135–136.

62. Jas. S. Knapp to Joseph Copes, New Orleans, October 23, 1861, Joseph S. Copes Papers.

63. J. D. B. DeBow, *The Interest in Slavery of the Southern Non-Slaveholder* (Charleston, 1860), 9; *Report*, 18. On slavery and Southern domesticity, see Barton, "'Good Cooks and Washers.'"

64. *New Orleans Daily Picayune*, 4 August 1858. *Gardner's Directory*, 63, lists Blanchard's office at 15½ Baronne, and his residence in Jefferson City. The 1860 slave schedule for Jefferson Parish, Louisiana, records three slaves under Blanchard's name, including a thirty-five year old black woman, possibly De Hart's victim. Eighth Census of the United States, 1860, reel 428, p. 394.

65. *New Orleans Daily Picayune*, 19 August 1858.

66. William E. Wiethoff, *The Insolent Slave* (Columbia: University of South Carolina Press, 2002.) For a terse and illuminating explication of

insolence as a fuzzy legal category, see Thomas D. Morris, *Southern Slavery and the Law, 1619–1860* (Chapel Hill: University of North Carolina Press, 1996), 296–299 (Douglass quoted on 296). The cases Morris cites involve slaves tried for insolence, not white people tried for chastising slaves for insolence. Other states explicitly proscribed insolence by slaves, but not Louisiana, which only prohibited free people of color from insulting whites. This law did not authorize any white person to punish the offender, but white citizens often took the law into their own hands. See Bullard and Curry, *New Digest*, 66.

67. For rare cases involving assault against slaves, see *New Orleans Daily Picayune*, 30 May 1851, 10 September 1851, 18 August 1853 (by a free man of color), 11 December 1853, 7 July 1855. On caning, see Joanne B. Freeman, *Affairs of Honor: National Politics in the New Republic* (New Haven: Yale University Press, 2001), 172.

68. That Josephine was born early in 1861 is deduced from documentary evidence that when the family was sold yet again in August 1862, she was identified as twenty months old. *Report*, 7, 13.

69. *Report*, 18; Georges Herera to General N. P. Banks, New Orleans, January 14, 1863, Letters Received, ser. 1920, Civil Affairs, Department of the Gulf, pt. 1, R.G. 393, Document C-700, Freedmen and Southern Society Project, University of Maryland at College Park.

70. Eighth Census of the United States, 1860, reel 418, p. 776.

71. *Gardner's Directory for 1861*, 222. "F.m.c." stood for free man of color.

72. There were twenty-eight free black painters in New Orleans in 1850, according to J. D. B. De Bow, cited in Robert Reinders, "The Free Negro in the New Orleans Economy, 1850–1860," *Louisiana History*, 6 (Summer 1965), 275 (quotation on 285).

73. John Ethan Hankins and Steven Maklansky, eds., *Raised to the Trade: Creole Building Arts of New Orleans* (New Orleans: New Orleans Museum of Art, 2002).

74. *Report*, 18. A search of the marriage records of free people of color at the St. Louis Cathedral in New Orleans did not locate a marriage between George and Rose, but there are records of a Father Coste performing weddings between free people of color. See Marriages FPC 1844–1866, vol. 4, nos. 102, 104, 107, 108, 109, 120, 121, St. Louis Cathedral, New Orleans.

75. Rodolphe Lucien Desdunes, *Our People and Our History: Fifty Creole Portraits*, trans. and ed. Dorothea Olga McCants (Baton Rouge: Louisiana State University Press, 1973), 110. For a synthesis of the history of free people of color in New Orleans in the colonial era, see Lawrence Powell, *The Accidental City: Improvising New Orleans* (Cambridge, Mass.: Harvard University Press, 2012), 277–313, 335–339. A cross section of scholarship on New Orleans' free people of color in the nineteenth century includes the social history of Ira Berlin, *Slaves without Masters: The Free Negro in the Antebellum South* (New York: New Press, 1974); the intellectual history of Caryn Cossé Bell, *Revolution, Romanticism, and the Afro-Creole Protest Tradition in Louisiana, 1718–1868* (Baton Rouge: Louisiana State University Press, 1997); and the legal-cultural history of Shirley Elizabeth Thompson, *Exiles at Home: The Struggle to Become American in Creole New Orleans* (Cambridge, Mass.: Harvard University Press, 2009).

76. Statistics for Orleans Parish drawn from the Historical Census Browser, http://mapserver.lib.virginia.edu/index.html.

77. On the pressure against free people of color in the 1850s, especially in the Upper South, see Berlin, *Slaves without Masters*, ch. 11; William W. Freehling, *The Road to Disunion*, vol. 2, *Secessionists Triumphant* (New York: Oxford University Press, 2007), ch. 13. On proslavery ambitions in the Deep South, see Walter Johnson, *River of Dark Dreams*.

78. *New Orleans Daily Picayune*, 8 March 1856.

79. On the AME case, see Joseph Logsdon and Caryn Cossé Bell, "The Americanization of Black New Orleans," in Hirsch and Logsdon, *Creole New Orleans*, 212–214; Judith Kelleher Schafer, *Becoming Free, Remaining Free: Manumission and Enslavement in New Orleans, 1846–1862* (Baton Rouge: Louisiana State University Press, 2003), 145–146. The case is African Methodist Episcopal Church v. City of New Orleans, 15 La. Ann. 441, no. 6291 (1858). The original case files are available online through the Earl K. Long Library, University of New Orleans, http://libweb.uno.edu/jspui/handle/123456789/7765.

80. Schafer, *Becoming Free*, ch. 9.

81. For many examples, see Schafer, *Becoming Free*, ch. 6. On the enslavement of alleged runaways in Brazil, see Sidney Chalhoub, "Illegal

Enslavement and the Precariousness of Freedom in Nineteenth-Century Brazil," in *Assumed Identities: The Meanings of Race in the Atlantic World*, ed. John D. Garrigus and Christopher Morris (College Station: Texas A&M University Press, 2010), 93–100.

82. Loren Schweninger, ed., *The Southern Debate over Slavery*, vol. 2, *Petitions to Southern County Courts, 1775–1867* (Urbana: University of Illinois Press, 2008), 325. On the Perrine case and fears of enslavement, see Thompson, *Exiles at Home*, 81–87. For the original case, see Constance Bique Perrine v. City of New Orleans, Edward Planchard, appellant and als. no. 6036, 15 La. Ann. 133 (1859); for the original case files, see Earl K. Long Library, University of New Orleans, http://libweb.uno.edu/jspui/handle/123456789/7507.

83. PAR20885940, PAR20885941, in *Race, Slavery, and Free Blacks*, ser. 2, reel 18 (quotations from petition of Euphémie, PAR20885940). See also Schafer, *Becoming Free*, 125.

84. Desdunes, *Our People*, 112–114, for the 1858 Haitian emigration; Rebecca Scott and Jean M. Hébrard, *Freedom Papers: An Atlantic Odyssey in the Age of Emancipation* (Cambridge, Mass.: Harvard University Press, 2012), 117–118, for the Eureka colony in Mexico. For the *Rebecca*, see African Repository, January 1860, voyage ID 4323, Voyages: Transatlantic Slave Trade Database, www.slavevoyages.org.

3   WAR

1. William Howard Russell, *My Diary North and South*, ed. by Eugene Berwanger (Philadelphia: Temple University Press, 1988), 157–172 (quotation on 172).

2. "Friction and abrasion" comes from Abraham Lincoln's plea to representatives from the border slave states to accept compensated emancipation on July 12, 1862, *Collected Works of Abraham Lincoln*, ed. Roy P. Basler, vol. 5 (New Brunswick, N.J.: Rutgers University Press, 1953), 318. See James Oakes, *Freedom National: The Destruction of Slavery in the United States, 1861–1865* (New York: W.W. Norton, 2013), 288–293. For the collapse of slavery in New Orleans, see Ira Berlin, Barbara J. Fields, Thavolia Glymph, Joseph P. Reidy, and Leslie S. Rowland, *Freedom: A Documentary History of Emancipation, 1861–1867*, ser. 1, vol. 1, *The Destruction of Slavery* (New York: Cambridge University Press, 1985), ch. 4.

3. John Sacher, *A Perfect War of Politics: Parties, Politicians, and Democracy in Louisiana, 1824–1861* (Baton Rouge: Louisiana University Press, 2003), 288.

4. William N. Mercer to C. P. Leverich, 22 November 1860, Leverich Papers, New-York Historical Society. On the ties between Mercer and Leverich, see Alana K. Bevan, "We Are the Same people: The Leverich Family and Their Antebellum American Inter-regional Network of Elites" (PhD diss, Johns Hopkins University, 2009).

5. William N. Mercer to C. P. Leverich, 11 December 1860, Leverich Papers.

6. William N. Mercer to C. P. Leverich, 9 January 1861, Leverich Papers.

7. William N. Mercer to C. P. Leverich, 15 February 1861, Leverich Papers.

8. William N. Mercer to C. P. Leverich, 18 June 1861, Leverich Papers.

9. Charles P. Roland, "Louisiana and Secession," *Louisiana History*, 19 (Autumn 1978): 389–399.

10. B. M. Palmer, *Thanksgiving Sermon* (New York: George F. Nesbitt, 1861), 12–13, 17. Italics in original. For the impact of Palmer's sermon, see Haskell Monroe, "Bishop Palmer's Thanksgiving Day Address," *Louisiana History*, 4 (Spring 1963): 105–118.

11. Samuel Wilson Jr., ed., *Queen of the South: New Orleans, 1853–1862: The Journal of Thomas K. Wharton* (New Orleans: Historic New Orleans Collection, 1999), 277 ("troublous times"). On secession in Louisiana, see Sacher, *A Perfect War*, ch. 7. Manuscript returns indicate that secessionists won 52 percent of the vote across the state. See Charles Dew, "The Long-lost Returns: The Candidates and Their Totals in Louisiana's Secession Election," *Louisiana History*, 10 (Autumn 1969): 357–358 (total returns, 364–365; candidates from Orleans Parish, left bank).

12. *Official Journal of the Proceedings of the Convention of the State of Louisiana* (New Orleans: J. O. Nixon, 1861), 9 (1st quotation), 10–11 (2nd quotation), 11 (3rd quotation).

13. The Civil War Diary of Dora Richards Miller (typescript), n.d., 2, Manuscripts Collection 524 (67), Tulane University Libraries, New Orleans, Louisiana. George Washington Cable published the diary as "War Diary of a Union Woman in the South," in *Strange True Stories of Louisiana* (New York: Charles Scribner's Sons, 1889), 261–350.

14. Russell, *My Diary*, 160.

15. Terry L. Jones, "Wharf-rats, Cutthroats, and Thieves: The Louisiana Tigers, 1861–1862," *Louisiana History*, 27 (Spring 1986): 147–165. Jones estimates that about ten thousand Louisiana soldiers joined Lee in Virginia in the war's first year, and of these, one-third were creoles, one-third were Northern-born, and one-third were foreign-born. (147–148).

16. Jones, "Wharf-rats," 152.

17. Michael D. Pierson, *Mutiny at Fort Jackson: The Untold Story of the Fall of New Orleans* (Chapel Hill: University of North Carolina Press, 2008); James G. Hollandsworth Jr., *The Louisiana Native Guards: The Black Military Experience during the Civil War* (Baton Rouge: Louisiana State University Press, 1995), ch. 1. See *New Orleans Daily Picayune*, 23 April 1861, for Metcalf's arrest.

18. *Report*, 25–26; Arthur W. Bergeron Jr., *Guide to Louisiana Confederate Military Units, 1861–1865* (Baton Rouge: Louisiana State University Press, 1989), 182.

19. Adam Rothman, *Slave Country: American Expansion and the Origins of the Deep South* (Cambridge, Mass.: Harvard University Press, 2005), 148–149; Ari Kelman, *A River and its City: The Nature of Landscape in New Orleans* (Berkeley: University of California Press, 2003), 108.

20. Nathaniel "Natty" Palmer to Alexander Palmer, New Orleans, 21 April 1861, Palmer-Loper Family Papers, Library of Congress.

21. Anonymous, New Orleans Civil War Diary, 26 April 1861 and 8 May 1861, Mss. 4761, Louisiana and Lower Mississippi Valley Collections, Louisiana State University Libraries, Baton Rouge, Louisiana.

22. Elliot Ashkenazi, ed., *The Civil War Diary of Clara Solomon: Growing Up in New Orleans, 1861–1862* (Baton Rouge: Louisiana State University Press, 1995), 57. The same rumor was reported by the anonymous author of the "New Orleans Civil War Diary" on July 5.

23. *New Orleans Daily Picayune*, 25 July 1861; Pierson, *Mutiny*, 53–56.

24. *New Orleans Daily Picayune*, 26 July 1861.

25. See, e.g., the *Picayune*'s coverage of the slave insurrection panic in Texas in the summer of 1860, which alleged that abolitionists were encouraging slaves to commit arson. William H. White, "The Texas Slave Insurrection of 1860," *Southwestern Historical Quarterly*, 52 (January 1949): 277–285.

26. *New Orleans Daily Picayune*, 30 May 1861; Junius P. Rodriguez, "'We'll Hang Jeff Davis on a Sour Apple Tree': Civil War Era Slave Resistance in Louisiana," *Gulf Coast Historical Review*, 10 (January 1995): 9.

27. Martin Crawford, ed., *William Howard Russell's Civil War: Private Diary and Letters, 1861–1862* (Athens: University of Georgia Press, 1992), 65.

28. Russell, *My Diary*, 233.

29. Diary of Dora Richards Miller, 4.

30. Robert Reinders and Frank D. Harding, "A Wisconsin Soldier Reports from New Orleans," *Louisiana History*, 3 (Autumn 1962): 362; James Parton, *General Butler in New Orleans* (New York: Mason Brothers, 1864), 267.

31. David C. Rankin, *Diary of a Christian soldier: Rufus Kinsley and the Civil War* (New York: Cambridge University Press, 2004), 92.

32. John De Forest, *A Volunteer's Adventures: A Union Captain's Record of the Civil War* (New Haven, Conn.: Yale University Press, 1946), 17 ("Bress"), 31 ("our side").

33. Chester G. Hearn, *The Capture of New Orleans, 1862* (Baton Rouge: Louisiana State University Press, 1995); Pierson, *Mutiny*, ch. 4.

34. Pierson, *Mutiny*, 5. The classic study of federal rule over New Orleans in the Civil War is Gerald Capers, *Occupied City: New Orleans under the Federals* (Lexington: University of Kentucky Press, 1965). See also Chandra Manning and Adam Rothman, "The Name of War," *New York Times*, 17 August 2013, http://opinionator.blogs.nytimes.com/2013/08/17/the-name-of-war.

35. Ira Berlin, Barbara J. Fields, Steven F. Miller, Joseph P. Reidy, and Leslie S. Rowland, *Slaves No More: Three Essays on Emancipation and the Civil War* (New York: Cambridge University Press, 1992); Eric Foner, *The Fiery Trial: Abraham Lincoln and American Slavery* (New York: W. W. Norton, 2010); Oakes, *Freedom National*.

36. Silvana Siddali, *From Property to Person: Slavery and the Confiscation Acts, 1861–1862* (Baton Rouge: Louisiana State University Press, 2005), 52–54. For Butler's political career before the war, see Pierson, *Mutiny*, 156–160.

37. *Private and Official Correspondence of Gen. Benjamin F. Butler, during the Period of the Civil War* (Norwood, Mass.: Plimpton Press, 1917), 1:517–518 (hereafter cited as *BC*).

38. *War of the Rebellion: A Compilation of the Official Records of the Union and Confederate Armies* (Washington, D.C.: U.S. Government Printing Office, 1886), ser. 1, 15:446 (hereafter cited as *OR*). For the tussle between Butler and Phelps, see Berlin et al., *Destruction of Slavery*, 192–195. Phelps's controversial proclamation against slavery from December 1861 can be found in *OR*, ser. 1, 15:486–490. On Phelps's career, see William F. Messner, "General John Wolcott Phelps and Conservative Reform in Nineteenth Century America," *Vermont History*, 53 (Winter 1985): 17–35.

39. *BC*, 1:564–565. For other cases, see *BC*, 1:525–527, 553–554.

40. *OR*, ser. 1, 15:535.

41. *BC*, 2:109.

42. *OR*, ser. 1, 15:535.

43. For statistics on black military service in the Civil War, see Berlin et al., *Slaves No More*, 203. On Afro-Louisianians military service during the Civil War, see Hollandsworth Jr., *The Louisiana Native Guards*, 104 ("manhood"); Stephen J. Ochs, *A Black Patriot and a White Priest: André Cailloux and Claude Paschal Maistre in Civil War New Orleans* (Baton Rouge: Louisiana State University Press, 2000). For an overview of the history of black military service during the Civil War with a selection of marvelous sources, see *Freedom: A Documentary History of Emancipation, 1861–1867*, ser. 2, *The Black Military Experience*, ed. Ira Berlin, Joseph Reidy, and Leslie Rowland (New York: Cambridge University Press, 1982). On the "war within," see Thavolia Glymph, *Out of the House of Bondage: The Transformation of the Plantation Household* (New York: Cambridge University Press, 2008), esp. ch. 4.

44. Kate Masur, "'A Rare Phenomenon of Philological Vegetation': The Word 'Contraband' and the Meanings of Emancipation in the United States," *Journal of American History*, 93 (March 2007): 1050–1084.

45. On slaves' and freedpeople's "upstart claims," see Kate Masur, *An Example for All the Land: Emancipation and the Struggle over Equality in Washington, D.C.* (Chapel Hill: University of North Carolina Press, 2010), 7.

46. Ashkenazi, *Civil War Diary of Clara Solomon*, 384.

47. Eugene D. Genovese, *Roll, Jordan, Roll: The World the Slaves Made* (New York: Vintage Books, 1972), 97–113.

48. Ann Wilkinson Penrose Diary and Family Letters, 1861–1865, Mss. 1169, Louisiana and Lower Mississippi Valley Collections, Louisiana State

University Libraries (hereafter cited as *PD*), 2 June 1862 ("Retired & quiet"). On the Penrose's family, see Josiah Granvil Leach, *History of the Penrose Family of Philadelphia* (Philadelphia: D. Biddle, 1903), 89, 113. Joseph Penrose (25) and his mother Ann (51) appear in the 1860 federal census for Plaquemines Parish. Joseph is noted as having $25,000 in real estate and $10,000 in personal estate. They are adjacent neighbors to Ann Penrose's brother, Robert Wilkinson, a wealthy sugar planter who served as an officer in Louisiana's 15th Regiment and was killed at Second Manassas. The 1860 slave schedule lists eleven slaves under J. B. W. Penrose. The 1860 census for Jefferson Parish, Louisiana lists Joseph B. Wilkinson as a "gentleman" of seventy-four years and a personal estate valued at $40,000. On the experience of Confederate women in New Orleans, see George Rable, "'Missing in Action': Women of the Confederacy," in *Divided Houses: Gender and the Civil War*, ed. Catherine Clinton and Nina Silber (New York: Oxford University Press, 1992), ch. 8; Drew Gilpin Faust, *Mothers of Invention: Women of the Slaveholding South in the American Civil War* (Chapel Hill: University of North Carolina Press, 1996), 207–214; Jacqueline G. Campbell, "'The Unmeaning Twaddle about Order 28': Benjamin F. Butler and Confederate Women in Occupied New Orleans, 1862," *Journal of the Civil War Era*, 2 (March 2012): 11–30.

49. *PD*, 17 August 1862.
50. Ibid., 24 June 1863.
51. Ibid., 19 May 1862.
52. Ibid., 23 May 1862.
53. Ibid., 17 May 1862.
54. Ibid., 3 June 1862. The continuing story of Ben Travis, Grace, and their children may be followed at 16 June 1862, 27 June 1862, 10 July 1862. Penrose eventually recovered them and sent them to a plantation outside the city.
55. Ibid., 15 August 1862.
56. Ibid., 2 December 1862.
57. Ibid., 20 May 1862 ("Proclamation Phelps"), 7 August 1862 ("4000"), 25 September 1862 ("Our servants").
58. Ibid., 2 February 1863.
59. Ibid., 13 April 1863.
60. Ibid., 6 May 1863.

61. Ibid., 21 May 1863.

62. This story is cobbled together from *PD*, 21 December 1862, 6 January 1863, 10 January 1863, 28 February 1863, 5 August 1863. For another story of a mother "stealing" her child from her New Orleans mistress, see Kate Mason Rowland and Mrs. Morris L. Croxall, eds., *The Journal of Julia Le Grand, New Orleans, 1862–1863* (Richmond: Everett Waddey, 1910), 272, 282–286. In 1864 a black soldier in Missouri named Spotswood Rice wrote to his children to tell their owner "that She is the frist Christian that I ever hard say that aman could Steal his own child especially out of human bondage"; Ira Berlin et al., *The Black Military Experience*, 689–690.

63. *PD*, 5 October 1863.

64. *BC*, 1:434.

65. General Orders, no. 41, Department of the Gulf, *BC*, 1:575. On the operation of the Second Confiscation Act in Louisiana, see Oakes, *Freedom National*, 245–254 (Lincoln quoted on 250). For the complete letter and context, see Abraham Lincoln to Cuthbert Bullitt, 28 July 1862, *Collected Works of Abraham Lincoln*, 5:346.

66. The act of sale is included in *Report*, 13–15. The De Harts' landlord testified that he "never understood that she [Widow Roland] had any means or property"; *Report*, 31.

67. *BC*, 2:307.

68. See testimony of Dr. J. L. Riddell in *Report*, 31. Riddell claimed that De Hart left without paying him $1,500 or $1,600 in back rent. For cases of debtors squirreling away their slaves, see Judith Kelleher Schafer, *Slavery, the Civil Law, and the Supreme Court of Louisiana* (Baton Rouge: Louisiana State University Press, 1994), 174–175.

69. *OR*, ser. 1, 19:278.

70. Daniel E. Sutherland, "Looking for a Home: Louisiana Emigrants during the Civil War and Reconstruction," *Louisiana History*, 21 (Autumn 1980): 343–344; Diary of Dora Richards Miller, 26 July 1862. For other examples of Confederates leaving New Orleans after April 1862, see Mary Elizabeth Massey, *Refugee Life in the Confederacy* (Baton Rouge: Louisiana University Press, 2001), 33, 38–39, 73, 78, 85, 87, 91–93, 108, 164, 169, 175, 178, 254–256.

71. Michael C. Cohen, "Contraband Singing: Poems and Songs in Circulation during the Civil War," *American Literature*, 82 (June 2010): 292–295.

72. General Orders, no. 76, *OR*, 15:575–576. Campbell examines the controversy over this order in "Unmeaning Twaddle," 21–23. See also Parton, *General Butler in New Orleans*, 467–477; Capers, *Occupied City*, 86–7, 92–94; Massey, *Refugee Life*, 208–210.

73. See Testimony of P. A. Snaer in *Report*, 26.

74. On the city's disastrous wartime economy, see Capers, *Occupied City*, ch. 7.

75. *New Orleans Daily Picayune*, 8 January 1858 ("gay"). For ties between New Orleans and Havana, see Matthew Guterl, *American Mediterranean: Southern Slaveholders in the Age of Emancipation* (Cambridge, Mass.: Harvard University Press, 2008), 20–22. See also Louis A. Pérez Jr., *On Becoming Cuban: Identity, Nationality, and Culture* (Chapel Hill: University of North Carolina Press, 1999), 17–24. On Velazquez, see Richard Hall, "Loreta Janeta Velazquez: Civil War Soldier and Spy," in *Cubans in the Confederacy: José Augustín Quintero, Ambrosio José Gonzales, and Loreta Janeta Velazquez*, ed. Philip Thomas Tucker (Jefferson, N.C.: McFarland, 2002), ch. 3. Examples of mid-nineteenth-century travel narratives that encompass both New Orleans and Havana include John S. C. Abbott, *South and North; or, Impressions Received during a Trip to Cuba and the South* (New York, Abbey & Abbot, 1860); Fredrika Bremer, *Homes of the New World*, vol. 2, *Impressions of America*, trans. Mary Howitt (New York: Harper and Brothers, 1856); Henry A. Murray, *Lands of the Slave and the Free; or, Cuba, the United States, and Canada* (London: J. W. Parker, 1855).

76. For New Orleans' role in the Cuban filibusters, see Tom Chaffin, *Fatal Glory: Narciso López and the First Clandestine U.S. War against Cuba* (Charlottesville: University Press of Virginia, 1996); Robert E. May, *Manifest Destiny's Underworld: Filibustering in Antebellum America* (Chapel Hill: University of North Carolina Press, 2002); Walter Johnson, *River of Dark Dreams: Slavery and Empire in the Cotton Kingdom* (Cambridge, Mass.: Harvard University Press, 2013), chs. 11–12.

77. *Class A. Correspondence with the British Commissioners at Sierra Leone, Havana, the Cape of Good Hope, and Loanda, and Reports from British Vice-Admiralty Courts, and from British Naval Officers, Relating to the Slave Trade from April 1, 1859 to March 31, 1860* (London: Harrison and Sons, 1860), 2:279 ("celebrity"). On U.S. participation in the slave trade to Cuba in the nineteenth century, see David Eltis, "The U.S. Transatlantic Slave Trade,

1644–1867: An Assessment," *Civil War History*, 54 (December 2008): 371–377. Twenty slaving voyages originated in New Orleans from 1853 to 1861; Transatlantic Slave Trade Database, www.slavevoyages.org. Seven of these landed slaves in Cuba. Additional voyages are listed in Warren S. Howard, *American Slavers and the Federal Law 1837–1862* (Westport, Conn.: Greenwood Press, 1976), app. J ("Slavers Purchased at New Orleans, 1856–1860"), 253–254. Three of these vessels landed slaves in Cuba; *William D. Miller* (Slavevoyages. org, ID no. 4232), *Toccoa* (Slavevoyages. org, ID no. 4399), and *William R. Kibby* (Slavevoyages. org, ID no. 4356).

78. S. Ex. Doc. 49, 35th Cong., 1st Sess. (1858), 67–68. For data on the Jupiter, see Slavevoyages.org, ID no. 4246.

79. James Daniel Richardson, *A Compilation of the Messages and Papers of the Confederacy* (Nashville: United States Publishing, 1906), 2:81–82, 111 (quotation on 111). On Helm, see Erin Katherine Toler Landrum, "Charles J. Helm and the Confederate Agenda in Cuba, 1861–1865" (MA thesis, Louisiana Tech University, 2003).

80. Richardson, *Compilation*, 2:175. For the cat-and-mouse game between Union and Confederate agents in Havana, see F. C. Drake, "The Cuban Background of the Trent Affair," *Civil War History*, 19 (March 1973): 29–49.

81. Richardson, *Compilation*, 2:124–125, 147–149, 150, 175–180; *BC*, 2:361. Stephen R. Wise, *Lifeline of the Confederacy: Blockade Running during the Civil War* (Columbia: University of South Carolina Press, 1988), 74–80. Much evidence of blockade running between New Orleans and Havana during the first year of the war can be found in *Official Records of the Union and Confederate Navies in the War of the Rebellion* (Washington, D.C.: U.S. Government Printing Office, 1903), ser. 1, 16:530–869, 17:1–175, esp. 142–3, 18: passim. See also *BC*, 2:96–102.

82. *Official Records of the Union and Confederate Navies*, ser. 1, 16:746. For newspaper reports of Confederate activity in Havana, see *New York Times*, 17 June 1862, 10 May 1863.

83. *BC*, 2:368 ("nefarious traffic"), 387 ("running cotton").

84. *BC* 2:342–343; *OR*, ser. 3, 2:625–640. On Butler's quarantine measures, see Jo Ann Carrigan, "Yankee versus Yellow Jack in New Orleans, 1862–1866," *Civil War History*, 9 (September 1963): 251–253. Clifford L. Egan summarizes Butler's conflicts with the Spanish consul in "Friction in New

Orleans: General Butler versus the Spanish Consul," *Louisiana History*, 9 (Winter 1968): 43–52.

85. On the *Blasco de Garay*, see *BC* 2:324–325, 368–371, 374–375; Egan, "Friction," 48–50.

86. *Diario de la Marina* (Havana), 10 October 1862. "A su bordo trae cerca de 80 pasageros de ambos sexos, en su gran mayoría personas de la mejor posicion social que bajo el amparo de la bandera española han venido á buscar en nuestra isla la seguridad de que carecian en su propia tierra."

87. *New Orleans Daily Picayune*, 28 October 1862.

88. "Aviso al publico," *Diario de la Marina* (Havana), 4 November 1862. De Hart continued to advertise in the *Diario* until January 1866.

89. "Tambien hace presente que por medio de un procedimiento de su invencíon particular puede arreglar del modo mas satisfactorio todas las dentaduras artificiales que no sean del agrado de sus poseedores."

90. In October 1862, e.g., General Butler had refused to grant a passport to a woman who intended to take her slaves to Cuba against their will. Anonymous to Butler, October 4, 1862, Provost Marshal General, New Orleans, box 3, A 39 (1862), Letters Received, ser. 1390, pt. 4, R.G. 393, NARA, Doc. C-953, Freedmen and Southern Society Project, University of Maryland, College Park (hereafter cited as FSSP).

91. *Report*, 18.

92. *Report*, 26.

93. *Report*, 23.

94. *Report*, 24.

95. S. G. Howe, "Scene in a Slave Prison," *Liberty Bell*, 1 January 1843. On the New Orleans jail in the early nineteenth century, see Rashauna Johnson, "Confined Cosmopolitans: New Orleans Slavery during the Age of Revolution," manuscript in possession of the author.

96. Prisoners in the Parish Prison to Benjamin Butler, 6 May 1862, box 11, Benjamin Butler Papers, Library of Congress.

97. For Butler's General Orders, no. 88, see *BC* 2:437–438. For the continuing incarceration of slaves at the end of 1862, see *Report*, 26–27. Around the same time, a black sailor complained to Union authorities that his sister had been thrown in jail for nonpayment of rent. Ira Berlin, Thavolia Glymph, Steven F. Miller, Joseph P. Reidy, Leslie S. Rowland, and Julie Saville, *Freedom: A Documentary History of Emancipation, 1861–1867*, ser. 1,

vol. 3, *The Wartime Genesis of Free Labor: The Lower South* (New York: Cambridge University Press, 1990), 407–408.

98. *Report*, 18.

99. Peyton McCrary, *Abraham Lincoln and Reconstruction: The Louisiana Experiment* (Princeton, N.J.: Princeton University Press, 1978), 95–107 (congressional elections), 112–114 (impact of Emancipation Proclamation on Louisiana); Oakes, *Freedom National*, 313–328, 362–367.

100. Cecil D. Eby Jr., *A Virginia Yankee in the Civil War: The Diaries of David Hunter Strother* (Chapel Hill: University of North Carolina Press, 1961), 135 ("kindness"). For Banks's December 24 proclamation, see *OR*, 1:15, 619–621; Nathaniel P. Banks to Abraham Lincoln, 24 December 1862, Abraham Lincoln Papers, Library of Congress, http://memory.loc.gov/cgi-bin/query/r?ammem/mal:@field(DOCID+@lit(d2040200)). On Banks's arrival in Louisiana and his policy toward slavery, see James G. Hollandsworth Jr., *Pretense of Glory: The Life of General Nathaniel P. Banks* (Baton Rouge: Louisiana State University Press, 1998), ch. 7; McCrary, *Abraham Lincoln and Reconstruction*, ch. 11; Berlin et al., *Wartime Genesis*, 354–359.

101. "Diary and Correspondence of Salmon P. Chase," in *Annual Report of the American Historical Association for the year 1902* (Washington, D.C.: U.S. Government Printing Office, 1903), 2:346.

102. *Report*, 29.

103. *Report*, 28–29.

104. *Report*, 24–25.

105. *Report*, 21, 24.

106. Georges Herera to General N. P. Banks, New Orleans, January 14, 1863, Civil Affairs, Department of the Gulf, Letters Received, ser. 1920, pt. 1, R.G. 393, NARA, Doc. C-700, FSSP.

107. Christopher Hager, *Word by Word: Emancipation and the Act of Writing* (Cambridge, Mass.: Harvard University Press, 2013), ch. 5.

108. On New Orleans' free people of color's military service, see Hollandsworth Jr., *Louisiana Native Guards*. For the political activism of New Orleans' free people of color during the Civil War, see Caryn Cossé Bell, *Revolution, Romanticism, and the Afro-Creole Protest Tradition in Louisiana, 1718–1868* (Baton Rouge: Louisiana State University Press, 1997), ch. 7. An excellent introduction to *L'Union* and the *Tribune* is Jean-Charles Houzeau, *My Passage at the New Orleans Tribune: A Memoir of the Civil War*, ed. David

C. Rankin (Baton Rouge: Louisiana State University Press, 1984). For a critique of the sharp dichotomy between free people of color and slaves, see Ochs, *A Black Patriot and a White Priest*, 87.

109. Hager, *Word by Word*, 140, 282n3.

110. *Report*, 23–25. On the departure of the *Bio Bio*, see *New Orleans Daily Picayune*, 16 January 1863. The arrival of the *Bio Bio* in Havana on January 21 was noted in the *Gaceta de la Habana*, 22 January 1863. Three months later the *Bio Bio* returned to New Orleans, caught fire, and was destroyed (*New Orleans Daily Picayune*, 23 March 1863). I have drawn some details of the voyage from David Strother's account of his voyage from New Orleans to Havana in May 1863. See Eby, *Virginia Yankee*, 177–179.

111. Gobierno Superior Civil, Leg. 1293, Nu. 50408, Archivo Nacional, Havana, Cuba (hereafter cited as ANHC).

112. *Report*, 50. Michele Reid-Vazquez, *The Year of the Lash: Free People of Color in Cuba and the Nineteenth-Century Atlantic World* (Athens: University of Georgia Press, 2011), 39–40, 71–75; David R. Murray, *Odious Commerce: Britain, Spain, and the Abolition of the Cuban Slave Trade* (New York: Cambridge University Press, 1980), for Cuba's ineffective "Penal Law" of 1845.

113. Gobierno Superior Civil, Leg. 1037, Nu. 35999, ANHC. I am grateful to Adriana Chira for sharing a copy of this document with me. De Hart was not the only passenger on the *Bio Bio* to be accompanied by slaves. The Countess Marigny ("Condesa Marigny") also petitioned the authorities to let in her three colored servants, Quina, Cecilia, and Jorge. See Gobierno Superior Civil, Leg. 1293, Nu. 50388, ANHC. For similar cases, see Gobierno Superior Civil, Leg. 1293, Nus. 50387, 50382, 50390, 50393, 50400, 50402, 50405, 50407, ANHC.

114. Rebecca J. Scott and Jean M. Hébrard, *Freedom Papers: An Atlantic Odyssey in the Age of Emancipation* (Cambridge, Mass.: Harvard University Press, 2012), 65–69.

115. On the *criado* as a form of "tutelary servitude" that flourished in postemancipation Latin America, see Nara Milanich, "Degrees of Bondage: Children's Tutelary Servitude in Modern Latin America," in *Child Slaves in the Modern World*, ed. Gwyn Campbell, Suzanne Miers, and Joseph C. Miller (Athens: Ohio University Press, 2011), 104–123.

116. Clarence Mohr, *On the Threshold of Freedom: Masters and Slaves in Civil War Georgia* (Athens: University of Georgia Press, 1986), ch. 4.

See also John D. Winters, *The Civil War in Louisiana* (Baton Rouge: Louisiana State University Press, 1963), 158; Berlin et al., *Slaves No More*, 56–57.

117. Clara Walker, quoted in *Born in Slavery: Slave Narratives from the Federal Writers' Project, 1936–1938*, vol. 2, pt. 7, *Arkansas Narratives* (online transcript), 24, http://memory.loc.gov/ammem/snhtml/snhome.html. The Works Progress Administration's ex-slave interviews for Texas and Arkansas include many stories and recollections of slaves relocated from Louisiana during the war.

118. Sarah Morgan Dawson, *A Confederate Girl's Diary* (Boston: Houghton and Mifflin, 1913), 45–46.

119. Sarah Ann Dorsey, *Recollections of Henry Watkins Allen, Brigadier-General of the Confederate States Army Ex-Governor of Louisiana* (New York: M. Doolady, 1866), 250.

120. Frances Fearn, *Diary of a Refugee* (New York: Moffat, Yard, 1910), 27–32 (quotation on 30).

121. *Annual Message of Governor Henry Watkins Allen to the Legislature of the State of Louisiana, January 1865* (Caddo, La., 1865), 15, http://docsouth.unc.edu/imls/lagov/allen.html. A more extensive depiction of the Yankee abuse of slaves in Louisiana is presented in *Official Report Relative to the Conduct of Federal Troops in Western Louisiana during the Invasions of 1863 and 1864* (Shreveport, La., 1865).

122. Dale Baum estimates that at least 32,000 slaves were sent to Texas during the war, many from Louisiana; Dale Baum, "Slaves Taken to Texas for Safekeeping during the Civil War," in *The Fate of Texas: The Civil War and the Lone Star State*, ed. Charles D. Gear (Fayetteville: University of Arkansas Press, 2008), 83–103.

123. Ella Washington, quoted in *Born in Slavery*, vol. 16, pt. 4, *Texas Narratives* (online transcript), 132–133.

124. Fred Brown, quoted in *Born in Slavery*, vol. 16, pt. 1, *Texas Narratives* (online transcript), 159.

125. Jake Walker, quoted in *Born in Slavery*, vol. 2, pt. 7, *Arkansas Narratives* (online transcript), 40.

126. Andrew Smith, quoted in *Born in Slavery*, vol. 2, pt. 6, *Arkansas Narratives* (online transcript), 174.

4 JUSTICE

1. *Report*, 12. De Hart probably arrived on the steamship *Morning Star*, which arrived in New Orleans from Havana on January 3, 1865. See *New Orleans Daily Picayune*, 4 January 1865.

2. *Freedom: A Documentary History of Emancipation, 1861–1867*, ser. 1, vol. 3, *The Wartime Genesis of Free Labor: The Lower South*, ed. Ira Berlin, Thavolia Glymph, Steven F. Miller, Joseph P. Reidy, Leslie Rowland, and Julie Saville (New York: Cambridge University Press, 1990), 365, 373; *New York Herald*, 19 June 1864. On emancipation, civil rights, and Reconstruction in New Orleans, see Caryn Cossé Bell, *Revolution, Romanticism, and the Afro-Creole Protest Tradition in Louisiana, 1718–1868* (Baton Rouge: Louisiana State University Press, 1997), ch. 7; Rebecca Scott, *Degrees of Freedom: Louisiana and Cuba after Slavery* (Cambridge, Mass.: Belknap Press, 2005), ch. 2; Ted Tunnell, *Crucible of Reconstruction: War, Radicalism, and Race in Louisiana, 1862–1877* (Baton Rouge: Louisiana State University Press, 1984). For an overview of the social history of people of African descent in the Civil War and Reconstruction, see John Blassingame, *Black New Orleans, 1860–1880* (Chicago: University of Chicago Press, 1973).

3. On law, justice, and the Civil War, see most recently Stephen C. Neff, *Justice in Blue and Gray: A Legal History of the Civil War* (Cambridge, Mass.: Harvard University Press, 2010); John Fabian Witt, *Lincoln's Code: The Laws of War in American History* (New York: Free Press, 2012). For how revolutions change the very architecture of justice, see Katherine Fischer Taylor, "Geometries of Power: Royal, Revolutionary, and Postrevolutionary French Courtrooms," *Journal of the Society of Architectural Historians*, 72 (December 2013): 434–474.

4. *Report*, 18. St. Louis Cemeteries Death Records, nos. 1 and 2, 1857–1864, p. 176, New Orleans Archdiocesan Archives.

5. Stephen J. Ochs, *A Black Patriot and a White Priest: André Cailloux and Claude Paschal Maistre in Civil War New Orleans* (Baton Rouge: Louisiana State University Press, 2000), 1–5 (quotation on 5).

6. J. David Hacker, "A Census-based Count of the Civil War Dead," *Civil War History*, 57 (December 2011): 338.

7. *Liberator*, 8 July 1864.

8. Sanford B. Hunt, "The Negro as Soldier," *Anthropological Review*, 7 (January 1869): 48 ("scourge of the negro"). Tuberculosis was a major killer

in New Orleans during the war, far worse than the dreaded yellow fever. See Elizabeth Joan Doyle, "Civilian Life in Occupied New Orleans, 1862–1865" (PhD diss., Louisiana State University, 1955), 70; Jim Downs, *Sick from Freedom: African-American Illness and Suffering during the Civil War and Reconstruction* (New York: Oxford University Press, 2012), 157–158. Perhaps it was this illness that kept Herera out of military service. On tuberculosis among black Southerners in the nineteenth century, see Tera Hunter, *To 'Joy My Freedom': Southern Black Women's Lives and Labors after the Civil War* (Cambridge, Mass.: Harvard University Press, 1997), ch. 9.

9. Information on the history of this location (Lot Number 22933-D) can be found through the *Collins C. Diboll Vieux Carré Digital Survey*, www.hnoc.org/vcs/property_info.php?lot=22933-D (accessed December 12, 2013). The lot appears to have been owned by Edmond Albert Hoa from 1855 to 1872.

10. St. Augustine Baptisms PC, 1858–1871, vol. 3A, p. 148, New Orleans Archdiocese Archives. Louise Josephine was born August 15 and baptized on September 6, 1864.

11. I have not located Louis Forstall and Cecile Hypolite in any census or other records. The last recorded baptism of a slave at the St. Louis Cathedral in New Orleans took place on May 1, 1864. See St. Louis Cathedral Baptisms S-FPC, 1856–1865, vol. 33, p. 137, New Orleans Archdiocese Archives.

12. "Tomb of the Unknown Slave," www.staugustinecatholicchurch-neworleans.org/hist-slave.htm (accessed December 13, 2013). For free people of color and St. Augustine Church, see Shirley Elizabeth Thompson, *Exiles at Home: The Struggle to Become American in Creole New Orleans* (Cambridge, Mass.: Harvard University Press, 2009), 135–136. For events after Hurricane Katrina, see Trushna Parekh, "Of Armed Guards and Kente Cloth: Afro-Creole Catholics and the Battle for St. Augustine Parish in Post-Katrina New Orleans," *American Quarterly*, 61 (September 2009): 557–581.

13. Tines Hendricks, quoted in *Born in Slavery: Slave Narratives from the Federal Writers' Project, 1936–1938*, vol. 2, pt. 4, *Arkansas Narratives*, http://memory.loc.gov/ammem/snhtml/snhome.html (accessed December 17, 2013). See also Heather Andrea Williams, *Help Me to Find My People: The African American Search for Family Lost in Slavery* (Chapel Hill: Univer-

sity of North Carolina Press, 2012), chs. 5–6; Michael P. Johnson, "Looking for Lost Kin: Efforts to Reunite Freed Families after Emancipation," in *Southern Families at War: Loyalty and Conflict in the Civil War South*, ed. Catherine Clinton (New York: Oxford University Press, 2000), 15–34; Ira Berlin and Leslie Rowland, eds., *Families and Freedom: A Documentary History of African-American Kinship in the Civil War Era* (New York: New Press, 1988). Some historians have drawn attention to freed people's interest in recovering the labor of their children, but I have found no direct evidence that Rose Herera's desire to recover her children was motivated by economic self-interest.

14. L. P. Duval to Archbishop Odin, 30 December 1866, University of Notre Dame Archives, http://archives.nd.edu/search/calendar.htm (accessed December 17, 2013.) See also Robert Lope to Nathaniel Banks, 10 March 1863, Nathaniel Banks Papers, Library of Congress; and the case of William Ambrose documented in the *New Orleans Tribune*, 29 August 1865, 1 September 1865, and 2 September 1865.

15. George H. Hanks's endorsement of Thomas Conway to George H. Hanks, 13 April 1864, Nathaniel Banks Papers, Library of Congress.

16. Thomas Jefferson, *Notes on the State of Virginia* (New York: Penguin Books, 1999), 146. On slavery as a remedy against child abuse in proslavery doctrine, see Anna Mae Duane, *Suffering Childhood in Early America: Violence, Race, and the Making of the Child Victim* (Athens: University of Georgia Press, 2010), 156.

17. Quoted in Mary Niall Mitchell, *Raising Freedom's Child: Black Children and Visions of the Future after Slavery* (New York: New York University Press, 2008), 146.

18. Marie Jenkins Schwartz, *Born in Bondage: Growing Up Enslaved in the Antebellum South* (Cambridge, Ma: Harvard University Press, 2000), 163–172; Wilma King, *Stolen Childhood: Slave Youth in Nineteenth-Century America*, 2nd ed. (Bloomington: Indiana University Press, 2011), 239–242.

19. Tara Zahra, "'A Human Treasure': Europe's Displaced Children between Nationalism and Internationalism," supplement, *Past and Present*, 210, no. S6 (2011): S332–S350; Nara Milanich, "Degrees of Bondage: Children's Tutelary Servitude in Modern Latin America," in *Child Slaves in the Modern World*, ed. Gwyn Campbell, Suzanne Miers, and Joseph C. Miller (Athens: Ohio University Press, 2011), 104–123.

20. Mitchell, *Raising Freedom's Child*. See also Anya Jabour, *Topsy-Turvy: How the Civil War Turned the World Upside Down for Southern Children* (Chicago: Ivan R. Dee, 2010); James Marten, *The Children's Civil War* (Chapel Hill: University of North Carolina Press, 1998), 125–136.

21. Thomas Conway to George H. Hanks, 13 April 1864, Nathaniel Banks Papers, Library of Congress. On children expressing a preference for their owners over their parents, see Mitchell, *Raising Freedom's Child*, 174–177.

22. *Report*, 19.

23. *Report*, 3.

24. *OR*, ser. 1, 15:582.

25. Thomas W. Conway, *Report on the Condition of the Freedmen, of the Department of the Gulf . . .* (New Orleans: H.P. Lathrop, 1864), 6. For an overview of the city's court system during the war, see Thomas W. Helis, "Of Generals and Jurists: The Judicial System of New Orleans under Union Occupation, May 1862–April 1865," *Louisiana History*, 29 (Spring 1988): 143–162; Doyle, "Civilian Life," ch. 12.

26. *Report*, 3–4, 19–20.

27. *New Orleans Tribune*, 3 May 1865, 15 September 1865.

28. *Report*, 8, 12, 19; *Gardner's New Orleans Directory for 1866* (New Orleans: Charles Gardner, 1866), 442; *New Orleans Tribune*, 3 May 1865, 15 September 1865.

29. Joseph G. Tregle, "Thomas J. Durant, Utopian Socialism, and the Failure of Presidential Reconstruction in Louisiana," *Journal of Southern History*, 45 (November 1979): 485–512 ("thorough and practical reform" on 489–490, "evil" on 491, "rabid" on 492). See also Carl J. Gaurneri, *The Utopian Alternative: Fourierism in Nineteenth-Century America* (Ithaca: Cornell University Press, 1991), 261–267; Frank J. Wetta, *The Louisiana Scalawags: Politics, Race, and Terrorism during the Civil War and Reconstruction* (Baton Rouge: Louisiana State University Press, 2012), 19–24. It may have been Durant who introduced his law clerk Henry Hughes to what Hughes would later call "sociology." See Stephen Berry, *Princes of Cotton: Four Diaries of Young Men in the South, 1848–1860* (Athens: University of Georgia Press, 2007), 238.

30. Tregle, "Thomas J. Durant," 493–394 ("horrors" on 493). *Gardner's New Orleans Directory for 1861* (New Orleans: Charles Gardner, 1861), 152,

puts Durant's residence at Dryades and Canal, and the offices of Durant and Hornor at 18 Carondelet.

31. John D. Gordan III, "New York Justice in Civil War Louisiana," *Judicial Notice*, 8 (Spring 2012): 11–13.

32. Jon L. Wakelyn, ed., *Southern Unionist Pamphlets and the Civil War* (Columbia: University of Missouri Press, 1999), 366.

33. Thomas Jefferson Durant to Abraham Lincoln, 1 October 1863, New Orleans, Abraham Lincoln Papers, Library of Congress, http://memory.loc.gov/cgi-bin/query/r?ammem/mal:@field(DOCID+@lit(d2683900)) (accessed April 29, 2013).

34. Quoted in Tunnell, *Crucible of Reconstruction*, 37. See also Wetta, *The Louisiana Scalawags*, 56, 68–69.

35. "Tangible nucleus" from Abraham Lincoln to Nathaniel Banks, 5 November 1865, Abraham Lincoln Papers, Library of Congress, http://memory.loc.gov/cgi-bin/query/r?ammem/mal:@field(DOCID+@lit(d2783700)) (accessed January 22, 2014). Peyton McCrary, *Abraham Lincoln and Reconstruction: The Louisiana Experiment* (Princeton, N.J.: Princeton University Press, 1978) emphasizes the split over "the question of Negro suffrage" (209), whereas Tunnell, *Crucible of Reconstruction*, argues that Durant and Banks had similar ideas but "the issue was power" (50).

36. On the Fourierist origins of the Freedmen's Aid Association, see Caryn Cossé Bell, "'Une Chimère': The Freedmen's Bureau in Creole New Orleans," in *The Freedmen's Bureau and Reconstruction*, ed. Paul Cimbala and Randall M. Miller (New York: Fordham University Press, 1999), 148–149. Train and Durant's partner Charles Hornor were also officers of the Freedmen's Aid Association. See *New Orleans Tribune*, 3 May 1865.

37. Whitelaw Reid, *After the War: A Southern Tour: May 1, 1865 to May 1, 1866* (London: Sampson Low, Son, 1866), 232–233. See also John Niven, ed., *The Salmon P. Chase Papers*, vol. 1, *Journals, 1829–1872* (Kent, Ohio: Kent State University Press, 1993), 570.

38. *New Orleans Tribune*, 24 December 1865.

39. Proceedings of the Provost Court, New Orleans, August 1863–April 1866, Provost Field Marshal Organizations of the Civil War, Records of the U.S. Army Continental Commands, pt. 4, R.G. 393, NARA, 241:259–261. For a discussion of Virinda's case, see Mitchell, *Raising Freedom's Child*, 182–184.

40. *New Orleans Daily Picayune*, 4 October 1863.

41. Mitchell, *Raising Freedom's Child*, 183. For other child custody cases litigated in the provost court in New Orleans, see Proceedings of the Provost Court, 241:263–264, 244:154, 244:230, 264, 375, 245:394–396. On child custody cases in Southern law in the nineteenth century, see Peter W. Bardaglio, *Reconstructing the Household: Families, Sex, and the Law in the Nineteenth-Century South* (Chapel Hill: University of North Carolina Press, 1995), 79–106, 137–165.

42. Hurlbut was a South Carolinian who moved to Illinois in 1845, where he practiced law and was involved in politics as a Whig and then as a Republican. "Stephen Augustus Hurlbut," *Dictionary of American Biography* (New York: Charles Scribner's Sons, 1936).

43. *Report*, 18–19.

44. *Report*, 19.

45. Train's petition on behalf of "Rose Elyra" calls to mind Gayatri Spivak's famous question, "Can the subaltern speak?"; Rosalind C. Morris, ed., *Can the Subaltern Speak? Reflections on the History of an Idea* (New York: Columbia University Press, 2010).

46. *Opinion of Attorney General Bates on Citizenship* (Washington, D.C.: U.S. Government Printing Office, 1863), 4. Oakes, *Freedom National*, 355–360, conjectures that Bates's opinion was intended to bolster the case against the reenslavement of freedpeople. For struggles for citizenship in New Orleans during Reconstruction, see Bell, *Revolution*, ch. 7; Roger A. Fischer, "A Pioneer Protest: The New Orleans Street-car Controversy of 1867," *Journal of Negro History*, 53 (July 1968): 219–233; Eric Foner, *Reconstruction: America's Unfinished Revolution, 1863–1877* (New York: Harper and Row, 1988), 62–66; Rebecca J. Scott, *Degrees of Freedom: Louisiana and Cuba after Slavery* (Cambridge, Mass.: Belknap Press, 2005), ch. 2. See also Kate Masur, *An Example for All the Land: Emancipation and the Struggle for Equality in Washington, D.C.* (Chapel Hill: University of North Carolina Press, 2010), 7.

47. *Report*, 12, 44. Quotation from Mary Sophia Hill, *A British Subject's Recollection of the Confederacy while a Visitor and Attendant in its Hospitals and Camps* (Baltimore: Turnbull Brothers, 1875), 46. Hill's experience is discussed in Amanda Foreman, *A World on Fire: Britain's Crucial*

Role in the American Civil War (New York: Random House, 2012), 626–627. A petition from De Hart's lawyer indicates that De Hart was "now confined at No. 232 Julia street," which had been Mrs. E. C. O'Brien's boarding house in 1861. See *Gardner's Directory for 1861,* 338.

48. On Francis Lieber and the law of war, see John Fabian Witt, *Lincoln's Code: The Laws of War in American History* (New York: Free Press, 2012). The Lieber Papers at the Huntington Library contain few letters from Norman and none on the Herera case. Major G. Norman Lieber served on General Banks's general staff in the Department of the Gulf as judge advocate and assistant adjutant-general before being named to the provost court. See "BG Guido Norman Lieber," Lieber Collection, Library of Congress, www.loc.gov/rr/frd/Military_Law/Lieber_Collection/pdf/normanbio-more.pdf.

49. Oliver Otis Howard, *Autobiography of Oliver Otis Howard* (New York: Baker and Taylor Company, 1908), 2:253. For contrasting views of the provost courts, see Thomas Morris, "Equality, 'Extraordinary Law,' and Criminal Justice: The South Carolina Experience, 1865–1866," *South Carolina Historical Magazine,* 83 (January 1982): 15–33; and more favorably, Dylan C. Penningroth, *The Claims of Kinfolk: African American Property and Community in the Nineteenth-Century South* (Chapel Hill: University of North Carolina Press, 2003), 123.

50. For courts as theater in a slave society, see Ariela Julie Gross, *Double Character: Slavery and Mastery in the Antebellum Southern Courtroom* (Princeton, N.J.: Princeton University Press, 2000); Walter Johnson, "The Slave Trader, the White Slave, and the Politics of Racial Determination in the 1850s," *Journal of American History,* 87 (June 2000): 13–38. On trials as "social drama," see Michael Grossberg, *A Judgment for Solomon: The D'Hauteville Case and Legal Experience in Antebellum America* (New York: Cambridge University Press, 1996).

51. Thomas W. Conway, *The Freedmen of Louisiana* (New Orleans: New Orleans Times Book and Job Office, 1865), 17.

52. James Parton, *General Butler in New Orleans: History of the Administration of the Department of the Gulf in the year 1862* . . . (New York: Mason Brothers, 1864), 432.

53. Ibid., 432–433.

54. Ibid., 434.

55. On the invocation of "common sense" in the fight over slavery, see Sophia A. Rosenfeld, *Common Sense: A Political History* (Cambridge, Mass.: Harvard University Press, 2011), 233–235.

56. Parton, *General Butler*, 532. Parton does not name Montamal's wife or daughter.

57. *Report*, 9.

58. Note, 8 March 1865, Felix Limongi Papers, Library of Congress (hereafter cited as Limongi Papers). The Limongi Papers contain assorted papers of the law firm of Durant and Hornor, including original documents relating to the Herera case.

59. *Report*, 9.

60. Ibid., 9–11.

61. The trial record is included in *Report*, 20–43. The original trial record can be found in Proceedings of the Provost Court, 245:616–625, 246:2–9. Except for minor typographical differences, it matches the text in *Report*.

62. *Report*, 23–25.

63. Ibid., 26.

64. Ibid., 28.

65. Ibid., 29, 30.

66. Ibid., 29, 30.

67. Ibid., 27–28, 30, 31.

68. Ibid., 34.

69. Ibid., 39–40.

70. Ibid., 41.

71. Ibid., 29.

72. Ibid., 31–32.

73. Ibid., 29. See also p. 41 for a summary of the defense.

74. Ibid., 25–26. Snaer does not appear in the 1860 census for New Orleans or *Gardner's Directory for 1861*.

75. *Report*, 31; *Gardner's Directory for 1861*, 375. Riddell's name is misspelled with one *l* in the report. John Leonard Riddell invented the binocular microscope and wrote one of the first works of hard science fiction, *Orrin Lindsay's Plan of Aerial Navigation; With a Narrative of His Explorations in the Higher Regions of the Atmosphere, and His Wonderful Voyage*

Round the Moon (New Orleans: Rea's Power Press Office, 1847). In October 1865, Riddell would shock a Democratic Party gathering by condemning secession as "worse than a crime—it was a blunder." For Riddell's colorful life, see Everett F. Bleiler, "John Leonard Riddell, Pioneer," *Science Fiction Studies*, 36 (July 2009): 284–299 ("a blunder" on 291).

76. B. F. French, *Historical Collections of Louisiana, Embracing Translations of Many Rare and Valuable Documents Relating to the Natural, Civil and Political History of that State* (New York: D. Appleton, 1851), 3:94; L. Moreau Lislet, *A General Digest of the Acts of the Legislature of Louisiana* (New Orleans: Benjamin Levy, 1828), 101.

77. Walter Johnson, *Soul by Soul: Life Inside the Antebellum Slave Market* (Cambridge, Mass.: Harvard University Press, 1999), 122–123; Judith Kelleher Schafer, *Slavery, The Civil Law, and the Supreme Court of Louisiana* (Baton Rouge: Louisiana State University Press, 1994), 164–168. A sample of over 5,000 slave sales in New Orleans between 1804 and 1862 found that 40 percent of children age thirteen and younger were sold alone but asserts that whether they were "primarily orphans is unclear." Lawrence J. Kotlikoff, "The Structure of Slave Prices in New Orleans," *Economic Inquiry*, 17 (October 1979): 513. Contrast with Stanley Engerman and Robert Fogel, *Time on the Cross: The Economics of American Negro Slavery* (New York: W. W. Norton, 1989), 49–51.

78. *Report*, 34.

79. For a vivid account of another attempt to impose ex post facto justice in a revolutionary context, see David I. Kertzer, *The Kidnapping of Edgardo Mortara* (New York: Vintage Books, 1997), esp. chs. 18–21.

80. For the roots of the ban on ex post facto punishment in the United States, see Wayne A. Logan, *The American Criminal Law Review*, 35 (Summer 1998): 1275–1277. Article 1, Section 9, of the U.S. Constitution prohibits Congress from passing ex post facto laws, and Article 1, Section 10, prohibits states from doing so. See also Calder v. Bull, 3 U.S. (3 Dall.) 386. For the argument that the Northwest Ordinance violated the ex post facto taboo, see Paul Finkelman, "Slavery and the Northwest Ordinance: A Study in Ambiguity," *Journal of the Early Republic*, 6 (Winter 1986): 361–362.

81. *Report*, 37.

82. Ibid., 33–34. An 1855 state law made it a felony to forcibly seize and carry out of the state any free person without authority of law. As a side

matter, Durant also alleged that (1) Rose Herera had been jailed in violation of General Orders, No. 88, Department of the Gulf, November 1, 1862, which prohibited jailers from detaining slaves unless their owners were loyal; and (2) the children had been taken on board the *Bio Bio* in violation of General Orders, No. 44, Department of the Gulf, June 21, 1862, which prohibited ship captains from departing with colored persons on board, except under certain conditions. The defense argued that if these orders had been violated, they had been violated by the jailer and the captain, not Mrs. De Hart; *Report*, 33, 37.

83. *Report*, 36–37. Silvana Siddali, *From Property to Person: Slavery and the Confiscation Acts, 1861–1862* (Baton Rouge: Louisiana State University Press, 2005), 227–250.

84. A similar confusion led Annie Davis from Maryland to write to Abraham Lincoln in August 1864 to ask him "if we are free." Her poignant letter is included in Ira Berlin, Barbara J. Fields, Steven F. Miller, Joseph P. Reidy, and Leslie S. Rowland, eds., *Free at Last: A Documentary History of Slavery, Freedom, and the Civil War* (New York: New Press, 1992), 349.

85. *Report*, 35.

86. Tunnell, *Crucible of Reconstruction*, 59, 95–96 ("bug-eater"quotation on 59). For "the rankest kind of Copperheads," see S. W. Berhman to Nathaniel P. Banks, 23 April 1865, Nathaniel Banks Papers, Library of Congress. Abell's minority report against immediate emancipation can be found in *Debates in the Convention for the Revision and Amendment of the Constitution of the State of Louisiana* (New Orleans: W. R. Fish, 1864), 97–98. On Wells's right turn, see also Joseph G. Dawson III, *Army Generals and Reconstruction: Louisiana, 1862–1877* (Baton Rouge: Louisiana State University Press, 1982), 22, 29–30; McCrary, *Abraham Lincoln and Reconstruction*, 304–316. On civil-military relations in the South in 1865, see Michael Perman, *Reunion without Compromise, 1865–1868* (New York: Cambridge University Press, 1972), 132–143.

87. *New Orleans Daily Picayune*, 21 April 1865.

88. Albert Donnand to Mr. Durant, 27 April 1865, Limongi Papers.

89. *Report*, 12.

90. Ibid., 4, 22–23.

91. Ibid., 44.

92. Ibid., 4–5.
93. Edward Canby to T. J. Durant, New Orleans, 28 June 1865, Limongi Papers.
94. Note, 30 June 1865, Limongi Papers.
95. Edward Canby to T. J. Durant, New Orleans, 30 June 1865, Limongi Papers.
96. *Report*, 4, 47. The *New Orleans Daily Picayune*, 19 August 1865, mistakenly reported that the children had arrived back in New Orleans.

5 REUNION

1. Paul H. Bergeron, *The Papers of Andrew Johnson* (Knoxville: University of Tennessee Press, 1989), 8:212. For many other examples, see Heather Andrea Williams, *Help Me to Find My People: The African American Search for Family Lost in Slavery* (Chapel Hill: University of North Carolina Press, 2012), chs. 5–6.
2. For a seminal introduction to this problem, see Ira Berlin, Steven F. Miller, and Leslie S. Rowland, "Afro-American Families in the Transition from Slavery to Freedom," *Radical History Review*, 42 (Fall 1988): 89–121. See also Amy Dru Stanley, "Instead of Waiting for the Thirteenth Amendment: The War Power, Slave Marriage, and Inviolate Human Rights," *American Historical Review*, 115 (June 2010): 732–765.
3. "Social revolution" is from Bruce Levine, *The Fall of the House of Dixie: The Civil War and the Social Revolution That Transformed the South* (New York: Random House, 2013). For the "freedom generation," see Ira Berlin, *Generations of Captivity: A History of African-American Slaves* (Cambridge, Mass.: Belknap Press, 2003), 246–270.
4. *Report*, 2–3.
5. Ibid., 2.
6. Thomas Savage to William Seward, 29 July 1864, Despatches of U.S. Consuls in Havana, M899, NARA.
7. Thomas Savage to William Seward, Havana, 18 August 1864, Despatches of U.S. Consuls in Havana.
8. V. Sulakowski, Havana, 6 February 1865, Despatches of U.S. Consuls in Havana; F. W. Seward to W. T. Minor, 1 March 1865, Despatches of U.S. Consuls in Havana.

9. William T. Minor to Acting Secretary of State William Hunter, Havana, 15 June 1865, Despatches of U.S. Consuls in Havana; William T. Minor to W. H. Seward, Havana, 28 June 1865, Despatches of U.S. Consuls in Havana. Breckinridge arrived in Cuba on June 10. For Breckinridge's account of his hegira, see A. J. Hanna, "The Escape of Confederate Secretary of War John Cabell Breckinridge as Revealed by His Diary," *Register of the Kentucky State Historical Society*, 37 (October 1939): 322–333. For the reception of Confederate exiles in Havana, see James W. Cortada, "Spain and the American Civil War: Relations at Mid-Century, 1855–1868," *Transactions of the American Philosophical Society*, new series 70, no. 4 (1980): 86.

10. Thomas Savage to W. H. Seward, Havana, 28 June 1865, Despatches of U.S. Consuls in Havana. On Sarah Brewer and the Hotel Cubano, see Matthew Pratt Guterl, *American Mediterranean: Southern Slaveholders in the Age of Emancipation* (Cambridge, Mass.: Harvard University Press, 2008), 74–75, 208n101 ("head-quarters"). For Guterl's excellent account of the Eliza McHatton's slave Zell, who was sent to Cuba by the McHattons during the war, see pp. 89–90, 103–104, 109–112.

11. John Holland to Thomas J. Durant, New Orleans, 22 July 1865, Limongi Papers.

12. *Report*, 46–47. The letter was sent via a Mr. Dugué on board an English vessel sailing to Mobile, and Savage had instructed Dugué to deliver it to the authorities in New Orleans.

13. John Holland to Thomas J. Durant, New Orleans, 22 July 1865, Limongi Papers.

14. *Report*, 45–46. More on Delia's case can be found in pp. 51–54. For documentation of Delia's case in the Cuban National Archives, which describes her as a "joven de color" and indicates she arrived in December 1863, see Gobierno Superior Civil, Leg. 1293, Nu. 50402, ANHC. I am grateful to Adriana Chira for sharing a copy of this document with me.

15. *Report*, 46.

16. Thomas Savage to Thomas J. Durant, Havana, 26 October 1865, Limongi Papers.

17. "Octave Lahonfraye," 29 December 1865, Limongi Papers.

18. Laird W. Bergad, Fe Iglesias García, and María Del Carmen Barcia, *The Cuban Slave Market, 1790–1880* (New York: Cambridge

University Press, 1995), 41, 87, 91, 98. The authors' figures for slave sales define children as under the age of fifteen. Trends in the Havana slave market are discussed on pp. 85–94.

19. General Canby to Thomas J. Durant, 2 January 1866, Limongi Papers.

20. General Canby to Thomas J. Durant, 27 January 1866, Limongi Papers.

21. William Minor to T. J. Durant, January 1866, Limongi Papers.

22. *Report*, 47–48. It is not clear whether Durant received Savage's October 26 letter, or if he simply ignored it.

23. For Seward's Caribbean junket, see Walter Stahr, *Seward: Lincoln's Indispensable Man* (New York: Simon and Schuster, 2012), 454–457; Cortada, "Spain and the American Civil War," 87. Seward's son's memoir of the trip makes no mention of any discussion of the Herera children with Cuban authorities while Seward was in Cuba. Frederick W. Seward, *Reminiscences of a War-time Statesman and Diplomat, 1830–1915* (New York: G. P. Putnam's Sons, 1916), 328–343 ("charming tropical evening" on 331). While Seward was relaxing in the Caribbean in January 1866, his acting assistant secretary of state responded to Durant's New Years Day letter of inquiry. He told Durant that the case of the kidnapped children "has already received the attention of this department," and he forwarded him the same documents that Savage had sent to Canby in September, indicating that they were under Savage's control; *Report*, 48.

24. Seward, *Reminiscences*, 329.

25. *Report*, 49–50.

26. The only sustained analysis of the kidnapping rumor is José B. Fernandez and Jerrell H. Shofner, "Kidnapping of Freedmen from the United States for the Cuban Slave Trade," in *Homenaje a Lydia Cabrera*, ed. by Reinaldo Sanchez, Jose Antonio Madrigal, Richardo Viera, and Jose Sanchez-Boudy (Miami: Ediciones Universal, 1978), 295–302.

27. David G. Smith, "Race and Retaliation: The Capture of African Americans during the Gettysburg Campaign," in *Virginia's Civil War*, ed. Peter Wallenstein and Bertram Wyatt-Brown (Charlottesville: University of Virginia Press, 2005), 137–151; Margaret Creighton, *The Colors of Courage: Gettysburg's Forgotten History: Immigrants, Women, and African Americans in the Civil War's Defining Battle* (New York: Basic Books, 2005), 126–139.

28. *Official Records of the Union and Confederate Navies in the War of the Rebellion* (Washington, D.C.: U.S. Government Printing Office, 1912), ser. 1, 25:213. See also *Freedom: A Documentary History of Emancipation, 1861–1867*, ser. 1, vol. 3, *The Wartime Genesis of Free Labor: The Lower South*, ed. Ira Berlin, Thavolia Glymph, Steven F. Miller, Joseph P. Reidy, Leslie Rowland, and Julie Saville (New York: Cambridge University Press, 1990), 362, which asserts that Confederates captured "several thousand former slaves" in the June 1863 raids in the Lafourche region. On the "fragility of wartime emancipation," see also Ira Berlin, Barbara J. Fields, Steven F. Miller, Joseph P. Reidy, and Leslie S. Rowland, *Slaves No More: Three Essays on Emancipation and the Civil War* (New York: Cambridge University Press, 1992), 48–49. For comparison, see Laurent Dubois, *A Colony of Citizens: Revolution and Slave Emancipation in the French Caribbean, 1787–1804* (Chapel Hill: Omohundro Institute of Early American History and Culture / University of North Carolina Press, 2004), pt. 3.

29. David C. Rankin, *Diary of a Christian Soldier: Rufus Kinsley and the Civil War* (New York: Cambridge University Press, 2004), 94 (26 May 1862), 113 (27 November 1862).

30. James Parton, *General Butler in New Orleans: History of the Administration of the Department of the Gulf in the year 1862* . . . (New York: Mason Brothers, 1864), 536–538. This case resembles, and may be an embellished version of, the June 1862 case of a slave owned by a lawyer named Lotham, who tried to recover him from the service of a Dr. Pickman, who was working at the St. James Hospital in New Orleans. Lotham had hired out the slave to a barber shop when he began to work for Dr. Pickman. See *New Orleans Daily Picayune*, 21 June 1862; "Important Slave Case" clipping from the *New Orleans Delta*, June 1862 [n.d.], in New Orleans Civil War Scrapbooks, Manuscripts Collection B269, Tulane University Libraries, New Orleans, La.; and Journal of a Louisiana Rebel, June–August 1862, 19 June 1862, New-York Historical Society, New York City, N.Y. The journal identifies the owner as "W. Latham, lawyer of this city," and notes he was sentenced to two years in prison. *Gardner's New Orleans Directory for 1861* (New Orleans: Charles Gardner, 1861), 269, lists a "Latham, Wm. G." as a notary public at 118 Customhouse.

31. Berlin et al., *Wartime Genesis*, 518.

32. For a comparative perspective on the vulnerability of women and children to kidnapping in the age of emancipation, see Elisabeth McMahon, "Trafficking and Reenslavement: The Social Vulnerability of Women and Children in Nineteenth-Century East Africa," in *Trafficking in Slavery's Wake: Law and the Experience of Women and Children*, ed. Benjamin N. Lawrance and Richard L. Roberts (Athens: Ohio University Press, 2012), 29–44. For a first-person narrative of enslaved woman who was kidnapped with her family from St. Louis during the war and smuggled to Kentucky, see Dr. L. S. Thompson, *The Story of Mattie J. Jackson: Her Parentage—Experience of Eighteen Years in Slavery—Incidents during the War—Her Escape from Slavery* (Lawrence, 1866).

33. Berlin et al., *Wartime Genesis*, 415–416.

34. Ibid., 432–434.

35. Ibid., 434.

36. *New York Times*, 26 April 1864.

37. "The Shadow at New Orleans," *Independent*, 11 June 1863.

38. Berlin et al., *Wartime Genesis*, 456–458.

39. Ibid., 570–571.

40. *PD*, 6 April 1863.

41. Berlin et al., *Wartime Genesis*, 509.

42. Ibid., 520.

43. Ibid., 532.

44. John Burrud to Ocena Burrud, 1 January 1863, John B. Burrud Papers, Huntington Library, San Marino, Calif.

45. John Burrud to Ocena Burrud, 1 March 1863, John B. Burrud Papers.

46. *Freedom: A Documentary History of Emancipation, 1861–1867*, ser. 3, vol. 1, *Land and Labor, 1865*, ed. Steven Hahn, Steven F. Miller, Susan E. O'Donovan, John C. Rodrigue, and Leslie S. Rowland (Chapel Hill: University of North Carolina Press, 2008), 232. Apprenticeship became a particularly egregious cover for the kidnapping and enslavement of children. For examples, see Laura Edwards, *Gendered Strife and Confusion: The Political Culture of Reconstruction* (Urbana: University of Illinois Press, 1997), 47–48; Mary Niall Mitchell, *Raising Freedom's Child: Black Children and Visions of the Future after Slavery* (New York: New York University

Press, 2008), 150–160; Karin L. Zipf, "Reconstructing 'Free Woman': African-American Women, Apprenticeship, and Custody Rights during Reconstruction," *Journal of Women's History*, 12 (Spring 2000): 17–20.

47. For an analysis of labor recruitment in the postwar South, see *Freedom: A Documentary History of Emancipation, 1861–1867*, ser. 3, vol. 2, *Land and Labor, 1866–1867*, ed. René Hayden, Anthony E. Kaye, Kate Masur, Steven F. Miller, Susan E. O'Donovan, Leslie S. Rowland, and Stephen A. West (Chapel Hill: University of North Carolina Press, 2013), 791–795, 799, 802–803. Differences between the new labor agents and the old slave traders are emphasized in William Cohen, *At Freedom's Edge: Black Mobility and the Southern White Quest for Racial Control 1861–1915* (Baton Rouge: Louisiana State University Press, 1991), 119–127.

48. Hayden et al., *Land and Labor, 1866–1867*, 794.

49. James Scott, *Domination and the Arts of Resistance: Hidden Transcripts* (New Haven, Conn.: Yale University Press, 1990), 144–148. On the use of rumor to manipulate financial markets, see Richard White, "Information, Markets, and Corruption: Transcontinental Railroads in the Gilded Age," *Journal of American History*, 90 (June 2003): 19–43; Jessica Lepler, *The Many Panics of 1837: People, Politics, and the Creation of a Transatlantic Financial Crisis* (New York: Cambridge University Press, 2013), ch. 4. See also the analysis of rumor in Luise White, *Speaking with Vampires: Rumor and History in Colonial Africa* (Berkeley: University of California Press, 2000).

50. Note, 30 June 1865, Limongi Papers.

51. Caryn Cossé Bell, "The Common Wind's Creole Visionary: Dr. Louis Charles Roudanez," *South Atlantic Review*, 73 (Spring 2008): 10–25.

52. Steven Hahn, "'Extravagant Expectations' of Freedom: Rumour, Political Struggle, and the Christmas Insurrection Scare of 1865 in the American South," *Past and Present* 157 (November 1997): 122–158 ("political struggle" on 124, "dramatized" on 125). For rumor during the Civil War, see also Jason Phillips, "The Grape Vine Telegraph: Rumors and Confederate persistence," *Journal of Southern History*, 72 (November 2006): 753–758; Yael A. Sternhell, "Communicating War: The Culture of Information in Richmond during the American Civil War," *Past and Present*, 202 (February 2009): 175–205.

53. Patricia A. Turner, *I Heard It through the Grapevine: Rumor in African-American Culture* (Berkeley: University of California Press, 1993). After Hurricane Betsy in 1965 and Hurricane Katrina in 2005, rumors spread that the levees had been blown up. Edward F. Haas, "'Don't believe any false rumors ...': Mayor Victor H. Schiro, Hurricane Betsy, and Urban Myths," *Louisiana History*, 45 (Autumn 2004): 463–468, proves the rumor was false but fails to explain why anyone might have believed it.

54. *New York Times*, 18 December 1861.

55. *Liberator*, 20 December 1861.

56. John Blassingame, ed., *Slave Testimony: Two Centuries of Letters, Speeches, Interviews, and Autobiographies* (Baton Rouge: Louisiana State University Press, 1977), 383.

57. Elizabeth Hyde Botume, *First Days amongst the Contrabands* (Boston: Lee and Shepard, 1893), 13. Smalls and Botume are both quoted in the unparalleled Leon F. Litwack, *Been in the Storm So Long: The Aftermath of Slavery* (New York: Vintage Books, 1979), 58 (Smalls), 118 (Botume).

58. Ira Berlin, Barbara J. Fields, Steven F. Miller, Joseph P. Reidy, and Leslie S. Rowland, eds., *Free at Last: A Documentary History of Slavery, Freedom, and the Civil War* (New York: New Press, 1992), 108.

59. Whitelaw Reid, *After the War: A Southern Tour* (Cincinnati: Moore, Wilstach and Baldwin, 1866), 563. See also Guterl, *American Mediterranean*, 147–148.

60. Brig. Gen. Wager Swayne to Maj. Gen. O. O. Howard, Montgomery, Ala., 13 September 1865, Letters Received, ser. 15, Records of the Commissioner, R.G. 105, NARA, Doc. A-1577, FSSP. Emphasis in original. Swayne's father was Supreme Court Justice Noah Swayne.

61. Capt. William Kobbe, 178th New York, Commanding Post, to Assistant Superintendant of Freedmen, Greenville, Ala., 15 September 1865, Unregistered Letters Received, ser. 9, Office of the Assistant Commissioner, Ala., R.G. 105, NARA, Doc. A-2211, FSSP. On rumors of the kidnapping of freedmen who were employed to cut timber in Florida's forests, see Jerrell H. Shofner, "Negro Laborers and the Forest Industries in Reconstruction Florida," *Journal of Forest History*, 19 (October 1975): 184.

62. Bvt. Major General Charles R. Woods to Brig. General William D. Whipple, Mobile, Ala., 20 September 1865, vol. 1, Letters Sent, ser. 98, Department of Alabama, pt. 1, R.G. 393, NARA, Doc. C-53, FSSP.

63. Brooks D. Simpson, Leroy P. Graf, and John Muldowny, eds., *Advice after Appomattox: Letters to Andrew Johnson, 1865–1869* (Knoxville: University of Tennessee Press, 1987), 149.

64. H. G. Clagstone to Hon. E. M. Stanton, New York, 4 October 1865, endorsed by Max Woodhull, Assistant Adj. Genl. of the Freedmen's Bureau, 10 October 1865, Unregistered Letters Received, ser. 9, Office of the Assistant Commissioner, Ala., R.G. 105, NARA, Doc. A-2714, FSSP.

65. Col. T.W. Osborn to Maj. Genl. O.O. Howard, Tallahassee, Fla., 14 November 1865, Letters Received, ser. 15, Records of the Commissioner, R.G. 105, NARA, Doc. A-1435, FSSP. See also Major General J.G. Foster to Headquarters, Military Division of the Gulf, Tallahassee, Fla., 30 January 1866, vol. 235, Endorsements Sent, ser. 4485, Division of the Southwest and Department of the Gulf, pt. 1, R.G. 393, NARA, Doc. C-53, FSSP; G. Gordon Adam to Col. Samuel Thomas, Vicksburg, Miss., January 1866, Unregistered Letters Received, ser. 9, Office of the Assistant Commissioner, Ala., R.G. 105, NARA, Doc. A-2783, FSSP; *Report of the Joint Committee on Reconstruction*, 39th Cong., 1st Sess. (1865), no. 30, pt. 3, p. 43.

66. Joe M. Richardson, "A Northerner Reports on Florida: 1866," *Florida Historical Quarterly*, 40 (April 1962): 384.

67. Bob Dalehite, "Arch S. Dobbins," *Phillips County Historical Quarterly*, 4 (September 1965): 21.

68. Brvt. Major General Charles Woods to Brig. General W.D. Whipple, Mobile, Ala., 18 December 1865, Letters Sent, ser. 98, Department of Alabama, pt. 1, R.G. 393, NARA, Doc. C-53, FSSP.

69. Special Officer M.P. Hunnicutt to Brigd Genl F.T. Sherman, Provost Marshal General, New Orleans, La., 27 December 1865, Letters Received, ser. 4560, Provost Marshal, Division of the Southwest and Department of the Gulf, pt. 1, R.G. 393, NARA, Doc. C-1050, FSSP. Emphasis in original.

70. Special Officer M.P. Hunnicutt to Lieut. Col. Moore, Provost Marshal General, New Orleans, 8 January 1866, Letters Received, ser. 4560, Provost Marshal, Division of the Southwest and Department of the Gulf, pt. 1, R.G. 393, NARA, Doc. C-1050, FSSP.

71. Special Officer M.P. Hunnicutt to Major A.M. Jackson, Acting Provost Marshal General, Headquarters, Department of Louisiana, Office of the Provost Marshal General, New Orleans, La., 31 January 1866,

Provost Marshal General, Department of Louisiana, Letters Received, "H" 1866, Records of United States Army Continental Commands, 1821–1920, Record Group 393, NARA.

72. James Orton, *The Andes and the Amazon; or, Across the Continent of South America* (New York: Harper and Brothers, 1876), 252. On Confederate Louisianians who emigrated to Brazil, see Daniel E. Sutherland, "Looking for a Home: Louisiana Emigrants during the Civil War and Reconstruction," *Louisiana History*, 21 (Autumn 1980): 349–352.

73. *Works of Charles Sumner* (Boston: Lee and Shepherd, 1876), 10:101–103. On Sumner's role in Reconstruction politics, see Eric Foner, *Reconstruction: America's Unfinished Revolution, 1863–1877* (New York: Harper and Row, 1988), 229–230, and the more detailed treatment in David Herbert Donald, *Charles Sumner and the Rights of Man* (New York: Knopf, 1970), ch. 6.

74. Asuntos Políticos, Leg. 227, Nu. 19, ANHC. "Graves son los riesgos que surgen de este estado de cosas, no solo para los estados del Sur de este pais, sino lo que es todavia mas grave, para esas Antilles." On Dulce and the politics of the ending of the slave trade to Cuba, see David Murray, *Odious Commerce: Britain, Spain, and the Abolition of the Cuban Slave Trade* (New York: Cambridge University Press, 1980), ch. 14; Christopher Schmidt-Nowara, *Empire and Antislavery: Spain, Cuba, and Puerto Rico, 1833–1874* (Pittsburgh, Pa.: University of Pittsburgh Press, 1999), 104–106; Julián Moreno García, "El cambio de actitud de la administración española frente al contrabando negrero en Cuba (1860–1866)," *Estudios de Historia Social*, 1, no. 4 (1988): 271–284.

75. On ideological contamination and slave societies, see above all Julius Scott, "The Common Wind: Currents of Afro-American Communication in the Era of the Haitian Revolution" (PhD diss., Duke University, 1986). For late eighteenth- and early nineteenth-century efforts by the Cuban government to fend off Haitian and British abolitionist influences, see Ada Ferrer, "Cuban Slavery and Atlantic Antislavery," *Review*, 31, no. 3 (2008): 279–282, 289–292. For the impact of the Civil War on Cuba, see also Franklin W. Knight, *Slave Society in Cuba during the 19th Century* (Madison: University of Wisconsin, 1970), 56–58; 147–148; Schmidt-Nowara, *Empire and Antislavery*, 105.

76. Cortada, "Spain and the American Civil War," 76–77 ("stealing negroes" on 77); Murray, *Odious Commerce*, 313–314.

77. *Report*, 54.

78. *Congressional Globe*, 39th Cong., 1st Sess. (1866), 699. 852.

79. *Congressional Globe*, 39th Cong., 1st Sess. (1866), 1178.

80. Originals of many of the documents published in the report concerning the Herera case can be found in the Limongi Papers, which contains the papers of Durant and Hornor. These documents consistently refer to Herera as "Elyra," or just Rose.

81. For an example of newspaper coverage of the report, see the summary in the *New York Tribune*, 17 March 1866.

82. *Works of Charles Sumner*, 10:103 ("Yankees"); *Congressional Globe*, 39th Cong., 1st Sess. (1866), 2671, 2675, 2723, 2764; *Statutes at Large*, 39th Cong., 1st Sess. (1866), 50. For the rift between Johnson and the congressional Republicans, see Foner, *Reconstruction*, 239–261. The antikidnapping law might be compared to 1862 legislation against the "coolie trade." See Moon-Ho Jung, *Coolies and Cane: Race, Labor, and Sugar in the Age of Emancipation* (Baltimore: Johns Hopkins University Press, 2006), 36–38.

83. F. W. Seward to Thomas J. Durant, 21 March 1866, Limongi Papers.

84. William T. Minor to Thomas J. Durant, Havana, 9 March 1866, Limongi Papers; William T. Minor to William H. Seward, Havana, 20 March 1866; William T. Minor to William H. Seward, Havana, 12 April 1866, Despatches of U.S. Consuls in Havana. Minor refers to a letter from Durant dated March 19 reporting that the children had arrived on the *Evening Star* on March 17. The letter is not in the Seward Papers or the correspondence of the State Department, and I have not located it.

85. 1880 U.S. Census: New Orleans, Orleans, Louisiana, Enumeration District 050, Family History film 1254462, roll 462, p. 540B, image 0062.

86. James G. Hollandsworth Jr., *An Absolute Massacre: The New Orleans Race Riot of July 30, 1866* (Baton Rouge: Louisiana State University Press, 2001), although "race riot" as a misnomer. "Wholesale slaughter" is from Foner, *Reconstruction*, 263. Quotations from Durant are from his testimony to Congress in December 1866, published in *New Orleans Riots*, House Ex. Doc. 16, 39th Cong., 2nd Sess.(1867), Testimony, 7–11. The dentist A. P. Dostie was shot in the back as he left the Mechanics' Institute and died several days later; Hollandsworth, *Absolute Massacre*, 116, 130, 142–143.

87. *New York Times*, 10 October 1866. For the list of passengers, see *New York Times*, 17 October 1866. For Henry Palfrey's death, see Hannah Palfrey Ayer, *A Legacy of New England* (n.p., 1950), 2:337. I'd like to thank my student Olivia Huppman for bringing the *Evening Star* disaster to my attention.

88. "The Wave," *Harper's Weekly*, 8 December 1866.

EPILOGUE

1. Information about Juana la Americana comes from Asuntos Políticos, Leg. 74, Nu. 14, ANHC. For Queralta's affadavit, see *New York Tribune*, 23 April 1878. Leonard's death was a topic of gossip. See *New York Times*, 16 March 1878, 24 March 1878, 28 March 1878; *Washington Post*, 22 April 1878. For the concept of a "diving rumor," see Richard Allen Drake, "Construction Sacrifice and Kidnapping Rumor Panics in Borneo," *Oceania*, 59 (June 1989): 269–279.

2. On Cuba's Ten Years' War and the road to emancipation, see Rebecca Scott, *Slave Emancipation in Cuba: The Transition to Free Labor in Cuba, 1860–1899* (Pittsburgh, Pa.: University of Pittsburgh Press, 1985), pt. 1.

Acknowledgments

MORE PEOPLE than I can remember have helped me, one way or another, to write this book. The following are the people I do remember, with apologies to those I have forgotten: Elena Abbott, Ana Lucia Araujo, Tommaso Astarita, Ed Baptist, Carol Benedict, Denise Brennan, James Benton, Katie Benton-Cohen, Alan Berg, Jason Berry, Stephen Berry, Betsy Blackmar, Julia Butz, Daniel Cano, Marcia Chatelain, Adriana Chira, Emily Clark, Brian Costello, Chris DeLorenzo, Kate de Luna, Brian Distelberg, Mark Fernandez, Ada Ferrer, Barbara Fields, Eric Foner, Reinaldo Funes Monzote, Alison Games, Eric Gettig, Bob Groves, Sam Haselby, Judith Hunt, Maurice Jackson, Walter Johnson, Martha Jones, Michael Kazin, Ari Kelman, Emily Landau, Erick Langer, Amy Leonard, Lee Leumas, Chandra Manning, Kate Masur, Bryan McCann, John McNeill, Meredith McKittrick, Yusledis Mena, Jo Ann Moran Cruz, Amy Murrell Taylor, Brian Ostrander, Andres Pletch, Terry Pinkard, Larry Powell, Henry Richardson, Clay Risen, Mike Ross, Leslie Rowland, Jordan Sand, David Sartorius, Judith Schafer, Phil Schwartzberg, Joyce Seltzer, Shobana Shankar, Djuana Shields, Rebecca Shumway, Randy Sparks, Dale Tomich, John Tutino, Lea Vandervelde, Anna von der Goltz, Steve West, and Paul Young.

I must also thank the many helpful, knowledgeable archivists and librarians at the Archivo Nacional in Havana, the Baker Library at Harvard Business School, the Biblioteca Nacional de Cuba José Martí, the

ACKNOWLEDGMENTS

Freedmen and Southern Society Project at the University of Maryland College Park, Georgetown University's Lauinger Library, the Historic New Orleans Collection, the Huntington Library, the Library of Congress, Louisiana State University's Special Collections, the National Archives, the New Orleans Public Library, the New York Historical Society, and Tulane's University Howard-Tilton Library.

I had the opportunity to present drafts of portions of this book at Georgetown University's Americas Initiative Faculty Seminar and Normative Orders Collaborative; to history faculty and students at Loyola University New Orleans; at the Charles Warren Center for Studies in American History's "Emancipation @ 150" series; and at Howard University's "Slavery, Memory, and African Diasporas" seminar. The feedback I received at these venues enriched my thinking and gave me confidence that there might be an audience for this book. A rigorous manuscript workshop conducted by my colleagues in the History Department at Georgetown epitomized the ideal of constructive criticism among a community of scholars.

I would be remiss if I did not mention the many wonderful students I have taught in my time at Georgetown, who have taught me a great deal about what people truly appreciate in the study of history.

Finally, my love and gratitude for Marian Currinder and Frances Rothman cannot be expressed in words on paper.

Index

Note: Figures are indexed in italic.

Abell, Edmund, 147–148
Aimée, 169
Allain, Sosthene, 48–49
Allain, Valerian, 45, 47–49
Allen, Henry Watkins, 113
American Freedmen's Inquiry Commission, 164, 166–167
Argüelles, José Augustín, 180–181
Aristotle, 17
Atocha, A. A., 129–130

Badger, Roderick, 57
Banks, Nathaniel, 106, 109, 111, 115, 128, 148–152, 164
Baptismal records, 12–13, 117
Bates, Edward, 131
Bayne, Thomas (Nixon, Sam), 57–58
Becky, 87–88
Bell, Joseph, 133–134
Berlin, Ira, 154

Bio Bio, 4, 106–108, 111, 137–139, 141
Blanchard, Mrs. Albert G., 59
Blasco de Garay, 99–100
Botume, Elizabeth, 172
Bouligny, Alfred, 46
Brazil, 9, 18, 35, 162, 168, 170, 173, 177–179
Breckinridge, John Cabell, 155–156
Bremer, Fredrika, 41–42
Brewer, Sarah, 156
Brown, Fred, 113
Brown, William Wells, 8
Burrud, John, 167
Butler, Benjamin, 77–81, 85, 90–93, 99–100, 104, 106, 132–133, 163

Cable, George Washington, 3
Cailloux, André, 116
Camp Parapet, 79–81, 86
Canada, 27

257

INDEX

Canal Street, 33–34, 48, 54, 56, 66, 102, 126
Canby, Edward R. S., 150–151, 154–155, 157, 159–160, 169–170, 175
Catholicism, 12–14, 62, 117–118
Children: and emancipation, 85, 89, 93, 118–123, 129–130, 134–135, 153; in history, 121–122; mortality among, 18; slave children, 2, 4, 6–7, 10–13, 18–19, 22, 25, 36–37, 40–42, 46–50, 59–60, 91, 101, 120–121, 160, 188; slaves as children, 120; vulnerable to kidnapping, 28, 65, 164–165, 178. *See also* Slaves: children
Citizenship, 131–132
Civil War, 2, 4, 9, 67, 72–114 *passim*, 115, 162–163, 170–172, 179–180
Clara, 87–88
Clark, Daniel, 182
Code Noir, 13, 17
Colton's Rail-Road and Military Map of the United States, Mexico, the West Indies, 94
Congo Square, 3
Connor, James, 26–27
Consent, 137–141, 149–150
Conway, Thomas, 122–123, 133
Copes, Joseph, 43–44, 58
Cotton, 15, 34
Cougot, Madame, 122–123
Cuba: Herera children taken to, 3–6, 68, 101–102, 106–112, 123, 141; Confederate emigration to, 92, 94–100, 151, 155–156; links to New Orleans, 14, 35, 63, 66, 72, 94–100, 158–161; rumors of freedpeople sold in, 9–10, 161–162, 170–184, 187–189; slave trade, 94, 96–98, 179–181. *See also* Havana
Cugoano, Ottobah, 8

Davis, Garrett, 183
Death records, 18, 116
DeBow, J. D. B., 58–59
Debt, 30, 41, 45–46, 48, 55, 91–92, 135
De Forest, John, 77
De Hart, Amelie Valcour (Mary), 2–4, 50, 54, 59, 101–102, 106–109, 115–116, 123–125, 132, 151, 160, 169, 184; trial of, 136–152
De Hart, Edward, 2, 4, 59, 111
De Hart, James Andrew, 2, 48–52, 54–55, 59–60, 74, 90–94, 100–101, 145–146, 159–160
Delia, 158
Dentistry, 54–58, 100
Dobbins, Archibald, 176–178
Domestic service, 36–38, 58–59, 101, 160. *See also* Slaves: domestic
Dostie, A. P., 56, 73, 127
Douglass, Frederick, 5, 8, 11, 57, 59–60
Du Bois, W. E. B., 10
Dulce, Domingo, 161–162, 179–181
Durant, Thomas Jefferson, 70, 91, 125–129, 136, 140, 142, 144–146, 148–149, 151, 157, 159–161, 169, 182–183, 185, 189

INDEX

Emancipation: families, 119–123; mayhem, 7, 146, 166, 188–189; New Orleans, 67, 81, 85–90, 105–106, 115–116, 124, 128–129; reversal, 127, 163, 166–167; revolutionary, 9–10, 134, 154. *See also* Freedpeople

Emancipation Proclamation, 1, 105, 127

Evening Star, 184–186

Ex post facto punishment, 144

Fallon, J. G., 107, 138–139, 142
Fallon, Mrs. J. G., 108, 138
Farragut, David G., 77
Fearn, Frances, 113
Fort Jackson, 77, 85
Fourier, Charles, 126
Freedmen's Aid Association, 125, 128
Freedmen's Bureau, 168, 173–175
Freedpeople: fear of enslavement, 154, 168; insurrection scare, 170, 180; kidnapping rumors, 168–178; labor market for, 168, 172–173; law to prevent kidnapping of, 181–183; refuse to be enslaved, 167–168; search for family members, 118–120, 153; testify in court, 133. *See also* Emancipation

Free people of color: in New Orleans, 33, 36, 61–66, 73, 75–76, 110, 128, 169; in Pointe Coupée, 12, 20–21, 27–29; kidnapped/enslaved, 27–29, 65, 104, 153; political activity, 110, 128, 169; protest impressment, 165

"Free womb" principle, 18

Gardner's New Orleans Directory, 49, 51, 56, 59, 61
Gerstäcker, Frederick, 24–25
Godparents, 11–13, 117
Gramsci, Antonio, 2
Grapevine telegraph, 29, 169. *See also* Rumor
Guy, James, 85

Hahn, Michael, 105, 128, 147
Hahn, Steven, 170
Hanks, George, 120, 129, 163–164, 167
Harper's Weekly, 170–171
Havana, 2, 94–102, 106–112, 151, 178, 188; Confederate emigration to, 2, 92–94, 111–112, 142, 155–156; Herera children's arrival in, 111–112; slavery in, 160. *See also* Cuba
Hayes, Rutherford, 187
Helm, Charles, 92, 98, 102
Hendricks, Tines, 119
Herera, George, 2, 60–62, 65–66, 73, 107, 109–111, 116–117, 138–139
Herera, Joseph Ernest, 4, 48–49, 60, 109, 111, 114, 157, 159, 184
Herera, Joseph George, 3, 106, 184
Herera, Louise Josephine, 117, 184
Herera, Marie Georgiana, 4, 48–49, 60, 109, 111, 114, 157, 159, 184

Herera, Marie Josephine, 4, 60, 109, 111, 114, 157, 159, 184
Herera, Rose, 1–4, 12–13, 18–19, 30–33, 58, 60, 101–112, 115–119, 123, 130–131, 135–152, 159, 169–170, 182–184, 189–190; advertisement for sale, *47;* baptism, 12–13; birth, 11; case in provost court, 136–148; children of, 60–61, 104, 106–115, 118–119, 123, 137–146, 149–152, 154–161, 181–185; domestic servant, 36, 58–59; free, 115, 184–185; in jail, 1–4, 102–108; listed in 1880 census, 184–185; marriage to George Herera, 61–62, 130; mulatto designation, 19, 43; name spelled "Elyra," 130, 183; petition of, 11, 30, 102, 130–131, 193–197; refusal to go to Havana, 101–104, 107; slave status, 17, 115, 145–146; sold, 45–50, 91–92; taken to New Orleans, 30, 33, 35; threatened, 135
Holland, John, 140, 157
Houstoun, Matilda, 47
Howard, Oliver Otis, 132, 173–175
Hunter, Caroline, 121
Hurlbut, Stephen A., 130–132, 148
Hurricane Katrina, 30, 118

Immigrants, 33, 36, 50–54, 73–74
Insolence, 40, 59–60, 82, 86–88, 103

Jeff, 163–164
Jefferson, Thomas, 120
Jinnings, Thomas Jr., 58, 75
Johnson, Andrew, 148–149, 153, 174, 182–183, 185
Johnson, Arana, 164
Juana la Americana, 188–189
Jupiter, 97–98

Kidnapping, 8–9, 27–29, 162–166; case of Eulalie Oliveau, 27–29; case of Euphémie and Andrinette, 65; De Hart, Amelie Valcour tried for, 136–150; law to prevent, 181–183; rumors of, 9, 154, 162–163, 168–179, 187
King, Jennie, 176
Kinsley, Rufus, 77, 163
Kinsman, J.B., 135
Knapp, James, 58
Kobbe, William, 174
Kruttschnidt, V., 80

Lalaurie, Marie Delphine, 38–40
Leblanc, Octave, 12, 21–24, 30, 32–33, 45–46, 70
Leocadie, 12, 45, 47, 50, 107–108, 137–138, 184
Leonard, John, 187
Letton, J.A., 138
Leveque, George, 107, 138–139
Lieber, G. Norman, 132
Lincoln, Abraham, 1, 67–68, 91, 115, 123, 127, 148, 152
López, Narciso, 95–96
Lopez de Queralta, Fernando, 187
Lunsford v. Coquillon, 17
Lyddy, 87–88

INDEX

Margaret, 87–88
Martineau, Harriet, 39–40
Marx, Karl, 9
McDonough, John, 66
McKaye, James, 167
Mercer, William Newton, 48–49, 68–70
Microhistory, 5–6
Minor, William, 155–156, 160–161, 181
Mitchell, Mary Niall, 122
Montamal, John, 134–135
Morgan, Edwin, 182
Mulatto designation, 19–21, 43, 58, 62, 134

Natal alienation, 11
"Natural increase," 16–18
New Orleans, 2–3, 28, 30–66 *passim;* capture by Union forces, 2, 67, 77–78, 99; Civil War, 72–75, 77–78, 83–84, 90–94, 98–100; courts, 10, 123–124, 129–130, 147–148; end of slavery, 7, 67, 78, 81–91; free people of color, 61–66, 110; freedpeople search for family in, 119–120; freedpeople testify in court, 133; and Havana, 94–100, 116, 141, 158–159; immigrants, 53–54; jail, 3, 64–65, 102–104; Julia Street women's prison, 132, 148; kidnapping, 163–165, 176–178; Mechanics' Institute riot, 185; police, 102; slavery, 35–44, 57, 74–75, 78–92, 101; yellow fever, 30, 99
Northup, Solomon, 8, 29

Oliveau, Eulalie, 27–29
Olmsted, Frederick Law, 36

Palmer, Benjamin Morgan, 70
Panic of 1857, 45
Parlange, Charles, 26–27
Parsons, Lewis, 173–175
Parton, James, 133–135, 163
Partus sequitur ventrem, 17
Patterson, Orlando, 11
Penrose, Ann Wilkinson, 83–90, 166
Perrine, Constance Bique, 64–65, 104
Perry, William, 156
Persac, Marie Adrien, 22, *23*
Phelps, John Wolcott, 79–81, 86
Pierson, Michael, 77
Plessy, Homer, 118
Point Coupée, 2, 11–29 *passim;* cotton and sugar boom in, 15, 33; cultural divide, 28; growth of slave population in, 15–16; in 1850, 18–19; kidnapping of Oliveau family in, 27–29; Leblanc plantation, 18, 21–22; planters in, 18–19, 22–25; runaway from, 26–27
Poke, Alexander, 156
Porche, Simon, 27
Prescription, 29
Provost court, 102, 123–124, 129–130, 132–148, 151

261

Racial categories, 19–21, 117
Real Universidad, 100
Reconstruction, 127–128, 154, 183, 185, 189–190
Recorder's court, 124
Reid, Whitelaw, 128, 172
R.G. Dun & Co. credit reports, 33, 45
Richards, Dora, 76
Richmond, VA, 153
Riddell, John Leonard, 142–143, 169–170
Rockwell, Fenton, 136
Roland, Carmelite, 3, 91, 102–103, 106–107, 137, 139, 141–142, 156–158
Roudanez, Louis Charles, 169
Rumor, 84, 154, 168–179, 187
Russell, William Howard, 67, 72, 76

Savage, Thomas, 155–159
Schurz, Carl, 175
Scott, James, 169
Secession, 67–72, 78, 126
Second Confiscation Act, 80, 91, 93, 145–146
Seward, William, 154–155, 157, 161–162, 181, 183
Sheridan, Philip, 175
Slave dealers, 40, 49–51, 56
Slaveowners: baptize slaves, 13; during Civil War, 82–90, 112–114, 163–167, 170–172; paternalism, 12, 101, 120; Pointe Coupée, 19, 24; property rights, 6–7, 145; urban, 35–44, 58–59

Slaves: advertisements for sale of, 37, 38, 40–41, 46–47; baptism, 12–13; birthdays, 11–12; children, 6–7, 17–18, 40–41, 59–60, 89, 165; community, 31–32, 102; conspiracy and revolt, 14, 74–76; as "contrabands," 79, 82; domestic, 2, 33, 36–38, 40–44, 58–59, 83, 103, 111, 136; families, 11–12, 40–42, 90, 102, 120, 143; forced migration, 16–17, 112–114; fugitives, 26–27, 44, 79–80, 85, 104; insolent, 59–60, 82–83, 85–88; law, 17, 25, 29, 31, 38, 41, 66, 124, 134–135, 143–145, 149–151; loyal to owners, 2, 36–37, 41, 101, 111–113; manumitted, 126; marriage, 12; mortgaged, 32–33; mothers and fathers, 12, 22, 40–42, 45, 60, 89, 121, 143; "natural increase", 16–18; notarial acts, 31, 45, 47, 60; prohibition on sale of children apart from their mothers, 25, 41, 60, 143, 149–150; property, 31; "refugeed" during the Civil War, 112–114; rented, 42–44, 84, 108, 159–160; social relations, 31–32; sold, 18, 25, 26, 32, 38, 40–42, 45–50, 91, 135, 188; treated well, 139–140, 157–158; unionist, 76–77, 82; violence towards, 18, 26, 38–40, 59–60, 103–104, 164–165; women, 17–18, 36, 38, 85–90
Slave trade, Atlantic, 8, 35, 96–98, 111, 179–181

Slave trade, domestic, 16, 26, 28, 45–47, 143–144
Slidell, John, 98
Smalls, Robert, 172
Smith, Andrew, 113
Smith, Gardner, 38
Soloman, Joseph, 129–130
Solomon, Clara, 56–57, 75, 83
Soulé, Pierre, 96, 155
Stanton, Edwin, 154–155, 159
State Department, 154–162, 182–184, 189–190
St. Augustine Church, 117–118
St. Louis Hotel, 46–47
Still, William, 26–27, 57
Stinson, Joseph, 22, *23*, 32
Sulakowsky, Valery, 155
Sumner, Charles, 161–162, 178–179, 181–183
Swayne, Wager, 173–175

Tessara, Gabriel, 161–162, 180
Texas, 112–113
Thompson, Jane, 89
Tomb of the Unknown Slave, *118*

Train, Henry, 125, 129–131
Travis, Ben, 85
Tuberculosis, 116–117
Tureaud, A.P., 118
Turner, Vincent, 26

Underground Railroad, 26–27, 57
Union army, 7, 44, 81–82

Virinda, 129–130

Wadsworth, James S., 166–167
Walker, Clara, 112
Walker, Jake, 113
Washington, Ella, 113
Wells, James Madison, 147–148, 150
Woods, Charles, 175–176
Woolfley, F. A., 124–125
Women, contribution to emancipation, 3, 81–82; domestic labor, 36–44, 160; enslaved, 17–18, 21–22, 36, 38, 85–90; slave-owning, 38–40, 59, 82–90; and rumor, 169–170; vulnerable to kidnapping, 65, 164–165